Agrarian Reform Under State Capitalism in Algeria

Westview Special Studies

The concept of Westview Special Studies is a response to the continuing crisis in academic and informational publishing. Library budgets are being diverted from the purchase of books and used for data banks, computers, micromedia, and other methods of information retrieval. Interlibrary loan structures further reduce the edition sizes required to satisfy the needs of the scholarly community. Economic pressures on university presses and the few private scholarly publishing companies have greatly limited the capacity of the industry to properly serve the academic and research communities. As a result, many manuscripts dealing with important subjects, often representing the highest level of scholarship, are no longer economically viable publishing projects--or, if accepted for publication, are typically subject to lead times ranging from one to three years.

Westview Special Studies are our practical solution to the problem. As always, the selection criteria include the importance of the subject, the work's contribution to scholarship, and its insight, originality of thought, and excellence of exposition. We accept manuscripts in camera-ready form, typed, set, or word processed according to specifications laid out in our comprehensive manual, which contains straightforward instructions and sample pages. The responsibility for editing and proofreading lies with the author or sponsoring institution, but our editorial staff is always available to answer questions and provide guidance.

The result is a book printed on acid-free paper and bound in sturdy, library-quality soft covers. We manufacture these books ourselves using equipment that does not require a lengthy make-ready process and that allows us to publish first editions of 300 to 1000 copies and to reprint even smaller quantities as needed. Thus, we can produce Special Studies quickly and can keep even very specialized books in print as long as there is a demand for them.

About the Book and Author

Algeria is a former French colony where the state now owns and controls many key industries. However, the state also encourages enterprises in both the public and private spheres to adopt profit-oriented production relations. Looking at Algerian economic development in the last twenty years as a case study of state capitalism in the Third World, and drawing on research in twenty communities representing the country's major agricultural zones, Dr. Pfeifer investigates the institutional changes brought about by the agrarian reform of the 1970s.

The agrarian revolution had two explicit goals-- to increase production of basic foods and to put an end to the exploitation of man by man left as a legacy of colonial despoliation of the agricultural sector. But, Dr. Pfeifer argues, the reform also had other effects, including the eradication of subsistence production, the securing of non-absentee private ownership of land and of other means of production by capitalist farmers and commercial family farms, and the shift of surplus agricultural labor into wage employment both in the rural areas and in urban industry and services. Dr. Pfeifer concludes that the agrarian reform under state capitalism contributed to the transformation begun before independence from a pre-capitalist to a capitalist economic system.

Karen Pfeifer is assistant professor of economics at Smith College and a member of the Middle East Research and Information Project (MERIP). She is also a staff member and teacher at the Center for Popular Economics in Amherst, Massachusetts.

Agrarian Reform Under State Capitalism in Algeria

Karen Pfeifer

Westview Press / Boulder and London

Westview Special Studies on the Middle East and North Africa

Published in 1985 in the United States of America by Westview Press, Inc., Frederick A. Praeger, Publisher, 5500 Central Avenue, Boulder, Colorado 80301

Library of Congress Cataloging in Publication Data
 Pfeifer, Karen.
    Agrarian reform under state capitalism
 in Algeria.
    (Westview special studies on the Middle East
 and North Africa)
    Bibliography: p.
    Includes index.
    1. Land reform--Algeria. 2. Farm tenancy--Algeria.
 3. Agriculture and state--Algeria. 4. Agriculture--
 Economic aspects--Algeria. 5. Peasantry--Algeria.
 6. Agricultural laborers--Algeria. I. Title.
 HD1333.A4P46 1985   333.3'1'65   84-25606
 ISBN: 0-8133-7033-7

Composition for this book was provided by the author
Printed and bound in the United States of America

6 5 4 3 2 1

Contents

Map and Tables

Acknowledgments

I should like to express my gratitude to some of the people whose help and support made this work possible. Claudine Chaulet, Rachid Benattig, and the other staff members at the CREA institute in Algiers provided me with access to information for the original research and with an atmosphere of friendly encouragement and positive critical thinking. My friends, Dorothy and Mahfoud Bennoune, made my research trip to Algeria both pleasantly memorable and productive. Cynthia Taft Morris and James Paul provided badly needed critical commentary and encouragement on an earlier version of this work. The reformulation of that earlier work into this book subsequently benefited from critical readings by Robert Haddad and David Kotz. Betty Nanartonis and Letitia Sloan did a superb and dedicated job on the word processing. Ellen Dibble, Jackie Eghrari, and Lisa Ferrell performed vital editorial and secretarial services. And Mary Coppola created the map. Thank you, all, for your skill and patience.

K. P.

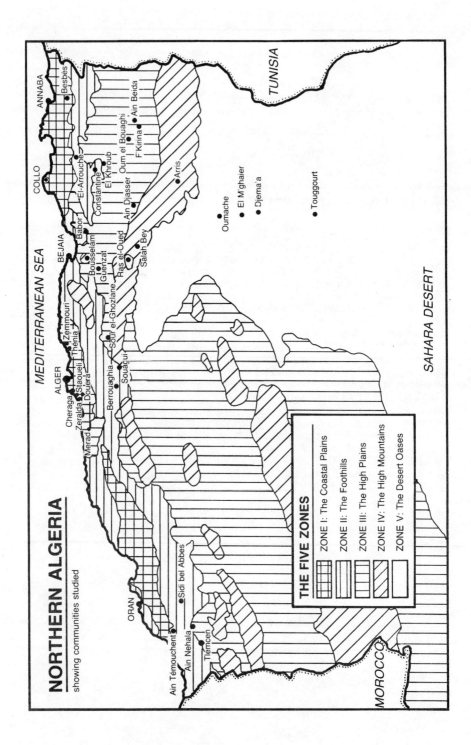

NORTHERN ALGERIA

showing communities studied

MEDITERRANEAN SEA

ANNABA

Besbes

Ain Beida

El Khroub

F'Kirina

Collo

El-Arrouch

Constantine

Oum el Bouaghi

Ain Djasser

Arris

Ain M'ghaier

Djema'a

Touggourt

Oumache

BEJAIA

Babor

Bousselam

Guenzat

Ras el-Oued

Salah Bey

Zemmouri

Thenia

Sour el-Ghozlane

ALGER

Cheraga

Zeralda

Staoueli

Douera

Merad

Berrouaghia

Souagui

ORAN

Sidi bel Abbes

Ain Témouchent

Ain Nehala

Tlemcen

TUNISIA

SAHARA DESERT

MOROCCO

THE FIVE ZONES

ZONE I: The Coastal Plains

ZONE II: The Foothills

ZONE III: The High Plains

ZONE IV: The High Mountains

ZONE V: The Desert Oases

1
State Capitalism and the Transformation of Agriculture

As compared to many other Third World countries in the period since 1960, post-colonial Algeria showed great promise for profound socio-economic transformation. Algeria had both the material resources, and leadership with a clear enough vision, to conduct a serious and rapid developmental program. In the 1970s especially, with the increase in hydrocarbon revenues, Algeria could have fundamentally reorganized the agrarian sector and raised rural living standards across the board, through investment in infrastructure, rural education, health, housing and improved agricultural techniques.

The achievements of this era in Algeria's history can be illustrated in a rough way using the criteria favored by agencies such as the World Bank. Real GDP grew at an annual rate of 4.3 percent in the 1960s and at 6.6 percent in the 1970s. Industry as a share of GDP increased from 35 percent in 1960 to 55 percent in 1982, while the percentage of the labor force in agriculture fell from 67 percent in 1960 to 25 percent in 1980. Major strides were taken in lowering the infant mortality rate and in providing access to education for the school-age population.[1]

It would be reasonable to expect the agricultural sector to play an integral role in this transformation. The announcement of an "agrarian revolution" in 1971 by the central government was therefore met with high expectations by both Algerian and foreign observers. However, many of these expectations went unfulfilled, and the "revolution" more properly may be called a "reform." Algerian economic policy makers did not pursue massive investment in agriculture and did not promote a profound reorganization of the agrarian sector after all.

The aim of this book is to examine Algeria's development program through the prism of the agrarian transformation of the 1970s. Delineating the achievements and limitations of changes in agriculture

provides some insight into the nature of Algeria's
social formation today, and into a developmental
process common to many Third World countries. This
social formation, state capitalism, and the process it
promotes, the construction of the capitalist mode of
production, are explained below.

In the analysis that follows, the interpretation
of the achievements and limitations of the reform is
sympathetically but critically differentiated from two
widely accepted alternative theories, those of
dependency and the non-capitalist way. Neither of
these theories is wrong in any absolute sense. Rather
each was useful for interpreting the Algerian social
formation in an earlier period, but is now inadequate.
The interpretation offered here is an attempt to
encompass and go beyond these earlier theories based on
evidence from the most recent period.[2]

HISTORICAL BACKDROP

In order to understand both the relative autonomy
of the Algerian state structure from domination by a
single class and the array of class forces which have
affected the state's developmental programming, it is
necessary to explain the transformation that took place
in the colonial era and in the immediate
post-independence era. Just how influential was the
"self-managed farm" workers' movement? Just how
prevalent were private commercial family farms in
general and capitalist farms in particular before 1970?
Just how did this array of social forces condition the
particular form taken by the "agrarian revolution" of
the 1970s?[3]

In several ways, the history of Algerian
agriculture up to 1960 substantiates the interpretation
of dependency theory.[4] Algerian agriculture was not
"underdeveloped" before the beginnings of French
penetration in 1830. Indeed, in the typical year,
surpluses of agricultural output were produced. These
were distributed by peasant producers through local
markets to non-agricultural producers such as
handicraftsmen. They were also distributed to a
traditional non-producing ruling class through the
tax-and-transfer mechanisms of the archaic state (under
the official suzereinty of the Ottoman Empire).

After 1830, as European political control was
extended and colonial capitalism implanted,
underdevelopment of the indigenous socio-economic
system gradually appeared and a subordinate dependency
of the colony on the French metropole was established.
Pre-colonial units such as villages, tribes, and guilds
were dismantled and their political and cultural

expressions degraded. Economic organization was altered to suit the needs of French capitalism: a European settler colony was established on 2.7 million hectares of the best lands, which were converted to the production of market crops for export, mainly wheat, wine, and dates. Only some of the former inhabitants of these lands were able to claim a share of the new system either through the purchase of land held now as alienable private property or through the favors of a colonial government seeking to win over a few strategic native allies. The majority of the population left in agriculture became either wage laborers on European estates or an impoverished peasantry squeezed into poorer quality reservation lands.

However, within the stringent constraints laid down by the European monopoly over the best lands and the means of production, important dimensions of socio-economic differentiation emerged within the native Algerian community. In the urban sphere a new set of privileged strata appeared, namely "businessmen, exporters of farm produce, brokers, wholesale and retail grain and tobacco dealers, oil manufacturers, landlords and innkeepers...land] intellectuals [such as] professors and teachers, Islamic judges, lawyers and interpreters", in other words, small but new classes which were both engendered and constrained by the colonial apparatus.[5] Furthermore, by 1954, a million-member non-agricultural wage-earning class had also materialized, about equally divided between those who were employed in Algeria and those who had migrated to France. The latter retained economic, social and political links to their homeland.

More directly significant for our purposes was the emergence of commercial agriculture among native Algerian farmers, including both simple commodity producers and a significant capitalist component. This development was stimulated by the growth of the home market for commercialized agricultural produce, such as wheat, as both wage labor on European farms and the non-agricultural classes mentioned above expanded. The 1920s in particular witnessed a burst of this type of transformation. By 1954, 60 percent of all native Algerian agricultural produce was marketed and there were 25,000 native farm owners holding more than 50 hectares each.[6] In some areas for which we have documentation, the class of capitalist farmers was very modern and very rich indeed.[7] The novel aspect of this line of reasoning, which goes beyond dependency theory, is that colonialism engendered not only rentier and feudal-like landlords and an impoverished subsistence agricultural sector, but also the capitalist/wage-labor relation in agriculture in company with rural markets in agricultural land, means of production, and labor.

The war of national liberation had contradictory effects on this array of class forces. On the one hand, the fortunes and misfortunes of war enhanced the rural class differentiation process, exacerbating differences in amounts of land held, in opportunities for investment and employment, and in income levels.[8] On the other hand, the National Liberation Front (FLN) the sole organization for the anti-colonial struggle, was an umbrella under which all class forces were gathered and which encompassed all political tendencies (except outright collaboration with the French). This included not only political parties, all illegal under colonial rule, but also the well-organized and powerful trade union federation which was under socialist influence. The balance among these forces was delicately maintained during the war by the FLN's failure to specify what its post-independence economic program might be, although several conferences in-exile were held to address that issue.

At the time of independence in 1962, economic disorder, due to the disruptions of the war itself and the mass European departures, was accompanied by political disorder as the suppressed conflict among the various social forces erupted into direct confrontation. Armed groups of peasant guerrillas, who had done most of the fighting against the French army within the boundaries of the country, still controlled parts of the countryside in an <u>ad hoc</u>, decentralized manner. On the other hand, the Army of National Liberation (created by the FLN and provisioned by sympathetic external forces) had been confined by the French army to the regions of Morocco and Tunisia adjacent to Algeria's borders. At independence, this well-armed military force, tightly organized under the authority of career officers, such as Houari Boumedienne, marched in to take command and impose order. The presence of the army made it possible for the Provisional Revolutionary Government (whose leaders, such as Ahmed Ben Bella, had been either in exile or imprisoned by the French) to create a new state apparatus and to fill its offices with civil servants who had served in the former colonial bureaucracy. Union militants within the FLN, as well as disgruntled guerrillas, immediately raised fierce objections to what they saw as a concentration of power and privilege in the hands of a potential new ruling class of army officers and state bureaucrats stepping into the still-warm shoes of the former colonial masters.[9]

In agriculture, as opposed to the situation in the state bureaucracy and the army, the union militants and guerrillas soon found a base from which to continue their struggle. As the European- held estates were

vacated, the wage workers formerly employed on them
stayed on to continue planting and harvesting crops.
Since there were no managers remaining to direct the
work, and economic chaos threatened the country as a
whole, these workers simply managed themselves. First
on an <u>ad hoc</u> basis, then on a larger scale and more
systematically via the leadership of the trade union
federation, this experiment became elevated to a
nation-wide movement. Algerian workers'
self-management was lauded both within Algeria itself
and internationally as the special form that Algerian
Socialism would take. It was then officially if
belatedly embraced by Ben Bella, now head of state, and
Boumedienne, the top army officer, as well.

The social formation that took shape in Algeria in
the 1960s, then, was an expression of the uneasy
balance that had been established among these various
social forces. Gradually the army and state apparatus
asserted more authority over both the political
structure and the economy. The last guerrilla
rebellion was suppressed by the army in 1967, and by
1969 all independent political parties and special
organizations (the trade union federation, the youth
and women's groups, the peasant associations) were
brought under the control of the FLN.

In agriculture, the national bank and the ministry
of agriculture were able to assert more and more
influence over the "self-managed" farms, which were
expected to conform uncomplainingly to the central
planners' assignments. Self-management did not die an
easy death, for the workers on the self-managed farms
retained a strong sense of organization among
themselves, a sense which they shared with the growing
working class segments in industry and services.
However, they could not prevent the encroachment of
bureaucracy on the economic operation of their
production units; thus the material base of their
political strength was eroded.[10]

In the private sector of agriculture, on the other
hand, the state did close to nothing through 1970. In
one sense this was benign neglect: the classes of
commercial family farmers and capitalist farmers were
left untouched by Algerian "socialism", despite vague
intermittent rumblings about land reform. In another
sense, the neglect was truly negligent in so far as the
state did little to encourage new investment.
Inconsistent credit, marketing and input-provision
policies led to confusion and to the withholding of new
investment. Perhaps most discouraging to farmers, the
internal terms of trade were allowed to turn against
agriculture, and average agricultural income fell
relative to urban income.

To understand how this state of affairs came to

pass, it is necessary to sketch the features that
distinguish the Algerian social formation, "state
capitalism," the economic development program pursued
in this era under state capitalist institutions, and
the role assigned to agriculture. The timing and shape
of the "agrarian revolution" can then be seen in
relief.

NATURE OF STATE CAPITALISM

Independent Algeria as it evolved in the 1960s fit
neatly into neither the pure "capitalist" nor the pure
"socialist" model of development. Yet the pattern it
manifested seems to be representative of a trend among
Third World countries at certain periods in their
histories. Comparable Middle Eastern cases are Turkey
from 1930 to 1950 and from 1960 to 1980,[11] and Egypt
from 1954 to 1970.[12]

Under "state capitalism", the state nationalizes
natural resources and asserts public ownership over the
major means of production. The state takes an active
role in directing the economy, through central
planning, investment in infrastructure (transportation,
communications, and utilities), and even direct
investment in manufacturing. It uses its control over
resources and credit to influence the decisions of
private enterprises in those arenas where it does not
actively invest in public enterprises, usually light
industry, services, and agricultural production. It
promotes social, educational and welfare policies that
aim to redistribute the population and modernize the
labor force. It may attempt to affect income
distribution as well, through wage policy and through
public subsidies for certain consumer goods. It may
also promote structural change in agriculture through
agrarian reform.

On the other hand, private enterprise remains
important in manufacturing, services and agriculture,[13]
and, indeed, may find new scope for growth in response
to the changed demands emanating from the state-run
sector for inputs, subcontracting of parts of the
production process, and distribution. Private firms
also constitute important markets for the output of
state enterprises. Market forces remain powerful in
governing these relationships, and are encouraged by
them as more complex forward and backward linkages
among sectors and industries develop. Furthermore, the
aim for all enterprises, public and private,
industrial, agricultural, financial and commercial, is
to maximize profit. The enterprises compete among
themselves to do so. The state does construct
multi-year central plans to guide economic development,

even administering prices to control the allocation of
resources. Yet, under the broad constraints set by the
central plan, economic activity is effected through
markets and individual enterprises are free to adjust
their employment of resources and labor, and their
offer of output, as they judge best to maximize
profit.[14]

Private enterprise in the form of international
corporations retains and even enhances its influence in
state capitalist countries. Although natural resources
are nationalized, the state contracts with foreign
firms to help develop, process and market them.
Although basic industry is publically owned and
operated, the state contracts with foreign firms to
build factories, train labor and management, and import
needed raw materials, capital goods and technology.
Foreign firms thus make high (and guaranteed) profits
and become indispensable to the fulfillment of the
state capitalist development program.

Algeria's leaders literally believe that "state
capitalism" (Boumedienne's own phrase) is the path to
Arab Socialism.[15] This opinion is shared by the leaders
of other Arab countries such as Iraq and Libya, who see
Algeria's path to development as a model for other
Third World countries to emulate, and by Soviet
theoreticians of the "non-capitalist way" (see footnote
2 above.) Algeria's leaders became influential and
vocal advocates of the Third World countries' interests
in international bodies such as the United Nations and
producer cartels such as OPEC, and in the debates over
the New International Economic Order.

The theory of the non-capitalist way is partly
correct, especially for Algeria in the 1960s, in that
the balance of class forces did not favor a clearly
pro-capitalist direction. This can be seen by contrast
with a comparable country such as Morocco, in which
pro-capitalist forces were undeniably in control of the
state and economic policy from the time of
independence. Many Algerian policies, such as the
adoption of the "self-management" movement, the
nationalization of resources and basic industry, and
the construction of multi-year central plans, were what
anyone would logically expect of a young "socialist"
government.

However, the theory of the non-capitalist way is
incorrect in so far as this pattern does not
necessarily lead to more socialization of the economy.
Although the working class is one important social
force that influences party and state decisions, it is
not the only one. In Algeria, a working-class-based
party has never come anywhere near attaining state
power. In fact, the only socialist opposition party
(the PAGS, mentioned in footnote 2 above) was declared

illegal in response to its criticism of the drift toward a more "free market" economic program after 1979. The course of recent Algerian economic history, like that of Turkey and Egypt before it, is for the balance ot class forces to shift in favor of a reduction in the role of the state in order to create more room for private enterprise. This occurs as the achievements and limitations of the state capitalist program become apparent.

Theory of state capitalism

Many Third World countries like Algeria, former colonies seeking to catch up with the industrial capitalist countries, follow a development path which entails a crucial role for the state and public ownership, yet which fosters institutions such as pursuit of profit and hierarchical social relations that are typical of other, more obviously capitalist societies. State capitalism is a social formation which builds the foundation for the emergence of the capitalist mode of production.

Capitalism is a mode of production based on the exploitation of wage labor. In bare schematic form,[16] there are two fundamental classes under capitalism: all value[17] is produced by one class, wage workers, who themselves own no means of production, and who only have access to the means of subsistence they produce by being paid wages with which to purchase them in the market. However, wage workers produce more value than the equivalent of what is necessary merely to reproduce themselves and their children; they also produce surplus value. The second class in a capitalist mode of production, then, is the class of appropriators of surplus value, the capitalists or bourgeoisie. Because they own or control the means of production, and are ultimately in charge of the production process, the bourgeoisie have the legal right to take the entire output and sell it, keeping what income remains after they have paid wages and other costs. "Exploitation" is the right of this latter class to appropriate what others produce, and their power to decide what to do with that surplus product (either to invest it in new means of production or to consume it).

State capitalism is a social formation which promotes the development of capitalism. Whether the appropriators "own" the means of production directly or merely control them, or in what proportions the two are combined, depends on the specific historical circumstance of the particular society. In many Third World countries, a nascent, but weak, national bourgeoisie is engendered by colonialism, and takes charge of the state apparatus after independence. Because it is weak relative to the bourgeoisies of the advanced capitalist countries, because it lacks the initial capital in large enough volume to build private enterprise directly, and because it must contend with other class forces that oppose it domestically, this bourgeoisie uses the state's monopoly on political power and economic resources (a heritage of the national liberation struggle) to promote a state capitalist development program. In the process, it both builds the material forces of production (contrary to the expectations derived from dependency theory) and fosters a reordering of the pre-independence social structure into clearly distinguishable "modern" classes, the bourgeoisie and the proletariat (contrary to the expectations derived from the non-capitalist-way theory).

This explanation takes into account the material fact that it is very difficult for a socialist mode of production (as defined in footnote 2 above) to be built on an economically underdeveloped base. It is the historic mission of capitalism to develop the forces of production in the base first, but capitalist development is fraught with the contradictions of inequality, unemployment, and economic and social insecurity that are now pervasive in both the industrial capitalist and former colonial capitalist countries. Contrary to the view of dependency theory, state capitalism abets this process, and, objectively, moves a society at a more rapid pace than colonial capitalism did toward the conditions in which a socialist mode of production becomes a viable alternative.

The theory of the non-capitalist way correctly sees state capitalism's contribution to creating the potential for the emergence of socialism. However, contrary to the theory of the non-capitalist way, state capitalism does not resolve class conflicts; it raises class conflict to a higher level through the transformation of the class structure. Any movement toward socialism is then not the smooth and frictionless choice of policy planners, however "revolutionary" they claim to be. Rather, movement toward socialism, or away from it (as in the 1980s), reflects the changing balance among the conflicting class forces brought to fruition by state capitalist development.

ALGERIA'S DEVELOPMENT PROGRAM

Algeria's economic development program evolved on the basis of the state capitalist institutional framework. The specified long-run goal was economic independence, that is, to be an internally articulated, industrialized economy liberated from subordination to the West European and other capitalist economies. The strategy followed, based on the work of G. Destanne de Bernis,[18] was in effect one of "unbalanced growth". The importance of the availability of oil revenues to finance this program cannot be overstressed, for they allowed major investments to take place without a reduction in the average standard of living. Indeed, the standard of living for some segments of the population rose.

The strategy entailed massive public investment first and foremost in state-owned enterprises in those industries which were believed to stimulate further industrialization automatically. These industries were iron metallurgy and other mineral processing, mechanical engineering, production of organic and inorganic chemicals, and of course hydrocarbon processing. Their transformation was then expected to serve as a transmission belt for new technology, to produce new capital goods, to process raw materials for use in other industries, and to raise productivity in other industries.

This policy then involved a deliberate decision to ignore the development of light industries and to put off the production of consumer goods. The development of these was considered to be of secondary importance and was expected to be taken up after the first stage was in full operation. It also involved a deliberate choice not to invest in agriculture in this stage, with the expectation that the stimulus from industrial development would induce the appropriate responses: farmers (both "self-managed" and private) would raise output to feed the burgeoning urban workforce and to supply raw materials to industry, and would increase productivity so as to free up "surplus" agricultural labor to shift to industrial and service jobs. These same farmers would also serve as a growing domestic market for those industrial products, such as tractors, threshers, fertilizer and irrigation pumps, that industry was to produce.

This strategy downplayed the negative aspects of the plan, and overestimated the planners' ability to deal with problems as they arose. First, there were the social problems. The unevenness of employment was ignored, and little planning for the distribution of the labor force or for equality in income-earning was considered. As growth engendered more inequality, this

problem grew worse over time. Furthermore, tensions
arose in the urban areas as some incomes rose, but the
supply of food and consumer goods did not rise in
tandem. Pressures grew to release the restrictions on
imports (which had favored heavy industry over light
industry and foodstuffs), and food imports in
particular began to rise rapidly.

Second, there were the problems in the basic
industrialization process itself. Indigenous
technologies never appeared. Instead, capital goods,
technology, technical personnel, and even whole
unassembled factories were imported from abroad.
Foreign firms made high profits fulfilling construction
and engineering contracts with the Algerian government.
The continued reliance on imports of capital goods,
plus the growth of food imports, led to increased
reliance on export of hydrocarbons to obtain foreign
exchange. This entailed a gamble that both world
demand for and prices of oil and gas would remain high.
Furthermore, as the new heavy industries began to come
on line, it was discovered that many, such as
petrochemicals and steel, could be economically viable
only if part of their output were exported. Yet
world-wide overcapacity was emerging by the 1970s.
Huge sunk costs could not necessarily be recovered, and
that meant that further investment was inhibited.

Third, problems in agriculture were exacerbated.
Due to the lack of investment and the fact that the
internal terms of trade were held against agriculture
throughout the 1960s, production in basic crops
stagnated. Only the uncontrolled products, like market
garden vegetables and poultry, responded well to the
growth in urban demand reflected in rising prices.

These problems began to become manifest by 1970.
It is in this crisis-prone context that the Agrarian
Revolution of 1971-78 should be seen. It was intended
to promote a set of institutional changes that would
force agriculture to respond in the manner necessary
for accumulation in industry to proceed and for the
development program to move ahead.

AGENDA FOR AGRARIAN REFORM

To bring the agricultural sector more into harmony
with the needs of the state's overall transformation
strategy, the "agrarian revolution" and agricultural
policy in general were assigned a complex agenda, with
hidden as well as explicit components.[19]

The explicit agenda included, first, the goal of
providing for national self-sufficiency in the
production of basic foods like cereals, fruits and
vegetables, poultry, dairy and meat products. This was

seen not only as a problem of quantity, but also as one
of diversification of agricultural produce, and as one
of provision of raw materials to food-processing
industries.

The beneficiaries of the reform and peasants in
the remaining private sector were to be reorganized
into production cooperatives, using technical processes
that were to raise land and labor productivity and
contribute to the growth of aggregate agricultural
output. This was necessary in order to feed the
growing urban labor force and to provide inputs to
industry, both at low prices. Aggregate agricultural
income was expected to rise nonetheless.

The hidden element here was the unstated but
essential requirement that Algerian agriculture become
fully commercialized. All peasants and cooperative
members would turn over all of their produce to be
marketed, and they would then purchase all of their
other needs out of their money income. This would
contribute to increased demand for industrial products,
both consumer goods and inputs to agriculture such as
fertilizer. Fertilizer provides a prime example
because it is a product of the petrochemical industry,
itself a spin-off of hydrocarbon production and
refining. It shows how inter-industry and
inter-sectoral linkages would be reinforced.

A second component of the explicit agenda was the
expropriation of "lands despoiled by colonization" and
their redistribution to landless and landpoor peasants.
This was to entail an end to "exploitation" of
sharecroppers and renters by absentee landlords, and,
thus, a reduction in inequality among segments of the
rural population.

There were two implicit elements in this part of
the agenda, which derive from the way in which
expropriable properties and exploitation were defined.
One was the de facto securing of non-absentee private
ownership of land and other means of production.
Commercial family farms and resident capitalist farms
were exempt from the reform. The other was the de
facto enhancement of wage-labor employment both in the
rural areas, and, more important for the overall
development program, in urban industry and services.
Surplus labor was to be effectively transferred from
underemployment in rural agriculture into more
productive sectors.

The body of the work that follows evaluates the
process and results of the pursuit of these various
agenda items during the agrarian reform of the 1970s.
In the final chapter, we return to the overarching
question of how the agrarian reform, and state policy
toward agriculture in general, illuminate the nature of
state capitalism as a social formation.

NOTES

1. World Bank, <u>World Development Report</u>, 1984, pp. 221, 223, 259, 263, 267. "Real GDP" refers to Gross Domestic Product, the total value of all goods and services produced in the economy in one year, corrected for inflation. The infant mortality rate fell from 165 in 1960 to 111 in 1982, still high by world standards. Life expectancy at birth was 57 years in 1982, and the daily calorie supply was only 89 percent of requirement, both figures still low by world standards. The number enrolled in primary school was 94 percent of the appropriate age group in 1981, up from 46 percent in 1960.

2. A comprehensive statement of dependency theory is Samir Amin, <u>Unequal Development</u> (New York: Monthly Review Press, 1976). Examples of work on the Middle East from this perspective are Samir Amin, <u>The Maghreb in the Modern World</u> (Baltimore MD: Penguin Books, 1970); Mahmoud Hussein, <u>Class Conflict in Egypt, 1945-1970</u> (New York: Monthly Review Press, 1973); Caglar Keyder, <u>The Definition of a Peripheral Economy: Turkey 1923-1929</u> (New York: Cambridge University Press, 1981); and Berch Bergeroglu, <u>Turkey in Crisis: from State Capitalism to Neo-Colonialism</u> (London: Zed Press, 1982).

Dependency theory views underdevelopment in Third World countries as the corollary to development in First World countries. The success of the latter was achieved by extracting surplus from the Third World, thus impoverishing it, and transferring the surplus back to be invested in the First World. "Surplus" applies to surplus product (the exploitation of Third World agriculture and natural resources) and to surplus labor (the payment of very low wages to obtain superhigh profits). This process does not end when direct colonialism ends, but is perpetuated through neo-colonialism and the continued integration of independent Third World countries on unequal terms into the international division of labor. The development of autonomous capitalism, that is, of a true national bourgeoisie,and of internally articulated economies in Third World countries, is impossible. The only route to real development is through socialism and severing the ties to the international market system, on the model of China in the 1950s and 1960s. In this view, Algeria does not have a socialist mode of production, but is still a dependent capitalist social formation.

The theory of the non-capitalist way, as laid out by Soviet development economists, is exemplified by: Yuri Popov, <u>The Developing Countries from the Standpoint of Marxist Political Economy</u> (Moscow: Novosti Press Agency Publishing House, 1977); Igor

L. Andreyev, The Non-Capitalist Way, Soviet Experience and the Liberated Countries (Moscow: Progress Publishers, 1977); and Vasily Solodovnikov and Victor Bogoslovsky, Non-Capitalist Development, An Historical Outline (Moscow: Progress Publishers, 1975).

The application of the theory directly to Algeria's case is exemplified by Ahmed Benabdelkrim, "Agrarian Revolution in Algeria," World Marxist Review 19 (October 1976): pp. 118-126. Benabdelkrim was a member of the Parti Avant-Garde Socialiste (PAGS), a loyal-opposition party that was allowed to operate legally in the 1970s. According to Jacob M. Landau, "Some Soviet Works on Algeria," Middle East Studies 17, 3 (July 1981), pp. 408-412, there are now works in Russian confirming the proposition that the non-capitalist road is leading to socialism in Algeria, by V. F. Volyanskiy and A. M. Traskunova (1976) and by Yu V. Potyomkin (1978).

In the theory of the non-capitalist way, some Third World countries do succeed in attaining true independence from the international capitalist system. In their political struggle for national liberation, a new leadership arises, a group of "revolutionary democrats", which aligns itself with the interests of the masses of peasants and workers. On taking state power, this leadership turns toward the Soviet bloc for trade and aid in order to ensure its independence from the capitalist countries. It promotes internal institutional changes that move the nation in a socialist direction, nationalizing natural resources and other sources of wealth, introducing central planning and state investment in infrastructure and industry, promoting agrarian reform and social welfare programs to benefit the masses, and shifting political institutions toward a workers' and peasants' democracy. In this view, Algeria is taking the non-capitalist road and will eventually have a fully socialist mode of production.

The differences among the theories of dependency, the non-capitalist way and state capitalism are explained in more detail in Karen Pfeifer, "Three Worlds or Three Worldviews? State Capitalism and Development," MERIP Reports No. 78 (June, 1979), pp. 3-11, 26.

3. These analyses are offered in detail, with synopses of case histories, in a forthcoming work: Karen Pfeifer, "The History of Algerian Agriculture, 1830-1970," in Paul Uselding (ed.), Research in Economic History, 11 (1986).

4. Amin, Unequal Development, for example p. 22. See also the chapters on Algeria in Amin, The Maghreb in the Modern World

5. Marnia Lazreg, The Emergence of Classes in

Algeria: A Study of Colonialism and Socio-Political Change (Boulder CO: Westview Press, 1976), p. 51.
6. Tami Tidafi, L'agriculture algérienne et ses perspectives de développement (Paris: Maspéro, 1969), pp. 146-147. See also Rezig Abdelouahab,"La reproduction du capital agraire au cours des années 1920"(Ph.D. dissertation, University of Algiers, 1977).

"Simple commodity producers" (or yeomen) are peasants who generally live and work on family farms, doing the labor themselves without systematically employing hired help, and who produce at least part of their output for sale on the market. They use the money proceeds to purchase other commodities they need but do not produce themselves. In Algeria, on average, a family could support itself using only its own labor on ten hectares of land.

"Capitalist farmers" (or gentry, sometimes also called kulaks or rich peasants) are also farmers who produce commodities for sale on the market. They differ from simple commodity producers in so far as they systematically employ wage labor and use their profits to invest in capital improvements on the farm, in the hope of being able to expand the size and success of their business. They generally hold more land than the farm family can work by itself.

7. For example, see Michael Launay, Les paysans algériens (Paris: Editions du Seuil, 1963), on the community of Ain Témouchent; Xavier Yacono, La colonisation des plaines du Chélif (Algiers: Imprimerie Imbert, 1955); and Hildebert Isnard, La reorganisation de la propriété rurale dans la Mitidja (Algiers: A. Joyeux, 1947).
8. Launay, Les paysans algériens, pp. 259-266, 396-402, provides some colorful examples.
9. Lazreg, Classes in Algeria, Chap 4. David Ottaway and Marina Ottaway, in Algeria, The Politics of a Socialist Revolution (Berkeley: University of California Press, 1970), devote an entire book to the political struggles of the immediate post-independence era.
10. These processes are described in Ian Clegg, Workers' Self-Management in Algeria (New York: Monthly Review Press, 1971); Lazreg, Classes in Algeria, Chapter 5; Tidafi, L'agriculture algérienne, pp. 89-111; and Keith Griffin, "Algerian Agriculture in Transition towards Socialism," Land Concentration and Rural Poverty (New York: Holmes and Meier Publishers, Inc. 1976), pp. 22-72.
11. See Bernard Lewis, The Emergence of Modern Turkey (London: Oxford University Press, 1968); Osman Okyar, "The Concept of Etatism," The Economic Journal, no. 297 (March 1965):98-111; Feroz Ahmed, "Military

Intervention and the Crisis in Turkey," MERIP Reports
No. 93 (January 1981):5-24; and Sevket Pamuk, "The
Political Economy of Industrialization in Turkey,"
MERIP Reports No. 93 (January 1981):26-32.

12. See Mahmoud Abdel-Fadil, Development, Income
Distribution, and Social Change in Rural Egypt
(1952-1970):A Study in the Political Economy of
Agrarian Transition (N.Y.: Cambridge University Press,
1975); and Mark N.Cooper, The Transformation of Egypt,
(Baltimore MD: The John Hopkins University Press,
1982).

13. The development of capitalism, of a private
capitalist class, and of "self-management" in industry
in Algeria will be touched on only tangentially here.
For fuller discussions, see: Georges Grandguillaume,
"Algeria," Commoners, Climbers and Notables, a Sampler
of Studies on Social Ranking in the Middle East, ed.
C. A. O. VanNieuwenhuijze (Leiden: E. J. Brill, 1977),
pp. 175-195; Lazreg, Classes in Algeria, especially
Chap. 5; Yusuf Sayigh, "Algeria," Economies of the
Arab World (New York: St. Martin's Press, 1978),
pp. 521-578.

14. The social consequence of this pattern of
economic organization may be the perpetuation of
inequality in employment and income distribution.
Overall unemployment remained high in Algeria: while
the rate of urban unemployment fell from 27 percent in
1966 to 8 percent in 1977, 75 percent of the rural
workforce were estimated to be underemployed and 18
percent fully unemployed. See Abdellatif Benachenhou,
L'exode rural en Algérie (Algiers, 1979), pp. 41-42,
and 53. Income distribution within the Algerian
community was more skewed by 1970 than it had been at
the time of independence (when the major distinction
between the European and Algerian communities held
sway), as Algerians moved up into the social ranks left
vacant by the departing Europeans and as economic
development proceeded. Evidence from the early 1970s
shows income shares to have been distributed unequally:
the top 30 percent of families received 74.5 percent of
national income, while the lower 70 percent received
only 35.5 percent. The top 9 percent alone received 38
percent of all income. See Revue algérienne du
travail, no. 13 (February 1974), as cited by Pierre
Jacquemot and Michel Nancy, "Chronique économique:
Algérie," Annuaire de l'Afrique du Nord, 1973 (Paris,
1974), p. 550.

15. For example, see Houari Boumédienne's
interview with the Egyptian magazine, Al-Ahram, as
quoted by the Foreign Broadcast Information Service
(Washington, D.C., 25 October 1974).

The philosophy of Algerian socialism is explained
in République Algérienne Démocratique et Populaire,

Front de Libération Nationale, La charte nationale (Algiers, 1976), pp. 9-10 and 21-31.

16. In any actual social formation where the capitalist mode of production prevails, other, "middle", classes exist (such as personal servants, civil servants, professionals, and the petty bourgeoisie, the latter producing commodities but without systematically exploiting wage labor). But the dynamics of these strata, while important, are secondary to the basic dynamic between capitalists and workers. In Third World social formations, other secondary classes such as poor and middle peasants, merchants and usurers may exist as well. The fate of these classes is one important question to ask about capitalist transformation.

17. "Value" is a measure of the output of the economy per some period of time, and can be expressed either in the labor hours required to produce it, counting both direct living labor and labor embodied in means of production, or in the monetary equivalent of those hours.

18. G. Destanne de Bernis' seminal work was L'Afrique, de l'independance politique a l'independance économique (Paris: Editions Maspéro, 1975). Its application in Algeria is treated by Abdurahman Hersi, Les mutations des structures agraires en Algérie depuis 1962 (Algiers: Office des Publications Universitaires, 1981), pp. 160-185; Aissa Bennamane, The Algerian Development Strategy and Employment Policy (Swansea, Wales: Centre for Development Studies, University of Wales, University College of Swansea, 1980).

19. The agenda for agriculture, state policy toward agriculture, and the fit of agriculture into the larger development program are expounded in Front de Libération Nationale, Charte nationale pp. 73-78 and 157-165, and Marc Ollivier, "Place de la révolution agraire dans la stratégie algérienne de développement," Annuaire de l'Afrique du Nord, 1975 (1976), pp. 91-114.

2
The Role of Algerian Agriculture in Economic Development, 1965–1980: Limitations and Contributions

Agriculture had been assigned a passive, supportive role in the state capitalist development program of the 1960s. With the institutional changes of the "agrarian revolution" of the 1970s, agriculture was expected to step forward and assume a more active, dynamic role. This chapter examines the situation in Algerian agriculture (in both the self-managed and private subsectors) in the period 1965–1971, with an eye to the specific features that led into the declaration of the agrarian reform and the creation of yet a third subsector.

A preliminary evaluation is then offered, first, of the evolution of the labor force and consumption and the demand for marketed agricultural output, and, second, of whether the three subsectors, separately and together, are moving toward meeting the growing production needs generated by that evolution in the 1970s.

SITUATION IN ALGERIAN AGRICULTURE, 1965–1971

In the 1965–1971 period, almost all of self-managed farm output and about 60 percent of private farm output was sold on the market. In 1968, approximately 25 percent of private farm units could be classified as "commercial" (that is, selling more than 70 percent of their output on the market), 44 percent were in "subsistence" (that is, selling less than 30 percent of their output on the market), and 31 percent were "in transition" (selling between 30 and 70 percent of their output on the market). The larger farms tended to use mechanical traction and wage labor more often and to sell more to the market. It appears therefore, that the commercial oriented farms must have been producing a disproportionately large share of total output.[1]

Raffinot and Jacquemot estimate that large-scale

private properties (over fifty hectares each) occupied three million hectares prior to the agrarian reform. Of this size category, at least one million hectares belonged to "modern" capitalist farmers engaging in productive investment and having returns comparable to those in the self-managed (former colonial) sector. This gave the capitalist class a strong but not overwhelming power base in agriculture prior to the reform. They argue (and some supporting evidence will be examined in Chapters 3 and 4) that this capitalist subset of large-scale properties remained intact after the reform.[2]

Further evidence of the extent of the capitalist sector can be seen in the distribution of wage workers in private agriculture, Table 2.1. First, the absolute number of permanent wage workers in private agriculture in 1968 was double the 47,000 reported for 1954,[3] a rapid pace of change. Second, there was a distinct tendency for both permanent and temporary, but especially permanent, wage labor to increase significantly as the size category of farm unit increased. In 1968, the average farm of one hundred

TABLE 2.1--Distribution of Wage Workers, by Size Category of Private Farm Unit, 1968

Size Category of Farm Unit	No. of Farm Units	No. of Permanent Workers	No. of Permanent Workers per Farm Unit	No. of Temporary Workers	No. of Temporary Workers per Farm Unit
0-<10 ha.	440,600	40,800	0.09	49,150	0.11
10-<50 ha.	89,300	30,500	0.34	51,300	0.57
50-<100 ha.	4,500	6,300	1.40	6,000	1.33
100 ha. and up	3,500	14,000	4.00	4,200	1.20
Landless	25,000	4,000	0.16	350	0.08
Not Determined	5,000	2,200	0.44	1,000	0.20
Total	567,900	97,800	0.17	112,000	0.20

SOURCE: Bourrinet, Travailleurs agricoles, p. 113 (adapted) based on Ministry of Labor data.

hectares and up employed four permanent workers.
However, Table 2.2 shows that in the same year (1968),
pre-capitalist tenures were still significant:
sharecropping and renting-in-kind occupied 14 percent
of the total land area.[4] Direct owner operation of
farms was highest on the fifty to two hundred hectare
farms, where we would expect to see capitalist
organization predominate due to the socio-economic
changes that occurred in the 1920s and during the
liberation war. Money-renting was most common on the
two-hundred-hectare-and-up farms, which may or may not
be capitalist depending on whether they were holdovers
from colonial grants to "traditional" landlords or were
absorbed into the modern sector in the 1920s or 1960s.

If it is correct that non-capitalist landlords
controlled about two-thirds of the land held as
large-scale properties (as Raffinot and Jacquemot
estimated above), and that as much as 60 percent of
that could have been organized on traditional
sharecropping and renting terms, then that would have
constituted a powerful constraint on the expansion of
the modern sector. Bourrinet argues that these
non-capitalist landlords preferred extensive
cultivation and indirect tenures because they did not
want to invest in agriculture. Neither they nor their

TABLE 2.2--Distribution of Agricultural Land, by Size Category of
Farm Unit and Method of Operation, 1968, in percent

Size Category of Farm Unit	Direct (owner or manager) Operation	Money-renting or Leasing	Renting-in-kind	Sharecropping	Total
< 5 ha.	76	11	11	2	100
5-< 50 ha.	66	19	11	4	100
50-< 200 ha.	79	10	8	3	100
200 ha. and up	40	47	. . .	13	100
Total	68	18	10	4	100

SOURCE: de Villers, Pouvoir politique, p. 294, based on
Ministry of Agriculture data.

tenants or sharecroppers could be sure that they would
individually reap the benefits accruing to improvements
on the land, because of the traditional crop-disbursal
arrangements. Therefore few improvements took place on
these properties.

A comparable set of constraints seems to have
existed on public agricultural lands rented out to
tenants of all types. While some of these tenants must
have been capitalist farmers (as the community studies
below illustrate), no estimates of their overall
relative strength are available. However, it has been
cogently argued that these lands were becoming
impoverished because the public land tenure system held
no one responsible for maintaining the quality of the
land. Furthermore, the myriad of very small-scale
holders were generally unable to save enough, or have
access to enough credit, to be able to invest in
improving the land as individuals, and the
fragmentation of their holdings meant that they could
rarely capture economies of scale.[5]

Overall, the capitalist agricultural system seems
to have had a strong but not yet overwhelming presence
in Algeria by 1970, as measured by the extent of its
share of the land, production, revenue and employment
of wage labor. Some sources of data minimize the size
of the capitalist sphere. For example, minimum
estimates of the use of advanced techniques are
provided by the Ministry of Agriculture survey of
1973.[6] The survey found that private farms owned 24,000
tractors and self-managed farms owned 23,000, but that
mechanical traction was used on 26 percent of private
farms (usually the largest, most extensive ones) and
fertilizer used on only 10 percent. Only 1.8 percent
of the private agricultural land was irrigated (usually
the smaller, most intensive units), and only 4 percent
was in permanent plantations such as orchards. The
private sector used only 15 percent of all fertilizer
applied in 1965, while the self-managed farms used 85
percent.[7]

Other sources of data show that the capitalist
sphere was not only present but also growing in the
post-independence years. Those farm units using
mechanical traction covered 55 percent of the total
cultivable land. Between 1968 and 1973, the number of
hectares under irrigation in the private sector
increased from 87,000 to 93,000, while 39,000 hectares
were added to fruit and vegetable plantations (an
increase of 15 to 20 percent) in the same five year
period. Production of market-garden crops, chicken and
egg farming and cattle raising all increased as well[8]
(see below for a fuller analysis).

A comparison of yields of various crops produced
by the private sector and the self-managed sector

provides confirming evidence that at least some parts of the private sector were fully modern. On the one hand, yields in private sector cereal production for the nation as a whole were generally much lower than in the former colonial sector, when one looks at averages alone. When the data are not broken down by size category of holding and controlled by method of production, the "average" obscures important variations. On the other hand, community studies, such as the ones done on Tlemcen and Beni Slimane cited below, do break the data down by size category and method of production. They consistently find cereal yields to be comparable between the medium and large commercial farms and the self-managed farms, with the small-scale subsistence farms showing very low yields. Furthermore, Table 2.3 illustrates that, even at the aggregate level, when one examines market crops alone (leaving out the hardy winter cereals that still serve as subsistence crops in the more remote areas), for example, summer cereals such as soft wheat, dry-farmed and irrigated vegetables, citrus fruits, and wine, yields in the private sector turn out to be generally comparable to, and sometimes better than, yields in the self-managed sector.[9]

Illustrative cases. For the regions of Tlemcen and Sidi-bel-Abbes, Prenant estimated that 20 to 25 percent of all private agricultural land was held by city dwellers (urban absentee landlords). While only

TABLE 2.3-Yields of Selected Crops, 1971-1972, by Sector

| | Quintals per hectare | | | |
| | 1971 | | 1972 | |
	Self-managed	Private	Self-managed	Private
Winter cereals	8.5	4.9	10.8	5.5
Summer cereals	8.3	7.0	11.3	8.5
Dry-farmed vegetables	5.2	6.8	4.1	5.3
Citrus fruit	115.4	95.8	120.7	97.8
Irrigated vegetables	61	58	61	65

| | Hectolitres per hectare | | | |
| | 1971 | | 1972 | |
	Self-managed	Private	Self-managed	Private
Wine	29	28	23	23

SOURCE: République Algérienne Démocratique et Populaire (R.A.D.P.), Ministère du Travail et des Affaires Sociales, Evolution des problèmes de l'emploi en Algérie (1976), Part II: 10-11; Raffinot and Jacquemot, Capitalisme d'état, p. 384.

10 percent of city dwellers held agricultural land, one-sixth of those held 75 percent of it, so this form of tenure was highly concentrated. This tiny class of landlords, he says at first, was appropriating 10 percent of the total agricultural output produced on private lands, and using it for conspicuous consumption rather than investment. However, he later rivets attention on an important subdivision both within this class and within the class of medium-sized landholders--a subdivision between traditional tenures and a set of capitalist units as we defined them in Chapter 1. The latter set had aggrandized their lands in the 1960s through purchase and usurpation of European lands and through leasing and foreclosure on other Algerians' lands. He observed that the smaller-scale marginal farms were being abandoned and rented out in the 1960s as their holders migrated seeking wage labor.[10]

TABLE 2.4 --Distribution of Property and of Revenue, by Type of Property, Tlemcen, 1967

	% of Properties	% of Land Area	Average Area (ha.)	% of Net Revenue of All Properties
Large-scale commercial farms	1	24	272	32
Large-scale traditional farms	2	27	160	22
Middle-sized farms	18	37	22	26
Small-scale commercial farms	30	8	2.7	18
Small-scale traditional farms	49	4	0.9	2
	100%	100%	. . .	100%
Total number in survey	917	9,938	. . .	3.1 mnDA

SOURCE: de Villers, Pouvoir politique, p. 304.

De Villers provides an estimate of the size of these various categories in a reworking of Prenant's data (see Table 2.4). While large-scale commercial and traditional farms each controlled about one-fourth of the land, the large-scale commercial farms had a larger average farm size and a much higher share of agricultural income. Middle-sized and small-scale commercial farms seem to have been doing well, in terms of the revenue they were earning relative to their landholdings, as compared to both the large-scale traditional farms and the small-scale traditional farms.

Another study of Tlemcen for the 1960s rigorously confirms the presence and expansion of commercial agriculture prior to the land reform. While large-scale commercial farms (what this study calls "the capitalist system") were only 12 percent of all farm units in this survey, they controlled 44 percent of the land area and produced 55 percent of the total output of the private sector, using intensive techniques and wage labor (61 percent of all work days) to produce cash crops such as vegetables, fruit, meat and dairy products. The smaller-scale commercial farms ("market system") had 39 percent of the farm units, controlled 31 percent of the land and produced 35 percent of the total output. This latter class could be graded among themselves, from more successful to less, and tended to be unstable, evolving up into the capitalist class or down into the subsistence and wage-labor class ("domestic system"). The poor peasants ("domestic system") were 49 percent of all units, held 25 percent of the land, and produced 10 percent of all output. Members of this last group all had to do wage labor in addition to working their farms in order to subsist.[11]

The same pattern was discovered in studies of Beni Slimane, Constantine, Oum el-Bouaghi and the Mitidja prior to the agrarian reform.[12]

IMPETUS FOR THE 1970s LAND REFORM

Overall, by the early 1970s, private commercial farmers found themselves in an increasingly uncomfortable situation, caught in a web of interrelated restraints. While they had been growing in terms of economic strength since before the war for independence, they found further expansion to be impeded not only by the continued importance of the pre-capitalist structures controlling land and labor in the countryside as described above, but also by state price and credit policies and by periodic labor shortages. We now turn to the latter two problems.

As part of the process of facilitating the rapid
development in industry in the late 1960s-early 1970s,
the state held prices of agricultural products down
while prices of inputs such as fertilizer rose. This
drove both the self-managed farms and private farmers
into debt.

Efforts were made to "decentralize" the
self-managed subsector after 1966 in order to induce
expansion of output: the farms were directed to
operate as autonomous units, making their own
purchasing and production decisions and distributing
profits between new investment and revenues to members
as they saw fit. Credit was made available to the
self-managed subsector in increasing amounts over the
1966-74 period to facilitate the new investment, as
displayed in Table 2.5.

However, between what many observers believed to
be the heavy hand of bureaucracy on the farms and the
unfavorable relative price structure of the period, the
efforts to stimulate new investment generally failed.
Net investment hovered near zero and self-managed farm
employees continued to hoard part of their output for
their own consumption and to refuse to increase work
effort. The ability to use the credit available was
rather limited, as the use rates in the last column of
Table 2.5 show.

After an initial spurt of credit aid to private
agriculture in 1965-1966, accompanied by deferments of
debt, exoneration from taxes, and provision of selected
seeds, the state suddenly reversed its practices.
Between 1966 and 1975, the BNA gradually decreased the
loans it granted to the private sector, on the argument
that private farmers were making too little use of the
funds available. This argument was accepted even
though a year-for-year comparison shows that the
private farms had use rates of credit comparable to,
and sometimes better than, the self-managed farms
(Table 2.6 versus Table 2.5), and even though the
credits had been granted mainly to low-risk, higher
income "peasants" having more than ten hectares of
land.

Observers contend that there were several
institutional constraints limiting the productive use
of credit by both sectors. For one thing, the BNA's
procedures often involved long delays and inappropriate
allocations to recipients who would then not be able to
use the grants. Another factor was that input prices
remained so high that, even with credit, few farms
could afford to buy them. Reported purchases of
tractors (wheeled and caterpillar) fell
precipitously.[14]

Not only were these two sets of factors, state
policies and pre-capitalist social relations, each

TABLE2.5 --National Bank Credits to and Used by Self-Managed Farms,
1966-1974

Year	BNA Credits (thousands DA) Awarded to the Self-managed Farms	BNA Credits (thousands DA) Used by the Self-managed Farms	% Used
1966	200,000	1,434	1
1967	236,499	9,694	4
1968	190,000	17,184	9
1969	252,607	113,182	45
1970	210,000	170,974	81
1971	315,000	228,315	72
1972	423,100	311,700	74
1973	485,000	105,031	27
1974	485,000	245,004	51

SOURCE: Karsenty, "Investissements dans l'agriculture," pp. 126-
127, 130-131 (adapted); Tidafi, Agriculture algérienne, pp. 125-126.

TABLE 2.6 --National Bank Credits to and Used by Private Farms,
1966-1973

Year	BNA Credits (thousands DA) Awarded to Private Farms	BNA Credits (thousands DA) Used by Private Farms	% Used
1966	120,000	84,974	74
1967	115,000	112,983	98
1968	118,000	109,965	93
1969	110,000	102,138	92
1970	90,000	54,015	60
1971	60,000	45,399	75
1972	40,000	22,526	56
1973	60,000	12,224	20

SOURCE: Karsenty, "Investissements dans l'agriculture," p. 138.

operating individually, but also they interacted to impede the further development of commercial agriculture. First, credits were not accompanied by training or technical help for the recipients, who, if they were embedded in archaic landlord/sharecropper social relations, would not be able to get that training or new technology for themselves. Second, the social relations between the landlords and sharecroppers and renters were such that neither would take the risk of using credit to finance improvements on the land, since benefits would have to be shared with the other party, while failure would be borne individually. The consequence was that frequently local notables would use the credits to purchase consumption goods or to purchase farm equipment to rent out to others (at exorbitant rates), rather than investing in improvements on their own farms.[15]

Furthermore, the expansion of the urban wage labor force, with a decline in the urban rate of unemployment (discussed below), and consequent periodic local labor shortages in the countryside (discussed in Chapters 3 and 4 below), had aroused the militancy of agricultural workers' demands for wage increases. This threatened to cut into the capitalist farmers' accumulation fund. Something had to be done which would, on the one hand, encourage increased mechanization and raise labor productivity, thus reducing the relative demand for wage labor, and, on the other hand, increase the supply of wage labor.

Finally, it seemed to some observers[16] that the threat of land reform, announced in 1966 by Boumédienne but never executed, must have worried some commercial farmers. The very presence of the "self-managed" farm sector, the result of the last "land reform," constituted a continual reminder that private ownership of the land was not absolute.

All of these factors caused private commercial farmers to hold back on investment in new equipment and modern technology, and to reduce output. This slowed down the aggregate rate of growth in the agricultural sector. The consequence was that imports of food had to be increased every year in this period in order to feed the growing industrial workforce. But inflation in the food exporting countries was driving up the prices of food imports, putting upward pressure on the urban cost of living. The rising cost of the imports could only be covered by either wages directly (which meant wage increases to match inflation) or state subsidies for basic necessities like bread and cheese (which meant transfers from other budget categories). Either alternative ultimately implied a crimp in the rate of accumulation (a reduction in the aggregate surplus available for new investment) in the industrial sector.

In order to restore the rate of accumulation in both agriculture and industry, then, it became imperative that an agrarian reform of some sort be called into being which would address the constraints on agricultural production in fundamental ways.

TRENDS IN THE EVOLUTION OF THE LABOR FORCE AND CONSUMPTION

Table 2.7 compares the total population and the distribution of the labor force for the years 1966 and 1977, the period between these years being one of very rapid overall economic growth. While the Algerian population as a whole was growing at an astoundingly fast rate (3.2 percent per year), the urban portion was growing much faster than the rural portion, as the column "Ratio of 1977 to 1966" shows (1.8 versus 1.2 respectively). The non-agricultural labor force was growing faster than the agricultural (1.9 versus 1.2 respectively), and, within the non-agricultural category, the fastest growing sectors were industry (3.4), construction (4.3), transportation (2.2), and government (2.2). The highest growth (11.0), among university and technical students, was due to the attempt to compensate for the dearth of educational facilities available under the colonial regime.

Expressed as percentages, the non-agricultural labor force, 48.2 percent in 1966, had risen to 58.7 percent of the total labor force by 1977. Industrial workers, 4 percent in 1966, had risen to 9 percent of the total workforce by 1977. Table 2.8 shows the breakdown of the industrial workforce alone by type of industry. Noteworthy is the more rapid rise of heavy industries (hydrocarbons, steel) than of light consumer-goods industries (food processing, textiles and leather), but all at least doubled in the eleven years under consideration.

Furthermore, the expansion of the urban wage labor force, and the concomitant decline in the rate of urban unemployment, encouraged an increased militancy on the part of those workers employed, culminating in waves of strikes in the early and mid-1970s over the issues of wages and working conditions. There were over three hundred strikes in 1977, the most important among truckers and dockworkers.

The state responded to the growing importance of the urban wage-labor force, and to the pressure for wage increases, in several ways. First, it stopped making data on strikes and workdays lost due to strikes available to the public.[17]

Second, the state reversed the long-standing

TABLE 2.7--Population and Labor Force in Algeria, 1966 and 1977

	1966	1977	Ratio of 1977:1966
Total Population	12,420,000	17,660,000[a]	1.4
Abroad	600,000	800,000	1.3
Urban	3,900,000	7,060,000	1.8
Rural	7,920,000	9,800,000	1.2
Agricultural	5,700,000	7,150,000	1.3
Non-agricultural	2,220,000	2,750,000	1.2
Total labor force	2,450,000	3,740,000	1.5
Labor force in agriculture	1,270,000	1,545,000[c]	1.2
Males, 18-59 yrs.	970,000	1,245,000	1.3
Others	300,000	300,000	1.0
Full-time	450,000	570,000	1.3
State farm	180,000	190,000	1.05
Reform	. . .	100,000	. . .
Private	280,000	280,000	1.0
Part-time	820,000	975,000	1.2
Non-agricultural labor force	1,180,000	2,195,000	1.9
Industry	100,000	343,000	3.4
Construction	70,000	301,000	4.3
Transportation	50,000	109,000	2.2
Trade	190,000	282,000	1.5
Services	140,000	260,000	1.9
Handicrafts	40,000[b]	45,000	1.1
Government	180,000	390,000	2.2
Students (college)	10,000	110,000	11.0
Other active	120,000	180,000	1.5
Unemployed (non-agricultural)	320,000	175,000	0.55
(as % of non-agric.)	(27%)	(8%)	

SOURCE: World Bank, Memorandum on the Economic Situation and Prospects of Algeria (1978), Tables 1-1, 1-2, and 1-3.

[a]The United Nations Statistical Yearbook (1978), p. 893, cites an estimated total population of 17,910,000 in 1977.

[b]This figure is for 1973, not 1966.

[c]Chaulet, Bilan, pp. 44-45, estimates the total active agricultural workforce at 2.26 million, because she counts the work of women and other "family helpers" in the private sector, groups not included in the official counts.

liberal policy for emigration of Algerian workers to France.[18] In the mid-1970s, remittances from these emigre workers averaged 200 million dinars a year; while this represented a welcome infusion of foreign exchange, it also provoked an infusion of demand for goods and services by the recipients of the remittances without contributing to increased production.

Third, the state allowed wages to rise somewhat in order to redress the inequality in income distribution among wage workers. In 1977, a 30 percent increase in the minimum wage was legislated for industry, services and agriculture, and smaller increases were allowed for wage-income categories already above the minimum. However, as civil servants, medical personnel and professors also got 30 percent or higher increases, the marked distinction between wage and salary income shares was retained.[19]

This growing body of non-agricultural workers expecting increases in their standard of consumption constituted the "home market" for the cash crops produced by Algerian farmers, and for the wage goods produced by Algerian light industries. Indeed, total private household consumption grew 57 percent between 1970 and 1976 (in constant 1969 prices), an annual compound rate of increase of about 7.8 percent.[20]

TABLE 2.8 --Employment in Industry, Algeria, 1966 and 1977

	1966	1977	Ratio of 1977:1966
Industry	99,276	342,730	3.4
Food processing	19,850	50,520	2.5
Textiles & leather	12,813	59,570	4.6
Steel	3,553	22,000	6.2
Mechanical & electrical	14,859	53,480	3.6
Chemical & petrochemical	6,545	23,600	3.6
Miscellaneous	12,739	26,280	2.1
Construction materials	7,490	24,430	3.3
Hydrocarbons, refining	6,863	47,000	6.8
Energy	5,032	13,500	2.7
Mining & quarrying	9,532	22,350	2.3
Construction	70,000	301,200	4.3
Total	169,276	643,930	3.8

SOURCE: World Bank, Prospects of Algeria, Table 1-4 (adapted).

TABLE 2.9--Aggregate Agricultural Production, Algeria, 1962-1981,
by Product (in 1000s of quintals, unless otherwise
indicated)

| Product | 4-Year Averages | | |
	1962-1965	1966-1969	1970-1973
Cereals			
Hardy wheat	10,846	8,286	8,296
Soft wheat	3,007	3,603	5,619
Barley	5,408	3,684	4,903
Oats	296	201	469
Dry legumes	373[a]	378	421
Market garden crops			
Potatoes	2,103[b]	2,166	2,758[c]
Tomatoes	990[b]	822	994
Melons	1,386[b]	1,626	1,733
Onions, carrots, greenbeans and other	1,020[b]	1,492	2,003
Industrial Crops			
Canning tomatoes	–	–	423
Sugarbeets	77[b]	579	561
Fruit			
Citrus	4,363[a]	4,313	5,144
Dates	1,100[a]	1,450	1,318
Figs	816[a]	417	663[f]
Olives	196	183	1,528[f]
Other tree fruits	385	337	697
Table grapes	247[b]	275	369[c]
Wine (1000s hectolitres)	12,339	7,982	7,401
Animals (1000s head)			
Cattle	553[a]	795	892
Sheep	4,502[a]	7,012	8,288
Goats	1,587[a]	2,291	2,467
Horses	110[a]	129	143
Donkeys & mules	380[a]	487	539
Camels	171[a]	175	174

SOURCES: République Algérienne Démocratique et Populaire
(R.A.D.P.), Direction des Statistiques, Annuaire statistique de
l'Algérie, 1970, p. 91 (for 1962-1969), Algeria in Numbers, 1972,
pp. 38-39 (for 1970), Tableaux de l'économie algérienne, 1973,
pp. 131-141 (for 1971-1972), Annuaire statistique de l'Algérie,
1975, pp. 161-162 (for 1973-1974), Annuaire statistique de
l'Algérie, 1976, pp. 133, 134, 191, 192 (for 1974-1975),
L'Algérie en quelques chiffres, 1977, p. 8 (for 1976), L'Algerie
en quelques chiffres, 1977, p. 8 (for 1976), L'Algérie en
quelques chiffres, 1978, p. 12 (for 1977); L'Algérie en quelques
chiffres, 1982, pp. 10-11 (for 1978-1981).
[a]1963-1965   [b]1964-1965   [c]1970 and 1973
[d]1974-1975   [e]1978-1980   [f]1971-1973

TABLE 2.9--Continued

| 4-Year Averages | | Ratio:<u>1978-1981</u> |
1974-1977	1978-1981	1962-1965
8,552	8,156	.75
4,937	4,801	1.60
4,808	6,896	1.28
670	872	2.95
666	457	1.23
4,837	5,632	2.68
1,177	1,426	1.44
1,899	2,136	1.54
2,251[d]	4,407[e]	4.32
701	1,210	-
578	630	8.18
5,101	4,104	.94
1,509	2,013	1.83
817	780[e]	.96
1,769	1,580	8.06
1,124	1,069	2.78
493[d]	629	2.55
4,233	2,774[e]	.22
1,014	1,323	2.39
9,524	13,111	2.91
2,344	2,763	1.74
148	173	1.57
641	716	1.88
152	150	.88

Food purchases represented 55 percent of urban private consumption and 61 percent of rural private consumption in 1973.[21] The volume of marketed cereals (both public and private spheres) tripled in ten years, from 8.7 million quintals in 1963 to 27 million quintals in 1973. National consumption of _processed_ wheat flours (farina and semolina), which must pass through the marketing network, increased from 9.13 quintals per year in the 1963-69 period to 13.74 million quintals per year in the 1970-73 period.[22]

Whether this indicates a rise in the standard of consumption, or merely a shift in the proportion of marketed relative to unmarketed foodstuffs, is not clear. Mokrane seems to think it is the latter. Karsenty, arguing for the former, provides these estimates of total (marketed plus unmarketed) consumption for the comparable time period.[23]

	1964 total (tons)	Increases in Consumption: 1963-65 per head per year (kg)	1974 total (tons)	1972-74 per head per year (kg)
cereals	1,840,000	184.6	2,970,000	194.1
legumes	35,000	3.2	65,000	4.3
fruits	515,000	33.4	754,000	49.3
vegetables	504,000	37.3	778,900	50.9
meats	67,000	6.3	100,000	6.5

PRODUCTION TRENDS

Evolution of aggregate production

Table 2.9 shows the long-term trends in physical production of all significant crops and in numbers of animals held by all sectors in Algeria, including both marketed and subsistence production. Only the most profitable market crops show a growth pattern equal to or surpassing the rates of increase of the population as a whole (40 percent between 1966 and 1977) and of the labor force (50 percent for the whole labor force, 90 percent for the non-agricultural labor force). There is a decline in hardy wheat, the basic "subsistence" cereal. Soft wheat, a more profitable market crop, had a better showing: in 1978-1981, it was 60 percent higher than in 1962-1965. Barley, dry legumes, tomatoes and melons all presented respectable growth, but, like soft wheat, at rates too low to keep up with growing demand.

TABLE 2.10--Production of Processed Agricultural Products,
        Algeria, 1969-1981

	1969-1971	1975	1979	1980	1981
meat production					
(1000s m. tons)	73	84	97	108	111
wheat flour					
(1000s m. tons)	430	662	1,418	1,565	NA
sugar (1000s m. tons)	5	18	15	15	15
cigarettes (millions)	6,063	10,559	14,000	15,150	NA
cotton fabric					
(million sq. metres)	44	49	59	61	NA
milk (1000 m. tons)	504	667	783	813	836
eggs (1000 m. tons)	12.5	15.5	18.6	19.1	19.7

SOURCE: United Nations, Statistical Office, Statistical
Yearbook, 1981, pp. 532, 535, 624, 641, 651, 653.

Other crops grew at much faster rates: oats (used
as fodder for the growing herds of meat-providing
animals), potatoes and other market garden vegetables,
dates, tree fruits, and table grapes. The crops
showing the most dramatic growth patterns were canning
tomatoes (which will be important in our case studies
in Chapter 4), olives for oil as well as for eating
directly, and sugarbeets, all critical inputs for the
food processing industries. The decline in wine
production reflected the conversion of the vineyards to
other types of crop production. The two surprises were
the declines in citrus and fig production, which might
be expected to be as attractive to profit-oriented
producers as the other fruits. Cattle have increased
by two and one-half times in the eighteen year span,
and sheep have almost tripled, while goats, horses, and
donkeys and mules have just kept pace with population
growth, and camels have fallen far behind.
    The point is that subsistence crops and animals
have declined or barely kept up with the growth in
demand,while the more profitable fruits and vegetables
and animals have grown strongly in response to that
demand.[24] The agricultural inputs to industry have
grown in the same manner. Except for the basic human
food grains, then, Algerian agriculture does seem to
have responded to the call for increased production
sounded by the state development planners. This is
surely part of the explanation for the increased
production of processed food products such as milk (up
85 percent from 1970 to 1981), eggs (up 58 percent),
meat (up 52 percent), and sugar (up by a factor of
three). The growth in selected processed agricultural
products is presented in Table 2.10.

TABLE 2.1↓-Distribution of Total Registered Agricultural Land, Season 1976-1977, by Sector and Use (in hectares)

	Self-Managed Sector	(%)	Private Sector	(%)	Reform Sector	(%)	Total All Sectors
Perenially worked lands							
Herbaceous crops	1,099,640	(33)	1,707,010	(52)	486,130	(15)	3,292,780
Fallow lands	651,820	(18)	2,479,820	(69)	459,290	(13)	3,590,930
Subtotal	1,751,460	(25)	4,186,830	(61)	945,420	(14)	6,883,710
Permanent Cultures							
Grasslands	7,750	(38)	10,050	(50)	2,500	(12)	20,300
Vineyards	183,780	(80)	34,940	(15)	9,800	(4)	228,520
Fruit tree orchards	121,370	(30)	240,400	(59)	47,880	(12)	409,650
Subtotal	312,900	(48)	285,390	(43)	60,180	(9)	658,470
Total agriculturally useful land	2,064,360	(27)	4,472,220	(59)	1,005,600	(13)	7,542,180
Grazing lands	233,940	(0.7)	31,018,760	(98)	361,450	(1)	31,614,150
Unproductive lands	65,460	(17)	268,710	(71)	45,870	(12)	380,040
Total all lands	2,363,760	(6)	35,759,690	(90)	1,412,920	(4)	39,536,370

SOURCE: R.A.D.P., Direction des Statistiques, L'Algérie en quelques chiffres, (1978), p. 13

However, the growth of domestic agricultural output has by no means been sufficient to supply all the needs of Algeria's processing industries. Cattle, raw sugar, dry milk powder, tobacco, cotton, wool, wood, and, most important, wheat are all imported to be processed in Algerian factories. Some products, such as butter and cheese, are produced in Algeria only in very small quantities, so that domestic demand is met almost entirely by imports.

While there seems to have been important growth in some particular areas of agricultural production, then the demand for marketed foodstuffs has grown faster.[25] The consequence has been that imports of food and other agricultural products have risen, both in absolute terms and in terms of percentage of total imports (See Appendix A). The average index of food production per capita in 1980-1982 was 75, as compared to a base of 100 in 1969-1971. Agricultural imports rose at the rate of 23.5 percent per year between 1969-1971 and 1978-1980, as compared to 10.8 percent for all merchandise imports. Agricultural imports as a percentage of imports were 21 percent in 1981 (as compared to 26 percent in 1960, 10 percent in 1970).[26]

Shares of the three sectors in agricultural production

If the agrarian reform is ultimately to get at least part credit for increasing the rate of agricultural production in the long run, it will not be primarily because of the size of the cooperative sector, since, as Tables 2.11 and 2.12 show, the cooperative sector holds no more than 15 percent of any type of land (it holds only 13 percent of total agriculturally useful land) and less than 2 percent of any type of animal. Tables 2.13 and 2.14 show that the cooperative sector produced only a small fraction of most crops in the 1976-1977 season (15 percent of cereals, 14 percent of legumes, 9 percent of market garden crops, 20 percent of industrial crops, 5 percent of citrus fruit, 7 percent of other fruit). In fact, the private sector remains the largest sector, both in terms of land area held and share of total crops produced (46 percent of cereals, 38 percent of legumes, 57 percent of market garden crops, 67 percent of tree crops, but only 20 percent of industrial crops and 9 percent of citrus fruit).[27] The private sector produced 88 percent of all meat, 84 percent of all milk, and 98 percent of all eggs produced domestically in 1975.[28]

Therefore, if the reform is to have a significant impact, it will have to be through the new institutions it created that affect all subsectors of agriculture, not just the reform production cooperatives. Chapters

TABLE 2.12--Animals Held, 1975, by Sector (in heads)

	Reform Sector, No.	(%)	Self-Managed Sector, No.	(%)	Private Sector, No.	(%)	Total
Cattle	2,460	(0.2)	70,280	(7)	929,690	(92.7)	1,002,430
Sheep	158,360	(1.6)	536,890	(5.4)	9,007,300	(92)	9,772,550
Goats	410	(0)	1,580	(0)	2,267,080	(100)	2,269,070
Horses	370	(0.2)	2,830	(2)	150,940	(98)	154,140
Mules	940	(0.5)	5,300	(2.7)	189,240	(96.8)	195,480
Camels	10	(0)	190	(0.1)	154,670	(99.9)	154,870
Donkeys	740	(0.2)	510	(0.1)	427,600	(99.7)	428,850

SOURCE: R.A.D.P., Direction des Statistiques, Annuaire statistique de l'Algérie, (1976), p. 192.

TABLE 2.13--Fodder Crop Production, 1975, by Sector (in quintals)

	Reform Sector No.	(%)	Self-Managed Sector No.	(%)	Private Sector No.	(%)	Total
Artificial	454,660	(8)	4,409,680	(75)	1,005,080	(17)	5,869,420
Natural grasses	38,660	(8)	209,300	(42)	254,660	(50)	502,620
Fallowed lands	72,540	(2.5)	384,420	(13)	1,921,330	(66.7)	2,880,910

SOURCE: R.A.D.P., Direction des Statistiques, Annuaire statistique de l'Algérie, (1976), p. 148.

TABLE 2.14—Production of Principal Crops, 1976-1977 Season, by Sector (unit: 1000s of quintaux)

Crop	Reform Sector, No.	(Percent)	Self-Managed Sector, No.	(Percent)	Private Sector, No.	(Percent)	Total
Cereals	1,671	15	4,486	39	5,268	46	11,425
Hard wheat	1,003	17	1,999	35	2,731	48	5,733
Soft wheat	326	13	1,591	63	621	24	2,538
Barley	258	10	600	23	1,745	67	2,603
Oats	81	16	255	51	161	32	497
Summer cereals	4	7	41	76	9	17	54
Dry legumes	89	14	312	48	245	38	646
Market garden including	930	9	3,503	34	5,911	57	10,344
Potatoes	428	9	1,799	38	2,495	53	4,722
Tomatoes	88	8	378	35	627	57	1,093
Melons	122	9	460	33	799	58	1,381
Industrial including	306	20	936	60	317	20	1,559
Tomatoes (canning)	140	18	357	47	265	35	762
Tobacco	2	8	10	42	12	50	24
Sugarbeets	. . .	0	562	93	40	7	602
Cotton	. . .	0	1	100	. . .	0	1
Citrus fruits	230	5	4,357	87	432	9	5,019
Tree fruits	308	7	1,103	26	2,814	67	4,225
Dates	166	14	99	8	910	78	1,175
Figs (fresh)	17	2	23	3	728	95	768
Olives	61	5	410	35	692	60	1,163
Wine (1000 Hl.)	106	4	2,171	85	272	11	2,549

SOURCE: R.A.D.P., Direction des Statistiques, L'Algérie en quelque chiffres, (1978), p. 12 (% calculated by me).

three and four examine the impact of the reform on the private subsector and in the new cooperative subsector. Chapter five returns to the question of state policies and institutional changes as they affect all subsectors.

NOTES

1. Jacques Bourrinet, Salaires et revenus des travailleurs agricoles en Tunisie et en Algérie (Geneva: International Labor Office, 1975), pp. 121-123.

2. Marc Raffinot and Pierre Jacquemot, Le capitalisme d'état algérien (Paris: Maspéro, 1977), pp. 314, 355-356.

3. Tami Tadafi, L'agriculture algérienne et ses perspectives de développement (Paris: Maspéro, 1969), pp. 146-147.

4. Some authors, for example, Marnia Lazreg, The Emergence of Classes in Algeria: A Study of Colonialism and Sociopolitical Change (Boulder, Colorado: Westview Press, 1976), pp. 61-62; and Gauthier de Villers, Pouvoir politique et question agraire en Algérie (Louvain, Switzerland: Université Catholique de Louvain: Institut des Sciences Politiques et Sociales, 1978), p. 43, argue that sharecropping was defunct for all practical purposes by the 1960s.

5. Bourrinet, Travilleurs agricoles, p. 128.

6. As quoted by Omar Bessaoud, "Le mouvement coopératif dans le processus de la révolution agraire en Algérie," (Master's thesis, University of Algiers, 1976), p. 129; and by Claudine Chaulet and anonymous others, "Bilan de la révolution agraire," (Algiers, 1979, mimeographed), p. 72.

These are minima because the survey was undertaken as part of the process of evaluating properties for total or partial expropriation under the land reform, a situation in which proprietors had every motivation to downplay the extent and value of their farms and the improvements they had made on them.

7. Tidafi, L'agriculture algérienne, p. 82.

8. Jean Claude Karsenty, "Les investissements dans l'agriculture algérienne," Annuaire de l'Afrique du Nord, 1975 (1976):141. See also Abdurrahman Hersi, Les mutations des structures agraires en Algérie depuis 1962, (Algiers:Office des Publications Universitaires, 1981).

9. For more discussion of this point, see Raffinot and Jacquemot, Capitalisme d'état, pp. 314-315.

10. André Prenant, "La propriété foncière des citadins dans les regions de Tlemcen et Sidi-bel-Abbès," Annales Algériennes de Géographie 3 (1967):2-94.

11. Association Algérienne pour la Recherche Démographique, Economique et Sociale (AARDES), Etude sur le secteur privé agricole, Wilaya de Tlemcen, 3 vols. (Algiers: Secretary of State for Planning, 1975), vol. 3:6-13, 78-94, 159-181, 219-241.

12. De Villers, Pouvoir politique; Centre Nationale de Recherche sur l'Economie et le Sociologie Rural (CNRESR), "Etude socio-économique de la zone de modernisation rurale de Beni Slimane" (Algiers, 1971); Centre Universitaire de Recherche, D'Etude, et de Réalisation (CURER), "La propriété foncière des habitants de Constantine" (Algiers: Organisme National de la Recherche Scientifique [ONRS], 1973); CURER, "Structures foncières et sous-emploi rural dans le secteur privé de la commune de Oum-el-Bouaghi" (Algiers: ONRS, 1974); and Georges Mutin, La Mitidja, décolonisation et espace géographique (Algiers: Office des Publications Universitaires, 1977).

13 Marc Ollivier, "La politique agraire de l'Algérie," (Ph.D. Dissertation, University of Grenoble, 1972), pp. 229-232; Mourad Boukella, "Le thème du dualisme dans la politique agraire en Algérie," (Master's Thesis, University of Algiers, 1976), p. 114; see also Raffinot and Jacquemot, Capitalisme d'état, p. 319.

14. The decline in tractor purchases can be seen thus:

Year	No. of Tractors Purchased in Private Sector
1962-1966	4400
1967	1830
1968	1733
1969	1271
1970	792
1971	62
1972	77
1973	18

Some of this fall in reported purchases may be due to the fear of the land reform. See Karsenty, "Investissements dans l'agriculture," pp. 123, 133.

15. Boukella, "Thème du dualisme," pp. 114-115. In 1969, the amount of money rent (which does not include a monetized value for payments in kind) paid by peasants to landlords equalled about 200 million dinars. See Ahmed Lotfi Boukhari, "Stratégie de développement et financement de la révolution agraire,"

(Master's Thesis, University of Algiers, 1976), pp. 58-62, 67-68.

This amount was almost twice the value of BNA credits awarded to private agriculture in that year. No one knows what proportion went to landlords' consumption as opposed to investment, but it is generally believed to be mostly for consumption (see Prenant, "Propriété des citadins" for example).

16. For example, Claudine Chaulet, Paule Fahme, Rachid Benattig, interviews held at Centre de Recherche en Economie Appliqué (CREA), Algiers, April-May 1979.

17. See the blank spaces starting in 1974 in the International Labor Organization, Yearbook of Labor Statistics (Geneva: 1979), p. 590.

18. In 1964, there were 500,000 Algerians living in France. By 1973, this had risen to 800,000. The official count for 1977 was 650,000, but other sources put it still at 800,000, because the government was able only to halt, not reverse, the migratory tide.

19. Michel Nancy, "Chronique économique: Algérie," Annuaire de L'Afrique du Nord (1977), p. 549.

20. These calculations are based on World Bank, Memorandum on the Economic Situation and Prospects of Algeria,1978, Tables 2-3, 2-4, and 9-1. The Greater-Algiers Consumer Price Index (base 1969) was used because no overall GDP deflator was available.

21. World Bank, Prospects of Algeria, Tables 9-2 and 9-3.

22. That would yield an annual per capita purchase of .77 quintals of marketed cereals in 1963, as compared to 1.74 quintals in 1973. Per capita average annual consumption of processed wheat flour was 83.9 kilograms in 1963-69 and 114.8 kilograms in 1970-73. Arab Si Mokrane, "Analyse des relations OAIC-SN SEMPAC" [Office Algérien Interprofessionel des Céréales - Société Nationale des Semolines, Pâtes Alimentaires et Couscous] (Master's Thesis, University of Algiers, 1977), pp. 20-23.

23. Jean Claude Karsenty, "La politique agricole algérienne," Maghreb/Machrek No. 77 (1976), p. 37.

24. An index of production for fodder crops shows them to have increased 259 percent between 1969 and 1975, an expansion which meets the demand for feed arising from the growing cattle and sheep herds. Furthermore, an index of production for poultry shows it to have risen by 216 percent between 1969 and 1975, an expansion which explains the rising production of eggs shown in Table 2.10. R.A.D.P., Direction des Statistiques, Annuaire statistique de l'Algérie (1976), p. 195. No absolute figures for fodder crops or poultry were available.

25. It is beyond the scope of this presentation to estimate the relative weights of all factors possibly

influencing this demand, factors such as population growth, the shift from subsistence to wage labor production, and a rise in average income.

26.World Bank, <u>World Development Report</u>, 1984, pp. 229, 235 and 239. See analysis by Kevin M. Cleaver, "The Agricultural Development Experience of Algeria, Morocco, and Tunisia" (Washington, D.C.: World Bank, <u>Staff Working Papers Number 552</u>, 1982), pp. 7-10.

27.The private sector tends to be more important for the domestic market, while the state farms produce more for export. All dates, half of fresh vegetables, and about a third of citrus fruit marketed in Algeria itself come from private agricultural production. Paule Fahme, "Mecanismes et portée des prix dans l'agriculture algérienne" (Master's Thesis, University of Algiers, 1976), pp. 120-129, 138.

28.R.A.D.P., Secrétariat d'état au plan, "Elements de synthèse sur les secteurs agricoles," <u>Balances regionales</u>, Document II, (1978), no pagination.

3
Change and Continuity in Rural Economic Organization Under the Reform

       The aim here is to delineate the impact of the agrarian reform as of 1978 on land tenure, the organization of the labor force, and the rural socio-economic structure on the level of the nation as a whole. The focus is on the second part of the reform agenda, in both its explicit and hidden aspects. The actual achievements of the reform will be matched against the goals set for it by the government, and an evaluation offered of just how "revolutionary" it turned out to be in the period 1971-1978.

       Interpreting the actual effects of the reform is complicated by several features specific to Algerian society. First, the national government announced that it was to be an "Algerian Socialist Agrarian Revolution," and that it was to "put an end to the exploitation of man by man." Many landowners felt threatened by this radical rhetoric and responded by resisting the land reform wherever they could. Some researchers who, like the landowners, took the rhetoric at face value (see note on method below), saw such resistance as evidence that the privileged classes allegedly attacked by the reform were able to deflect it, and argue that the reform was therefore a failure. The aim in this chapter is to argue the contrary, namely that a careful reading of both the terms of the reform and its actual effects shows that private property in land and other means of production and the capital/labor relation were carefully protected, and that this was built into the fabric of a "successful" reform all along.

       Second, Algeria has had a history of fierce social conflict around the issue of land tenure. There was, of course, the long colonial period in which the French armies forcibly took the land, crushed determined resistance from the native population, and redistributed the land to the Europeans and to a small group of privileged natives. But, more immediate, the self-management movement had begun in the agricultural

sector at the time of independence in 1962 as a
struggle between wage laborers and private capitalist
farmers over who would take possession of the abandoned
colonial land. The 1970s reform was treated by many
parties as a replay of that struggle, with self-managed
farmworkers and student and military volunteers helping
to organize the poor and landless peasants vis-a-vis
the private owners of land and the renters of public
land. In some regions, these coalitions posed a real
threat to the gentry farmers, who were genuinely
frightened that they would lose their land. These
rural bourgeois underestimated the ability of the
state, operating through the Ministry of Agriculture
(MARA) and the local popular assemblies (APCs), to
channel the reform in ways that would generally not
alter their power base. Indeed, the majority of lands
finally reorganized by the reform were public rather
than private, and among the latter, small-scale
absentee-held rather than directly-worked farms.

Third, in order for the reform to succeed even
within the narrow confines of dismantling
pre-capitalist tenures but not capitalist or
medium-sized commercial tenures, some gentry farmers
were bound to be individually affected, because of the
interrelation of these two types of tenures. For
example, those who leased public land or private land
belonging to absentee landlords, even if they worked
the lands directly themselves as commercial farms, lost
some lands to expropriation. That some of their
material base was eroded does not mean that the reform
failed to promote capitalist and medium commercial
farms. In any capitalist society, the role of the
state is not necessarily to protect individual
capitalists, but to maintain the system as a whole,
which may sometimes require the sacrifice of some
particular interests. Commercial farmers as a group
benefitted from the land reform, though some
individuals may have suffered from it.

Methodological note

Much of the information used in this chapter and
the next comes from published and unpublished studies
and interviews provided by Claudine Chaulet and her
colleagues at the Centre de Recherche en Economie
Appliquée (CREA) in Algiers.[1] Searches of the
literature on Algerian agriculture and their reputation
among scholars in France and the United States who do
work on Algeria, as well as in Algeria itself, confirm
that this is a singularly well-informed and reliable
group of people.
However, the perspective on the significance of

the land reform held by the CREA researchers is rather different from mine. They had believed in the socialist goals of the "agrarian revolution" of the 1970s, anticipating that it would finally remove the colonial-molded shackles on the small and poor peasants still excluded from Algeria's rapid modernization project. They were disappointed in the results provided by their own research projects, and thus tend to focus on the limits and failures of the reform relative to socialist aims.

The CREA researchers see Algeria as neither capitalist nor socialist but "etatist," a massive and inefficient bureaucratic morass, stagnating in the stranglehold of privileged civil servants and special interest groups with personal ties to the government, such as landholders, and becoming resubordinated to the international imperialist system. They do not think that Algeria is being transformed into a capitalist society.

GOALS AND METHODS OF THE LAND REFORM

One major task of the land reform as stated in the reform documents[2] was to capture as much land as possible from the "colonial" tenure structures. Land expropriation took place in two waves, beginning in 1972. In the first wave, all lands owned by public agencies and operated by leaseholders or sharecroppers were required to be turned over to the National Fund for the Agrarian Revolution. These included state-owned properties inherited from the French colonial government, land owned by the communes, tribal lands, and habous lands (owned by local religious orders in public trust). This was to finish the process undertaken by the former colonial government of abolishing all forms of traditional Muslim land tenure. In the second wave, the "property rights of those who do not directly and personally work their land" were to be abolished, through the full expropriation of all absentee owners and the partial expropriation of those who owned more land than they could directly work.[3] Sharecropping was legally abolished and all debts owed by croppers to landlords were cancelled.

A second task of the reform was then to reorganize the liberated lands and labor power into more productive forms. The land remained state property, but was distributed to the beneficiaries of the reform as individual plots (on average fourteen to twenty hectares of non-irrigated land) under a tenure of perpetual usufruct, which could be inherited by the beneficiaries' heirs, but which could not (in theory) be sold, leased or mortgaged. The beneficiaries were to have come mainly from the ranks of those already working the expropriated lands, former sharecroppers, poor peasants, and landless agricultural workers (veterans of the war of national liberation were to have next priority), and to have no income other than what they earned on that land. They were required in most cases to join state-organized cooperatives, and guaranteed a minimum annual income of 3,000 dinars (about U.S. $750 in 1973), equal to the lowest rung on the scale of full-time state farm workers' incomes.

The intrusion that this strategy of agrarian reform imposed on the private agricultural sector was restrained. Private property in land was specifically guaranteed and the right, nay the need, to employ wage labor was recognized and condoned. Considerable inequality continued to be allowed. While the cooperative member received an income of 3,000 dinars per year, the private holder was allowed as much land as would yield his immediate family a yearly income of up to 13,500 dinars, and he was not precluded from having as much income again from extra-agricultural sources, nor from using that income to employ wage labor or to accumulate other forms of property (such as livestock, machines, tools, buildings and transport) which were not subject to nationalization. Middle-sized properties were thus officially left intact, as was the possibility of unfettered capital accumulation.

Furthermore, even given the maximum possible fulfillment of the goals of the reform, the program proposed in the reform document could not possibly have provided a full allotment to more than a minority of poor peasants and agricultural workers. Of the economically active private agricultural population at the outset of the reform,[4] there were approximately 424,000 poor peasants with holdings of less than ten hectares (on average, the minimum necessary to support a family), and 500,000 landless agricultural workers, 924,000 in all supporting a population of more than five million. But the maximum number of hectares that could possibly be expropriated in both phases of the nationalization was about three million (much of which needed to be enriched before becoming agriculturally useful anyway). If, on average, it takes ten hectares to support a family, then only 300,000 peasants and workers could possibly have become full beneficiaries on the most favorable assumption. Therefore, the existence of wage labor in agriculture and the rural-to-urban migration flow could be expected to continue. Indeed, since sharecropping and renting had been eliminated, the remaining 600,000+ peasants and workers had their options narrowed further in the direction of wage labor, and the pace of the rural exodus would have accelerated.

LAND DISTRIBUTION AND REDISTRIBUTION

The agrarian reform was to be implemented in three phases. Phase One entailed the nationalization and partial redistribution of public lands, beginning in January 1972. Phase Two entailed the partial nationalization and redistribution of lands and palmgroves owned by absentees and large-scale proprietors, beginning in June 1973. Phase Three was to entail the nationalization of all public pasture lands, after June 1975.[5] The discussion here will be confined to the successes and limitations of the first two phases involving agricultural lands.

Phase one

There is some ambiguity concerning, first, the amount of usable agricultural land actually existing on the public holdings, and, second, the proportion of the usable land that was actually transferred to the beneficiaries of the reform. Before the reform, the public lands were generally leased and worked under the auspices of rich farmers, either in association with middle and poor peasants,[6] or through the employment of wage labor or sharecroppers. After the announcement of the reform, significant holdings that were locally known to be under the control of rich farmers were erased from the registry. But there are no numerical estimates of the extent of this phenomenon.[7] Second, since the reform, some beneficiaries have abandoned their lots and withdrawn from the cooperatives, so that the amount of land allotted has fluctuated.

As of January 1974, it was reported by the Ministry of Agriculture that three million hectares of potentially cultivable lands (of which 800,000 hectares were currently usable) had been turned over to the land fund from the public sector. An additional 3.5 million hectares of pasture and 1.5 million hectares of forests and grasslands were also added to the fund. However, only eighteen months later, the count had fallen to 1.6 million hectares of potentially cultivable lands (of which no more than 600,000 were currently usable), apparently because some influential leaseholders had pressured their communes into refusing to actually give up the land. By the end of 1975, approximately 303,127 palm trees on public lands had also been nationalized.

Between 700,000 and 800,000 hectares of land and 294,029 palm trees were awarded to the beneficiaries by the end of Phase One in 1975; about 75 percent of the land was usable for agriculture, and the remainder was to be made into usable agricultural land by the beneficiaries themselves (who were to live on a stipend from the state in the meantime.)[8] The fate of the more than one million hectares that disappeared from the fund is undetermined in national statistics. At least some of these lands can be located through unofficial surveys of local communities, as Chapter 4 shows.

Phase two

The complications surrounding the private land question are even more onerous than those of the public lands, but generally follow the same patterns. The problem of agricultural land simply disappearing from one census to another seems to be due to more than soil erosion.

As the comparison among the censuses of 1950, 1966, and 1973 shows (Table 3.1), lands disappeared every time a census was taken, from a total of 7.3 million hectares in 1950 to 4.8 million in 1966 to 4.4 million in 1973. The first census, taken by the French colonial authorities, showed that there existed 25,000 native Algerian ("Muslim") landowners having fifty hectares or more each, for a grand total of 2.8 million hectares. The latter two censuses were each taken after a land reform had been announced (it never materialized in the first case). In the greater-than-one-hundred-hectare category where the biggest decreases were registered from one census to the next, there was a decrease in land area of 901,895 hectares (53.4 percent) between 1950 and 1966, and a decrease of 3,844 units (45 percent); the average size of the disappeared unit was 234.6 hectares. For the same category between 1966 and 1973, the decrease in land area was 219,104 hectares, and the decrease in units was 1,216; the average size of the disappeared unit was 180.2 hectares. Furthermore, in the conversion from colonial to self-managed farms at the time of independence, another 400,000 hectares of land simply disappeared, reputedly into private hands,[9] without ever being counted into the statistics. These calculations suggest that large-scale properties were at least half undercounted in 1973 and that therefore half of them remained entirely outside the reform framework.

Concentration of holdings may actually be much higher than the distribution of working units allows one to see because of the peculiarities of Algerian tenure institutions. The tradition of "indivision" allows one large farm, under one farmer's control, to be officially registered as a set of parcels each belonging to a different family member. The traditions of "chorka" and "association" allow parcels belonging to several poor peasants to be officially registered in their names, when they are leased to or worked in common with a neighboring rich peasant or farmer, whose ownership of more land, farm animals and tools and machinery give him the role of boss. There is no way to trace out these patterns with the aggregate statistics available at the national level. However, the increase in units of less than ten hectares between 1966 and 1973 suggests that the use of these types of land registry might have aided the larger proprietors to avoid detection and expropriation during the reform.

TABLE 3.1--Distribution of Privately Held Land in Algeria, 1950, 1966 and 1973

Size of Farm Unit (ha.)	Number of Units	Percentage of Units	Land Area (ha.)	Percentage of Land Area
1950				
less than 10	438,483	69.5	1,378,400	18.8
10 to 50	167,170	26.5	3,185,800	43.3
50 to 100	16,580	2.6	1,096,100	14.9
more than 100	8,499	1.3	1,688,800	23.0
Total	630,732	100.0	7,349,100	100.0
1966				
less than 10	423,270	72.1	1,318,125	22.6
10 to 50	147,043	25.1	2,967,545	50.8
50 to 100	11,875	2.0	765,585	13.1
more than 100	4,655	0.8	786,905	13.5
Total	586,843	100.0	5,838,160	100.0
1973				
less than 10	578,888	79.2	1,640,870	29.6
10 to 50	138,528	19.0	2,619,503	47.2
50 to 100	10,007	1.4	654,794	11.8
more than 100	3,439	0.5	628,978	11.3
Total	730,862	100.0	5,544,145	100.0

SOURCES: R.A.D.P., Direction des Statistiques, Tableaux de l'économie algérienne, 1960, p. 129 (does not include colonial sector), and 1973, p. 123; Raffinot and Jacquemot, Capitalisme d'état, p. 313; and R.A.D.P., Ministère du Travail, Evolution des problèmes de l'emploi (1976), p. 6.

This suggestion is borne out by the community studies in Chapter 4.

Finally, as the richer farmers are more likely to have better quality lands and more control over other means of production, their socio-economic position is not a simple function of the number of hectares they control. The size category of land distribution on the national level is just one indication of the inequality prevalent in the private agricultural sector. There is also inequality in the distribution of other means of production, which were not touched at all by the reform.

Given the major qualification that much privately held land was counted incorrectly or not counted at all in the 1973 census, the agrarian reform was still carried out on the basis of this census. Two surveys were taken, in which all people owning property in land (agriculturally useful or not) were to declare their residence and the type and extent of their holdings. The first survey, done in 1972-73, was a sample of about half of all persons having some claim to land.[10] They were ascribed to four categories (listes): (1) The non-concerned, those whose directly-worked holdings were too small to be considered in the reform. (2) The absentees, those whose properties were to be expropriated in full. (3) The limitable ones, those whose properties were judged to be larger than they could work themselves.[11] And (4) those not affected (non-touchés), those absentees and large-scale proprietors whose properties were exempted from the reform. The distribution resulting from this sample, and its extrapolation to the national level, is presented in Table 3.2.[12]

Based on this initial survey, the potentially nationalizable private lands were estimated to be about 900,000 hectares. The potentially affected of all proprietors (categories 2 and 3) turned out to be only about 5.2 percent of all proprietors, holding about 20.5 percent of all registered lands. This is a far cry from the pre-independence estimate of 2.8 million hectares held by 25,000 proprietors of fifty hectares or more. Yet not all of even this small fraction was to be affected by the reform.

The actual lists used to carry out the reform were modified by the local authorities (elected officials of the popular assembly in each commune) in 1974-75 to suit local conditions as they surveyed them. On average, across the country as a whole, 13 percent of all proprietors disappeared in this second survey, an epidemic comparable in magnitude to the erosion of the properties themselves in earlier surveys, so that they were simply left outside the framework of the reform altogether. Those to be affected (absentees and

TABLE 3.2--Lists of Property Holders in Algeria, Pre-Reform
(Recensement général de l'agriculture, 1973)

Lists (Type of property holder)	No. of property holders	Percentage of Property holders	Land Area Held (ha.)	Percentage of Land Area	Avg. Size of Land Area (ha.)
1. Not concerned	809,441	69.52	1,274,494	15.90	1.57
2. Absentees	34,096	2.93	243,057	3.03	7.13
3. Limitables	25,904	2.22	1,398,033	17.45	53.97
4. Not affected	294,937	25.33	5,099,467	63.63	17.29
Total	1,164,378	100.00	8,015,051	100.00	6.88

SOURCE: Chaulet et al., "Bilan," pp. 16-17 (adapted). These figures are the Ministry of Agriculture's extrapolations to the national level based on the sample of half of property holders taken as part of the pre-reform survey.

limitable ones) decreased to just 3.36 percent of all property holders, reducing the potentially nationalizable lands (extrapolated to the country as a whole and weighted by region) to under 600,000 hectares. Those not affected, 25 percent of the original survey in 1973, and 20 percent of the communal assembly lists, continued to hold onto over 63 percent of all private lands.[13]

Aside from the false or missing land declarations, there were many ways in which proprietors and lands came to be categorized as non-concerned and unaffected. The number of "limitable ones" was restricted by a series of exemptions allowed by the APCs. First, if the proprietor declared a total yearly income of between 18,000 and 27,000 dinars (dependents included), only half of which came from his/her agricultural property, (s)he was allowed to keep that property regardless of size. Second, large-scale proprietors took advantage of the system of indivision to register lands in the names of family members. Third, large-scale proprietors who knew expropriation was to happen made donations to the land fund, thereby being better able to deflect criticism, disguise holdings and to keep the better plots for themselves. Fourth, the land was undervalued by hiding evidence of technical improvements (for example, wells were covered over in the truck-garden areas of El-Asnam and Bordj Menaiel). And finally, when all else failed, the proprietors made legal appeal for revocation of the nationalization decrees. By June 1975, five thousand such appeals were being heard nationwide. In the wilaya of Sétif, for example, out of ninety-four appeals, twenty-six decrees were annulled, returning 1,007 hectares to their original proprietors.

The number of absentees ensnared on the lists was reduced by equally ingenious devices. First, and simplest, was to declare residence on the land and then proceed as above to avoid becoming a limitable one. Second, exemptions were granted to the elderly (sixty years old and older), the invalid, miners, emigré workers, youth in the national service, and veterans of the war of national liberation and their descendents. As most families could come up with members in one or more of these categories, they registered their lands in those names.

By 1977, approximately 500,000 hectares and 649,770 palm trees had been nationalized from the private sector and redistributed to beneficiaries of the reform. That brought the total for the new cooperative sector up to about 800,000 palm trees (11 percent of all palm trees) and about 1.2 million hectares of land from both phases of the reform, of which around 900,000 hectares were agriculturally useful[14] (36,000 irrigated), giving the cooperative sector about 13.3 percent of the total registered agriculturally usable land in the country. All in all, by 1977 21,826 private proprietors had been affected by expropriation. However, most of those, 15,271, were wholly expropriated absentees, while only 5,205 were limited. But the average size of the absentee property on the lists was only 7.13 hectares, while that of the limitable property was 53.97 hectares. It appears therefore that most of the nationalized lands were owned by small-scale absentees holding down jobs elsewhere[15] and that most of the large-scale landholders escaped major expropriation.

The major thrust of the agrarian reform on the task of redistribution of land has had two prongs: the agrarian reform forced a reorganization on those public lands which it was able to wrest from the control of renters, and it made a dent in the private sector, mainly on those lands it captured from small-scale absentees. The scope of the "revolution" remains narrow, at least as measured by its small share of agricultural land registered. However, if one of the major blocks to expanded modern cultivation was located on low-productivity publically-held lands and small absentee-held properties, while other properties, both large and small-scale, were generally either capitalist or simple commodity producing farms by 1970, then the reform would have gone some distance toward freeing up the former without disturbing the latter. The hidden agenda of increased commercialization would have been served.

REORGANIZATION OF THE LABOR FORCE

As of July 1973, in response to the implementation of Phase One of the reform, 200,284 peasants and workers applied to become beneficiaries. Although many more qualified applicants were to file in the following years, some to replace initial beneficiaries who withdrew from their allotments, less than half of all applicants were awarded allotments in either phase of the reform.[16] At the end of 1974, the first two phases of the reform counted a maximum of 85,788 beneficiaries, distributed as shown in Table 3.3. After that, due to the phenomenon of desistement (withdrawal) from the reform and the difficulty of finding replacements for those who withdrew in the prime agricultural areas, the total number of beneficiaries declined to about 82,500 in 1976, of which 76,500 were organized in cooperatives.[17]

Table 3.3 shows that the average number of hectares per beneficiary is relatively low, barely

TABLE 3.3.--Beneficiaries of the "Agrarian Revolution," as of 12/31/74

	Total No. Beneficiaries	No. of Individual Beneficiaries	% of all Beneficiaries	No. of Beneficiaries Organized into Cooperatives	% of all Beneficiaries	No. of Cooperatives	Avg. No. of Beneficiaries per Cooperative	Land Area Total (ha.)	Avg. Land Area per Cooperative[a]
Phase 1	55,990	2,316	4.1	53,674	95.8	2,921	18.4	788,281	269
Phase 2	29,798	3,907	13.1	25,891	86.8	2,340	11.1	353,196	151
Total Both Phases	85,788	6,223	7.2	79,565	92.7	5,261	15.1	1,141,477	217

SOURCE: Abdi, "Réforme agraire en Algérie," p. 38 (adapted).

[a] Calculation divided total land area by number of cooperatives without subtracting land of individual beneficiaries.

enough to meet a family's minimum subsistence needs as generally estimated. The average number of hectares per beneficiary is 14.07 in Phase One, and 11.85 in Phase Two, although Phase Two lands are generally of better quality than Phase One. The proportion of individual beneficiaries rises from 4 percent in Phase One to 13 percent in Phase Two. As of March 1977 there were 9,814 individual beneficiaries, having a total of 44,653 hectares among them, of which the usable agricultural lands are 40,214 hectares.[18]

Even adding in the landless herders organized into cooperatives on state lands in Phase Three (who had received 3,837 rams and 102,770 ewes by 1976), the total employed directly in agricultural production in the reform sector came to only 110,000 persons, about 7.2 percent of the rural active masculine population. As many of those persons were already working, the impact on total unemployment was minimal. As Table 3.4 shows, there were still 940,000 landpoor and landless agricultural workers untouched by the reform in 1976.[19]

Subemployment was still rife in the countryside in 1978: while 72 percent of non-agricultural wage workers worked 200 or more days per year ("full-time"), only 47 percent of agricultural wage workers did so.

TABLE 3.4--Rural Occupational Structure, Algeria, 1976
(Active masculine population only)

Type of Worker	Private Sector	Public Sector	Total
Permanent			580,000
State-farm		190,000	
Cooperative		110,000	
Farmers having 5 ha.+	280,000		
Seasonal			940,000
Farmers having <5 ha.	310,000		
Landless peasants	630,000	(200,000)[a]	
Total	1,220,000	300,000	1,520,000

SOURCE: Marc Ollivier, "La place de la révolution agraire dans la stratégie algérienne de développement," Annuaire de l'Afrique du Nord, 1975 (1976), p. 109.

[a]These 200,000 seasonal workers in the public sector come from among the 310,000 landpoor and 630,000 landless peasants of the private sector. They are not counted twice in the total.

It is estimated that over half of landless peasants
were still relying on non-farm wage employment and
remittances from emigré family members in order to make
ends meet.[20] Others relied on seasonal wage employment
in agriculture, in all three sectors, including the
cooperatives of the agrarian reform. Ironically, while
there were many workers who could not find work, there
were also jobs that could not find workers: the
Secretary of State's Planning Office (SEP) estimated
that the reform sector alone generated 19,900,000
potential days of work in 1976, but only 10,900,000
were actually filled, due to labor shortages in Blida,
Tizi Ouzou, Algiers and Oran. Two million, two hundred
thousand of those days were filled in by temporary
employment of non-cooperative members, and the rest
went unfilled.[21]

The total agricultural population was about 8.2
million in 1980, with a continuing outmigration of
50,000 to 100,000 per year. The state-farm sector and
agrarian reform sector combined affected the lives of
two million people at most, so the other 6.2 million
faced little change in their situation unless they were
commercial farmers or could find employment in wage
labor elsewhere. If intensification and mechanization
increase in all three agricultural sectors, a smaller
proportion of the workforce will be necessary in
agriculture in the long run. Only an increase in land
reclamation, irrigation and reforestation projects and
in non-agricultural jobs will absorb the rural
unemployed. Far from stemming the migratory tide, the
reform closed off the traditional options of renting
and sharecropping of public and private lands, and
channelled the flow of labor directly into rural and
urban wage employment, and its corollary, unemployment.

POLITICS OF LOCAL ADMINISTRATION OF THE REFORM

The direction actually taken by the agrarian
reform is due in part to the manner in which it was
administered on the local level. The authorities
responsible for implementing the reform were generally
not workers and poor peasants, but rather the landed
proprietors, merchants and other entrepreneurs, and
state and party officials, who formed the backbone of
support for the national ruling class. While the
reform was not officially made in the name of this
class, they, in addition to the minority of peasants
who have received reform lands, have objectively been
the major beneficiaries of the reform because it has
consolidated both their material and their political
power base.

The organs through which this gentry operated were

the communal popular assembly (APC, the elected body that locally governs each of the <u>communes</u> or townships),[22] the national peasant union (UNPA), the service and marketing network (Coopératives Agricoles Polyvalentes de la Commercialisation et Service, CAPCS), and the local branches of the national bank (BNA) which controlled the pursestrings and managed the accounts of the production units of the reform as well as providing credit to the private sector. They were also influential in local religious structures. They retained political influence over the poor and middle peasants of their community through their ties to the state and party and through their direct economic power. Specifically, they still held much land, often the best quality in the village, still employed wage labor, still lent money, still possessed farm implements to let out, and still invested in real estate and wholesale trade (including the black market), in addition to commercial farming.

The large-scale landed proprietors had ample time to prepare for the agrarian revolution, as it had been threatened and postponed for six years. They parcelled out ownership of lands to relatives and placed them juridically under "indivision." Many held back on new investment in tractors and harvesters (or reported that they did); some even destroyed citrus groves and slaughtered animals, following the precedent set by the Europeans on their exit from Algeria in 1962.[23] Some local notables in the FLN dragged their feet in instituting the reform. Other notables agitated against it among the middle peasants, saying that it would abolish private property, which is allegedly contrary to Islamic Law, and that the drought of 1973 and the floods of 1974 were evidence of God's anger. They threatened the poor peasants by telling them that they, like the self-managed farm workers, would become nothing but employees of the state. The notables forcibly prevented some potential beneficiaries from signing up for the reform, or allowed them to sign up on the agreement that the notables would then purchase the titles and destroy them.[24]

The APCs and APCEs, local organs of the reform

In theory, the popular assembly of the commune (APC) had significant economic as well as political power: it controlled the local application of the national four-year plan, owned nationalized enterprises in its territory, and controlled public utilities and its own police force. It was also charged with the administration of the land reform, nationalizing and redistributing lands, choosing beneficiaries (including admitting new ones and expelling old ones from the production units) and organizing them and their lands into various types of production units based on local conditions.

In practice, the local APCs were supervised closely by the wilaya administration, the National Commission of the Agrarian Revolution (CNRA, appointed by the Ministry of Agriculture), and by the Ministry of Agriculture itself. The elected representatives were mainly middle-level proprietors, shopkeepers, rural intelligentsia such as schoolteachers, and civil servants.[25]

The original APCs were sluggish in carrying out the reform. At meetings called to explain the reform, for example, the educated assembly members would sometimes speak in classical Arabic, which poor and landless peasants could not understand, or they would disseminate information in writing to illiterate peasants. When they did expropriate lands, they allowed generous exceptions to be made. Those who were most severely expropriated ' were the small-scale absentees, who were not present to defend their properties. Those few large-scale absentees who were threatened with expropriation were often allowed to sell out, while potentially limitable proprietors were allowed to choose which lands to give up. Furthermore, when doling out the expropriated lands, the APCs managed to give about 20 percent of them to middle peasants, and failed to respect the official guidelines of two-thirds of the land to the landless and one-third to small peasants. When setting up cooperatives they would sometimes deliberately choose the least qualified and least reliable candidates among the poor and landless, so as to ensure control of the new units by the middle and rich peasants.[26]

Under pressure from militant workers and peasants, the central government used three tactics to discipline the landowners and APCs. First, volunteers from the army and the universities were sent in to enforce the provisions of the reform. This was the source of the student reports quoted at length in many evaluations of the reform. Student support was largely spontaneous at first. The government leaders then marshalled and organized the students to go out to the countryside to explain the reform to the peasants in simple language, to form the production units and teach the cooperative members how to keep accounts and do common work, and even to do a token amount of manual labor with missionary zeal (in conscious emulation of the role of "Red Guards" of the Great Proletarian Cultural Revolution in China in the 1960s). The students themselves had no power base independent of the state with which to impose the reform on the APCs. So the

state abetted them by renovating local FLN cadres to
eliminate corruption, disbanding some of the more
outrageous APCs, and taking control of the UNPA from
the biggest landed proprietors.[27]
   The second tactic used by the state authorities
was to create by decree an expanded local authority in
each township (assemblée populaire communale élargie,
APCE). This temporarily replaced the APC, in order to
specially administer the reform, give advice to
cooperative members and set up production units. On
the one hand, this democratized procedures somewhat:
it was to be supervised at the wilaya level, and
disputes about the reform were to be adjudicated there,
thus bypassing local notables. Representation in the
APCE was officially broader than in the APC. It had to
include local members of the party, veterans of the
war, and representatives of the national labor union,
the national women's union, the national peasant union,
and the national youth organization. On the other
hand, its powers were carefully limited: the APCE was
advised by a committee consisting of representatives of
the APC, MARA, the Minister of Finance, and the
Secretary of Hydraulics, and was responsible to the
wilaya assembly and the MARA. The presidents of the
APCEs were appointed by the presidents of the APCs.
Furthermore, the same persons who controlled the local
APCs also controlled the wilaya level assemblies, which
is ultimately the national ruling class. The wilaya
governments had the power to overrule the APCE
decisions concerning the land reform, to grant appeals
made by landowners, and to restrict the extent of land
nationalizations.[28]

The UNPA, alleged watchdog of the reform

   The third tactic used by the state was to create,
again by fiat, a national peasant union (UNPA), with
local branches in every commune. Within the UNPA, or
as criteria of admission, no distinctions were made
between rich and poor peasants or between employing
farmers and wage laborers. The original UNPA, up to
1973, left out landless peasants and small herders
altogether. Of the first 110,000 members in that early
period: 2 percent had more than 100 hectares each, 12
percent had 50 to 100 hectares, 30 percent had 25 to 50
hectares, and 56 percent had 2 to 25 hectares.[29]
   Reforms were instituted after 1973 which required
that the UNPA include beneficiaries of the reform,
landless peasants who live from their own labor and
proprietors and herders not touched by the land reform.
They also required that the UNPA be included in the
local government (APCE), the service cooperatives

62

(CAPCS) and the marketing cooperatives (COFEL, except
when it came to decisions on finances and cultivation
plans!). As of 1974, the broadened UNPA had 750,000
members.[30]

However, this democratizing reform also turned out
to be limited. As in other organizations, the FLN
nominates candidates for office, so that leaders of the
UNPA go only as far down in the social structure as
middle peasants. In fact, when a political coalition
of UNPA poor peasants, workers and students showed
signs of being able to take over new APCEs, the central
government again changed the election rules, this time
to reduce the UNPA representation.[31]

The CAPCS

The local service cooperative (CAPCS) was a direct
supervisor of the reform beneficiaries, making sure
that each one farmed his allotted lands, conformed to
the production requirements of the national plan, and
participated in public works projects. Officially, the
CAPCS was to provide an input-supply and marketing
network to the reform sector to supplant the private
network (see Appendix B for details). In practice, the
two networks operated side-by-side (as captured by the
name marchés parallèles for the private network). In
part this complementary relationship was due to the
extensive overlap of personnel between the two spheres;
in part it was due to the structural limitations of the
CAPCS institution.

As of March 1977, there were 654 CAPCS serving 703
communes. The designated tasks of the CAPCS were:
1. To own matériel for mechanized farming
operations (cultivation, soil processing, and
harvesting) and supply it at cost to the member
production units as needed
2. to supply other inputs such as organic and
chemical fertilizers, plant and animal medications,
seedlings, seeds and animal feeds
3. to provide repair facilities, spare parts,
workshops and extension services, small tools, training
and technology, storage and packaging facilities, and
accounting services
4. to provide credit (through a national bank
branch office in each CAPCS) in a decentralized way to
both the reform production units and the small private
farmers
5. to plan and coordinate, at the commune level,
the production of all the cooperative units in the
commune
6. to organize work on nationalized lands which
have either not been allotted or been abandoned[32]

7. to market the production units' output locally
(they are technically not allowed to do it themselves)
and to convey the surplus product to a state marketing
agency at the wilaya level (COFEL), and thence at the
national level (OFLA).[33]

The leadership of CAPCS, like that of the APC, was
officially democratically chosen. However, while the
president and executive board (conseil de gestion) were
locally elected, the technical director and accountant
were appointed by the Ministry of Agriculture. This
was the same dual structure that was also
institutionalized within the self-managed farms and the
reform production units; it ensured the close
supervision by unelected local representatives of the
national government. As the provision of technical aid
by CAPCS was a serious problem (see below), the
presence of these supervisors seemed to serve more for
political control. Membership in the executive board
of the CAPCS was distributed as in Table 3.5.
Representatives of self-managed farms and CAPAM,[34] 22
percent, were included because CAPCS was supposed to
replace the state marketing agency that had previously
served them directly. Beneficiaries of the reform were
a larger proportion (46 percent) than any other group.
The private sector was significantly represented (23
percent), but tended to be limited by the requirement
that private farmers who chose to join agree to
coordinate their production with the communal and
national plan.[35] Given that the UNPA was under the
influence of rich and middle peasants, and that members
of the last two categories in the table were basically

TABLE 3.5--Members of CAPCS Executive Boards, 1977

Number	%	Occupation or Affiliation
2,271	46	Beneficiaries of reform (cooperative members and individuals)
1,148	23	Private peasants and herders
1,107	22	Representatives of state farms
156	3	Employees of state and local agencies (COFEL, CACG, etc.)
136	3	Representatives of UNPA
135	3	Artisans, merchants, members of APC, teachers, administrators
Total 4,953	100	

SOURCE: R.A.D.P., Ministère d'Agriculture, Enquête sur les
coopératives, pp. 49-51.

a rural middle class of non-producers, 9 percent of
CAPCS executive board members could not have been said
to represent poor and landless peasants at all. This
plus the fact that MARA appointed the director and
accountant raises the question of whom the CAPCS really
served. Some researchers directly observed cases in
which CAPCS personnel used its facilities for their own
private gain.[36]

The CAPCS were not properly equipped to fully
supply inputs to and conduct marketing for the reform
sector alone; yet they were expected to do so for the
self-managed farm and private sectors as well. The
first CAPCS did not seriously begin operations until
September 1975, and faced severe structural limits on
their operations. First, the physical distance between
the CAPCS office in the commune and the actual
production units was often prohibitive. Second, the
CAPCS often had inadequate supplies of inputs,
insufficient transportation, inconvenient storage
facilities, and lack of packaging supplies.[37] Third,
they lacked trained personnel to advise on the
technical aspects of production and to keep accurate
accounts. Some of this was due to the dearth of
trained agronomists and some was due to the political
nature of appointments to CAPCS offices. There was a
strong tendency for the directors of both CAPCS and
COFEL to treat their agencies as autonomous economic
units, using their own internal rate of profit as an
index of which production units and private farmers to
service and which to neglect.[38]

All of these factors, plus outright corruption
(hoarding, kickbacks) on the part of some state agency
bureaucrats, encouraged both private farmers and reform
beneficiaries (the latter illegally) to use private
suppliers and wholesale dealers as an alternative to
CAPCS. Private wholesalers, who are themselves usually
rich peasants or landowners, were paying agricultural
producers slightly higher prices than the state
agencies, paid in cash (the state paid by check), and
in turn charged higher prices in the urban markets.
But they did not compete with the CAPCS-COFEL-OFLA
network so much as they complemented it. In fact, the
major achievement of the state agencies after 1974 was
to keep the prices of inputs down while agricultural
product prices rose, allowing a potential rise in
income to all three sectors of agricultural producers,
and an apparent drop in the rate of profit to private
wholesalers.[39]

The potential benefits to be secured from an
efficient public input-supply and marketing agency that
is chartered to service the private as well as the
state sector were evident to the private commercial
farmers. As the CAPCS developed further, they could

help to rationalize all sectors--in the sense of
encouraging the more efficient units and squeezing out
the less efficient through the mechanism of
competition. As long as all units are run on the same
principles of unit-profitability and capitalist social
relations of production, then all could be accomodated
under the CAPCS-COFEL-OFLA umbrella.

THE BNA AND THE CREDIT STREAM

The manner in which the land reform encouraged
competition among farmers was most explicit in the
provision of credit. The central banks set up a
"credit envelope" for each wilaya as part of the
financing of the national four-year plan. Medium-term
credit (for machinery and construction of buildings)
was administered by the National Bank of Algeria (BNA)
in each wilaya, while long-term credit (for major
public works) was administered by the Caisse Algérienne
de Développement. These monies went to the CAPCS which
was responsible for purchasing the equipment and
conducting the construction.[40]
Productive units (either state or private) could
apply directly to the BNA at the wilaya level for
credit to purchase their own equipment, independent of
CAPCS, if they chose. The criteria for granting such
credits were whether the equipment already in place was
being used efficiently (that is, profitably), the level
of outstanding debt (if old debts were not repaid, new
credits were not forthcoming), and the maximum
profitability to be expected from the unit in the
future--the BNA was reputed to complain woefully about
some segments of the private sector not being
profitably run. Otherwise, the production unit was
dependent on the credit and/or equipment allocation
decisions of the CAPCS in its region. The BNA levied
an annual rate of interest of 4.75 percent in 1973, and
the production cooperative's income from harvest sales
could be directly garnished as it passed through the
CAPCS, in order to repay debts to the bank. This was
facilitated in so far as accounts were kept by another
agency related to the bank, the Coopérative Agricole de
Gestion et Comptabilité (CACG), not by the units
themselves. The CACG was supposed eventually to train
the reform beneficiaries in how to keep accounts,
estimate costs and revenue and measure profit.[41]
The BNA also granted money for short-term loans
(that is for one growing season) to the CAPCS, which in
turn doled it out to production units. Each unit was
required to make a yearly plan of operation, including
a budget (for costs of equipment use, soil improvement,
inputs of seeds and fertilizer, and labor).[42]

Table 3.6 shows that the amount of credit made available through these means increased steadily from 1972 to 1975. While the amount of credit used rose pretty much in tandem, the utilization rates varied from 45 to 70 percent and only about 50 percent of the available credit was actually used on the average. The result was a slow but sure growth of means of production and of use of improved techniques (see Appendix B).

The president of the national bank, Abdelmalek Temam, viewed the fiscal discipline imposed by the bank's credit policies on the agricultural producers as a way of promoting increased efficiency. In an article congratulating the bank on its contribution to the development of Algerian agriculture since the reform, he said:

The purification in progress in the agricultural sector and the realization of the agrarian revolution will open a new era characterized by the autonomy of management, [fiscal] responsibility and economic sanctions.[43]

This type of market discipline may well encourage increased efficiency as profit-maximizing production units compete among themselves to get access to credit and to sell their output in order to pay back their debts and stay afloat. However, such a banking system encourages capitalist development because inequalities among units are by no means redressed through the allocation of credit--on the contrary, they are reinforced. Only those which can survive the competitive process of getting access to the credits

TABLE 3.6--National Bank Credit Allocations to Agriculture, 1972-1975 (in dinars)

Season	Short-term Credits	Medium-term Credits
1972-73	63,964,112	185,219,866
1973-74	130,068,308	328,655,893
1974-75	313,613,528	418,398,614

SOURCE: Chaulet et al., "Bilan," pp. 101 and 104 (based on national bank data (adapted).

NOTE: Other sources which break the data down differently but lead to the same conclusions are: Karsenty, "Investissements dans l'agriculture," pp. 136-137, and Boukhari, "Financement de la révolution agraire," p. 109.

and to the unevenly-provided CAPCS services can become
profitable. Units which are better-endowed to start
with, and can demonstrate to the national bank either a
history or a promise of profitability, have a better
chance to receive credits and thus to improve their
capital endowments further and to become yet more
profitable. These units are both tied to and dominated
by rich peasants in the private sector.

On the other hand, some units may be poorly
endowed to start with; they may be made up of small
peasants and former landless peasants and workers who
bring nothing but their own labor to the cooperative,
and who are at the sufferance of the APC and CAPCS to
provide them with means of production. Such units
operate under the same structural disadvantages as
their counterparts in the private sector. They wind up
in the same straits: they may be forced to turn to
hoarding and subsistence consumption (practices which
do not endear them to the agencies), and they may be
forced to take up wage labor in order to have an
adequate money income. The profit-maximizing criterion
of credit allocation contributes to class
differentiation in the cooperative sector just as in
the private sector.

FORMATION OF PRODUCTION COOPERATIVES

Almost 90 percent of all beneficiaries of the
reform were organized into production cooperatives. In
most cases the Ministry of Agriculture required this in
order to reorganize production on more rational lines
and thus raise output. The cooperatives were created
like the reform itself, by the local popular
assemblies, under the close supervision of the Ministry
of Agriculture. In the years up to 1975, the
cooperatives lacked both autonomy from the state and
internal coherence. The cooperatives' production was
designed to feed into the national plan,[44] and they had
very little input into the construction of that plan.
Their job was to compete among themselves to fulfill
their share of the planned production. Accounts were
kept by the national bank (BNA) and national accounting
agency (CACG) to prevent cheating on work time and
pilfering of product for home consumption. The
proceeds from the sale of output (both salary and
profits) were distributed by the daïra (county)
administrators under bank and accounting agency
supervision to each beneficiary individually.[45]

The choices of membership and of type of
cooperative were made by appointees from the popular
assemblies at the local and provincial levels (APCs and
APWs), not by the cooperative members themselves. The

APC retained the authority to admit new members and expel old ones from the cooperative unit. Five types of cooperatives were established by the reform planners.

First, with much fanfare, the coopérative agricole de production de la révolution agraire (CAPRA) was officially designed to be the "most advanced" form. While beneficiaries who already owned lands were allowed to keep them, each cooperative member was assigned his or her "own" plot of reform land; the lands were all to be worked as a unit with a common production plan, all labor in common, means of production held in common and finances calculated in common, with profits shared equally. This form was planned for those situations in which agricultural wage workers and former sharecroppers were used to doing social labor. As in the self-managed farm sector, the members were to elect their own president and executive board (conseil de gestion) from among themselves; but the Ministry of Agriculture was to appoint a technical director and supply an extension agent, while the national bank was to assign an accountant to audit the finances. As we shall see below, this unit came to function as a business farm.

Second, the coopérative agricole d'exploitation en commun (CAEC) was to be the next most advanced form, in situations where the former poor and landless peasants were believed to have neither the experience nor the social outlook that would allow full cooperative labor, and this form was to serve as a transition to educate them for CAPRA-style work. In the CAEC, the beneficiaries held their land separately and could work it separately if they wished, but would pool their labor for common tasks (at sowing time and harvest time) and rotate means of production, under a common plan, with state-provided technical and economic guidance. Profits would be taken individually, with the class of small independent peasants left intact.

Third, the groupement pré-coopérative de mise en valeur[46] (GMV) was also considered a transitional form to move people toward full CAPRA status. It was organized in situations where the land was of such poor quality that it could not be farmed, so the beneficiaries would work together to reclaim it under the direction of a state-appointed technician, and receive a monthly stipend from the state. Such groups also engaged in common herding and building of public works, for example, irrigation. In addition to the stipend, members were allowed to keep the proceeds from any crops grown on their individual land.

Fourth, the groupement d'entraide paysanne (GEP) was to be a mutual-aid organization among small holders, both beneficiaries of the reform and in the

private sector, with no obligations but to lend each
other labor at various times during the year. This was
designed to attract the small peasants to the potential
gains to be gotten from larger units of organization
and thus to move them to join the reform voluntarily
(that is, to donate their land and sign up as members
of a more advanced cooperative).[47]

Fifth, the groupement agricole indivisaire (GI)
was conceptually the same as the GEP, but for small
holders whose land was held in the traditional tenure
of indivision.

Very few small peasants in the private sector
voluntarily joined the cooperatives, even at the level
of the GEP and GI. Their lands were often of better
quality, even if smaller, than the reform lands, and
they preferred to hold onto them as long as they could
for whatever security they could provide. Although the
total money income of small peasants was often lower
than that of the reform beneficiaries, they had the
freedom to consume their own product instead of selling
it, which members of cooperatives did not legally have
the right to do, and they had the flexibility to move
into and out of wage labor as their needs changed.[48]

Table 3.7 shows the numbers and percentages of
these various forms at three points in time, during the
first blush of the reform in Phase One in mid-1973, and
its peak at end-1974, and the 1977 results after the
dust settled. Variations across wilayas seemed to be
based mainly on the nature of the local terrain and
agricultural possibilities, but the evolution over time
and within homogeneous eco-zones seemed to be due more
to social and political factors.[49]

The tiny fraction of cooperatives in the GEP and
GI categories (only 3.2 percent of all cooperatives,
grouping only 4 percent of all beneficiaries) was due
to failure of the reform to attract small and middle
peasants to voluntarily join it. These groups seemed
to have been left by the wayside in the progress of the
reform. This is not surprising in a reform that
favored the formation of larger, more productive and
more profitable units.

The relative decline of the transitional form,
CAEC (number 2 above), and the relative rise of the
fully developed form, CAPRA (number 1 above), seems
also to be due to this systematic bias, as four years
is hardly enough time for a majority of CAEC members to
have been re-educated to the virtues of the CAPRA
organization. On the one hand, some CAEC were
pressured by the Ministry of Agriculture to become
CAPRA quickly, because their members continued to
operate as independent peasants, refusing to do shared
work among themselves and refusing to raise marketable
output, consuming the increased product themselves.

TABLE 3.7--Formation of Cooperatives, 1973-1977

	CAPRA[a]		CAEC[b]		GMV[c]		GEP[d]		GI[e]		Total Coops.	Individual Allotments
	No.	(%)	No.	(%)	No.	(%)	No.	(%)	No.	(%)		
Phase 1												
7/31/73	1,391	(54)	825	(32)	398	(15)	...	...	...	...	2,614	1,120
12/31/74	1,748	(60)	601	(20)	572	(20)	...	...	...	...	2,921	2,316
Phase 2												
12/31/74	1,854	(79)	214	(9)	186	(8)	86	(4)	...	...	2,340	3,907
Total, both phases												
12/31/74	3,602	(68)	815	(15)	758	(14)	86	(2)	...	...	5,261	6,223
Total, both phases												
3/31/77	4,203	(72)	528	(9)	930	(16)	170	(3)	10	(.2)	5,841	9,814

SOURCES: Abdi, "Réforme agraire en Algérie," p. 39; R.A.D.P., Ministère d'Agriculture, Enquête sur les coopératives, pp. 13-14.

[a]CAPRA = Coopérative agricole de production de la révolution agraire.
[b]CAEC = Coopérative agricole d'exploitation en commun.
[c]GMV = Groupement pre-coopérative de mise en valeur.
[d]GEP = Groupement d'entraide paysanne.
[e]GI = Groupement agricole indivisaire.

These problems occurred in CAPRA too (see below), but could be handled by the authorities more effectively in that form of organization.

On the other hand, many CAEC, and even some CAPRA,[50] had to be converted to the land reclamation type of cooperative (number 3 above), because the lands they were assigned were of such low quality that they could not support their beneficiaries. Thus the percentage of cooperatives of this third form remained constant, instead of decreasing as originally forseen by the authorities.

THE COOPERATIVE UNIT AS A BUSINESS ENTERPRISE

Because of the politics of the administration of the reform, in particular because of the overrepresentation of the rich peasants and rural gentry in the APCs, most of the cooperatives established experienced structural problems and class conflicts that generated competitive pressures both within and among them. The consequence was that only some could succeed, a process which continually drove some members to abandon their assigned lands and seek wage employment.

Differentiation and class conflict within the cooperative

Persons from several distinct rural classes (wage workers, sharecroppers, landless peasants, small and middle peasants, and rich peasants), whose material interests are frequently directly opposed, were mixed together as beneficiaries in the production units. A sample survey[51] of 2,370 households of beneficiaries in 140 communes in the northern parts of the country found the following distribution of previous occupations among the beneficiaries:

Renters of land	26.5%
Permanent wage workers	26.1
Small peasants	17.2
Temporary wage workers	15.8
Other activities	8.2
Unemployed	5.0
Sharecroppers	1.1

What is striking about this distribution is the low percentage of sharecroppers and the unemployed: together they were only 6.1 percent of all beneficiaries, although they were officially the object of the reform. The "other activities" category, which means non-agricultural occupations such as government functionaries, commercial and service workers, was higher at 8 percent. Wage workers (permanent and temporary) were 41.9 percent, while small peasants accounted for only 17.2 percent and sharecroppers 1.1 percent. This shows the relative rise in importance of wage and salary employment and the ongoing decline of small-scale independent production prior to reform.

Renters (on public lands, since these data are for Phase One beneficiaries) were 26.5 percent. This is an ambiguous category because the data were not broken down by size category of holding, income level, possession of other means of production, or employment of wage labor. Yet other sources (such as Chaulet, et al., "Bilan,") suggest that significant class differentiation exists within this category.

Benattig and de Villers also analyzed the AARDES data on 41,109 beneficiaries taken in 1977 (including beneficiaries of both phases of the reform). They found that agricultural wage workers, sharecroppers or "no occupation" formed 32 percent of reform beneficiaries, while 25 percent came from non-agricultural wage workers. In addition, 18 percent were farmers and herders having less than five hectares before the reform, but 25 percent were farmers and herders having more than five hectares before the reform.[52]

Analysis of first hand empirical studies suggests that those production units which were succeeding best in developing collective discipline were the ones in which former wage workers, sharecroppers and landless peasants predominated. Presumably, their life and work experience doing social labor had prepared them well for it. Such units were constituted on former large-scale holdings, in extensive cerealculture in Sétif, Tiaret and Constantine, and in modern intensive truck farms in Alger, Tlemcen, Oran and El-Asnam.[53] These also happened to be situated on better quality lands in more economically developed regions. The effects were contradictory: it was here that the highest rates of withdrawal occurred, because the beneficiaries were most disillusioned over the direction taken by the reform--their class background and the political support of the self-managed farm workers had provided them with a higher degree of political consciousness. By the same token, because of their land endowments and better skills, it was also here that some reform units were most likely to succeed as business enterprises.

In those situations in which small and middle peasants predominated, usually in cases where the reform alloted lands to them that they had previously been renting, they resisted the CAPRA form of work discipline, held onto their own individual property, and maintained their ties to the large landowners through "association." They tried to appropriate collective equipment and pasture land for their private use, had a high rate of absenteeism, did not challenge the unit president or rich peasants' decisions, failed to fulfill cooperative obligations and continued to employ seasonal wage labor on their own lands.[54]

The rich peasants, who became reform beneficiaries because they had formerly been farmers, managers or renters of the nationalized public and private lands, tended to use the cooperative unit as a base to further their own interests. They continued to monopolize the best lands among those that were nationalized, using privately owned or rented means of production which were unavailable to fellow cooperative members (as machines and tools were not expropriated along with the land). While they continued to work alongside the former wage workers and sharecroppers whom they had supervised on the very same land in the pre-reform period, they were able to use their profits (earned from their own land, plus their share of cooperative revenues) to purchase more means of production and extend their commercial and processing operations. They often had significant incomes from extra-agricultural activity in the parallel markets, in renting out their means of production, or in selling meat and milk products from their private herds.[55]

The relative security of the rich and middle peasants enabled them to survive the initial lean years in the cooperative unit better than the poor peasants and workers. They also had more choice over whether to sell or consume their output, or simply to hold out for a better price.

The relative advantages of the richer peasants over the poorer were reinforced by the non-democratic, hierarchical social organization internal to most of the cooperatives. Most commonly, the president of the unit, who was required to be literate and have some education, was a farmer or rich peasant with outside contacts who tended to run the unit in an authoritarian manner. He and the members of the managing council often did no physical labor themselves, but directed the labor of the others. The division of labor within the unit was purely its own affair--the otherwise loquacious reform authorities offered no administrative guidance on this subject--so that it most often followed patterns existing in the pre-reform period. The technical director appointed by the Ministry of Agriculture was beholden to no one in the cooperative, as he reported directly back to the planning authorities at the wilaya level.[56]

Differentiation among the cooperatives

Differentiation among cooperatives, even within homogeneous eco-zones, was not due to differences of effort on the part of the beneficiaries in general, but rather to differences in initial endowments in location, land, personnel, and material, and to the uneveness of CAPCS services. These were all reflected in variable revenues among cooperatives, as measured in their rates of profit, the sole criterion of success. The state did nothing to redress these revenue variations, on the argument that failures were due to a lack of effort and seriousness of commitment by the beneficiaries.

The reform sector, like the private sector, was endowed with lands that, on the average, were of poorer quality and produced lower yields than the self-managed farms. Two-thirds of reform lands were in herbaceous cultivation, most of those in non-irrigated cereal production. Only 5 percent were in perennial cultivation (such as orchards), while the rest (about 29 percent) was either unproductive or in the process of being reclaimed.

Although the fourchette system of land allotment (lot size being determined by potential revenue) was supposed to minimize differences between and within cooperatives, some cooperatives were established "by mistake" by the APCs on unproductive lands, or where the use of mechanical means of production was not practical (for example, on steep slopes). Many of these units were bound to fail from the beginning, and could only save themselves by being converted from production to reclamation cooperatives (GMV). In other cases, the lands actually available were not equal to the official allotments, because proprietors did not vacate them and the local authorities failed to enforce the expropriation. Elsewhere, cooperative lands were fragmented, scattered, and lacked water entirely, because the previous owners were allowed to choose which parcels to give up. Cooperatives based on Phase One public lands often found their holdings to be the most overworked and eroded in the commune, with the least access to irrigation. Furthermore, often the beneficiaries found their land to be located at great distances from their residences, which made daily labor and cooperation impracticable.[57]

In addition, there were technical problems. Former sharecroppers, renters, and wage workers often did not have enough knowledge of modern farming, particularly in intensive cultivation, to avoid making costly errors in soil preparation, seed planting, and plant growth supervision. Their limited education made it harder still for them to pick up this knowledge on

their own. The AARDES study mentioned above found that
38 percent of male beneficiaries were illiterate.
Furthermore, almost one-third were fifty years old or
older, which complicated the retraining of the
beneficiaries.[58]

CAPCS was supposed to provide extension services
to compensate for this lack of knowledge. But CAPCS
performance was uneven, favoring some cooperatives and
ignoring others. Delays in delivery of material and
equipment and problems of marketing output lowered the
ability of marginal cooperatives to stay afloat. This
contributed to a competitive shaking out of the weaker
cooperatives.

When surveyed, the cooperative members themselves
gave the following list of problems they felt
influenced their ability to hold out. Seventy percent
said work conditions were bad (poor pay, too far to
travel to work, too few members to do the work,
absenteeism, internal misunderstandings, and too little
seasonal labor). Sixty-one percent complained of
insufficiency of materials and equipment (either
non-existent, delayed, or in ill-repair). Forty-one
percent complained of an insufficiency of inputs such
as seeds and fertilizer (prices too high, delivery
delayed, poor quality, inadequate quantity).
Thirty-nine percent said their rented equipment arrived
too late to be useful. Thirty-six percent complained
of poor soil or an inhospitable climate. Thirty-four
percent said that bank credits were insufficient or
granted too late to be used. Finally, 20 percent said
that they had insufficient technical information.[59]

The unevenness of revenues

When the cooperatives were set up, the state got
them started with an installment subsidy (prime
d'installation) of 150 dinars per month in cash and one
hundred dinars per month worth of food per beneficiary.
This adds up to the three thousand dinars per year in
income set as the goal of the reform in order to give
each beneficiary a minimum subsistence. The subsidies
were to stop of course once the cooperatives became
economically self-sufficient.[60]

The reform sector was different from the
self-managed farms in that the cooperatives' members
all received exactly the same (low) monthly pay, no
matter how much they worked, and in that they would
(they hoped) someday share out their unit's profits
equally and directly. In contrast, the self-managed
farm workers got a more handsome daily wage, graded by
skill levels and directly related to the number of days
worked, but rarely did they see the profits they were

TABLE 3.8.--Number of Cooperatives and of Beneficiaries Showing Profit and Loss, 1972-73 and 1973-74

	1972-73 Number	%	1973-74 Number	%	% Change
Total cooperatives	1,988	100	3,164	100	. . .
Cooperatives showing profit	665	33.5	1,233	39	+5.5
Cooperatives in deficit	1,323	66.5	1,931	61	-5.5
Total beneficiaries	30,682	100	47,429	100	. . .
Beneficiaries receiving profit	9,521	31	17,868	37.6	+6.6
Beneficiaries in deficit	21,161	69	29,561	62.3	-6.7
Revenues of beneficiaries receiving profit					
More than 5,000 dinars	620	6.5	1,410	8	+1.5
3,000-5,000	1,256	13	1,677	9.4	-3.6
2,000-3,000	992	10.4	2,149	12	+1.6
1,000-2,000	1,695	17.8	3,726	21	+3.2
100-1,000	3,588	37.6	7,154	40	+2.4
Less than 100	1,370	14.3	1,752	10	-4.3

SOURCE: Chaulet et al., "Bilan," pp. 128, 129 (based on BNA report, September 1975).

TABLE 3.9 --Distribution of Production Cooperatives, 1974-75 By Type of Unit and Level of Profit

Type of Unit	Zero	Level of Profit (in dinars)[a] Less than 1,000	1,000 to 1,999	2,000 to 4,999	5,000 and up	Total
CAPRA	2,893	526	365	344	75	4,203
CAEC	444	36	26	19	3	528
GMV	885	24	15	3	3	930
GEP	162	1	3	2	2	170
GI	10	. . .	. . .	. . .	. . .	10
Total	4,394	587	409	368	83	5,841

SOURCE: Ministry of Agriculture, Enquête sur les coopératives, p. 29.

[a]"Profit" is measured as total revenue minus total costs, including payments to creditors, before any income is returned to the cooperative members. CUV (1978), p. 74, claims that more than 60 percent of CAPRAs were making profits in 1976, but this figure must not include what is owed to creditors ("profit" to the BNA and CAPCS, if not to the production unit) as part of total costs.

supposed to share.[61]

The constraint that many of the cooperatives faced is that their initial endowments of land and skills and their subsequent provision of inputs were inadequate to allow them to become self-supporting through the sale of their output. While the state exhorted them in the national press to work harder, they resorted to many other activities in order to make ends meet. Many cooperative members engaged in illegal subsistence consumption (eating their output instead of selling it to state agencies) much to the fury of the state planners. They kept their own animal herds (also illegally) independent of the cooperative's, although they used cooperative land to graze on when they could do it with impunity. Others arranged to lease out the cooperative's land and equipment to the private sector for hard cash. Still others sought temporary wage employment outside the cooperative, which caused a conflict in their time commitments and led to absenteeism. Finally, a sizable minority abandoned their rights to the land in the cooperative altogether and joined the rural-urban migratory stream. Of course revenues were expected to increase after 1975, when the state allowed agricultural prices to begin to rise, and when improved seeds, fertilizer and techniques were adopted in the cooperatives.[62]

In Table 3.8, based on a national bank survey for the 1972-73 season, 33.5 percent of all cooperatives were showing a "profit," (that is, covering debts and out-of-pocket costs) and 31 percent of all beneficiaries were earning some income from their participation in the cooperative. Among the latter, only 20 percent earned an income of three thousand dinars or more; these were 6 percent of all beneficiaries together. Things improved the next year, 1973-74: 39 percent of all cooperatives were operating in the black, and 37.6 percent of all beneficiaries were earning some income from the cooperatives. Among the latter, while their absolute numbers increased, the percentage earning three thousand dinars or more fell to 17 percent; these were again only 6.5 percent of all beneficiaries together.

There did not seem to be any association between profitability and the variation in the overall harvest. 1972 was a better-than-average year, 1973 and 1974 were worse than average, and 1975 and 1976 were better again. Table 3.9 shows how few cooperatives were showing a profit after the 1974-75 growing season, only 25 percent overall (31 percent of all CAPRA).[63] Table 3.10 shows how few cooperatives were yielding a minimum income of three thousand dinars per cooperative member after the 1975-76 growing season, again only 31 percent (23.7 percent for CAPRA).

The evidence on the wide disparity in revenues among cooperatives, combined with the knowledge that some cooperatives have already been disbanded or become practically inoperative, and that withdrawal of beneficiaries is common, is a strong prima facie argument that differentiation was occurring among the cooperatives. They were unequally endowed to start with, and the inequalities became exacerbated over time. The successful cooperatives were becoming business enterprises with capitalist characteristics, such as the internal hierarchy of authority and the division between mental and manual labor. The failures, operating in a predominantly capitalist environment, were spewing their members into the wage labor force.

This bifurcation cannot be attributed merely to differences in initial endowments, but also must arise out of the mechanisms of competition. It is logical that the successes would occur more frequently among fruit and vegetable producers in the richer regions (like Alger, Tlemcen, Constantine, and Saida), and failures would occur more frequently in the cereal and pasturage regions. However, even within localities or zones, where initial endowments were relatively equal, first hand studies show that there was a wide and growing variation among cooperatives.[64]

WITHDRAWAL AND THE DISPOSSESSION OF THE SMALL AGRICULTURAL PRODUCERS

Many poor and landless peasants resisted joining the reform from the start. About half of those agricultural workers and sharecroppers who would have

TABLE 3.10--Distribution of Cooperatives, 1974-75
  By Type of Unit and Income of Beneficiaries

| Type of Unit | Income of Beneficiaries (in dinars) | | | | | Total |
	Less than 2,000 ·	2,000 to 2,999	3,000 to 3,999	4,000 to 4,999	5,000 and up	
CAPRA	477	2,729	487	184	326	4,203
CAEC	301	181	27	10	9	528
GMV	80	50	53	499[a]	248[a]	930
GEP	155	8	3	1	3	170
GI	8	2	...	...	...	10
Total units	1,021	2,970	570	694	586	5,841

SOURCE: Ministry of Agriculture, Enquête sur les coopératives, pp. 29-30.

[a]The large number of GMVs having beneficiaries with high incomes is due to the GMV workers being paid a salary directly by the state, in relation to the number of days worked, as most of them do not yet produce a marketable output.

had priority to receive title to the lands they were working chose to abandon them and become wage workers elsewhere rather than to become beneficiaries. In fact, the economically active population on the public lands was halved by the reform's first phase--this was the first wave of dispossession resulting directly from the reform.[65]

But withdrawal continued to be a pattern even among those who accepted to become reform beneficiaries, a total of 4,885 from the first phase and 3,156 from the second phase (8,041 in all, or about 10 percent of all beneficiaries). As of September 1976, only 4,665 replacements had been found.[66]

There was a great deal of regional unevenness in the rates of withdrawal,[67] mainly depending on the availability of alternative employment, as can be seen in Table 3.11. In the Mitidja, in Alger, in Annaba, in Sidi-bel-Abbès, in Oran, anywhere that industry was growing rapidly, there was a dearth of candidates for allotments and a high rate of withdrawal. Alger was

TABLE 3.11--Withdrawals of Beneficiaries, by Wilaya, 1973 and 1974

Wilaya	Number of Withdrawals	
	As of September 30, 1973	As of September 30, 1974
Alger	907	1,186
Annaba	380	801
Aurès	581	961
Constantine	28	624
El-Asnam	38	177
Médéa	4	23
Mostaganem	20	105
Oasis	30	266
Oran	1,870	1,939
Saida	101	188
Saoura	. . .	. . .
Sétif	46	154
Tiaret	364	570
Grande Kabylie	28	75
Tlemcen	. . .	. . .
Total	4,397[a]	7,211[b]

SOURCE: Chaulet et al., "Bilan," p. 133 (based on BNA report, September 1975).

[a]This is 9 percent of the 46,910 beneficiaries surveyed.

[b]This is 11 percent of the 64,754 beneficiaries surveyed.

three thousand candidates short in 1974--its withdrawal rate was up to 40 percent by the summer. In March 1976, 1,432 hectares of land in the Mitidja (prime agricultural land), and 1,600 hectares in El-Hadjar (plain of Annaba) went begging for beneficiaries. But in less developed areas, there were more candidates than there were lots to attribute. This led to interregional transfers of beneficiaries, for example, from Guelma (where there was a surfeit of eleven thousand candidates) to Annaba, from Médéa to Alger, and from Tiaret and Batna to Oran.[68]

Intentionally or not, the reform accelerated the pace of conversion of the small producers into wage laborers, except for the minority who became successful entrepreneurs in the cooperatives that showed a profit. This process took place both directly through land redistribution and indirectly as the cooperatives became way stations on the rural-urban migratory route. Furthermore, the cooperatives themselves became employers of wage labor. They did so in rapidly developing regions in order to make up for the dearth of beneficiaries. They did so in the less developed areas as well because the cooperative members did not want to dilute their own revenues by having to share profits among more members. They resisted the admission of new members, preferring instead (with the blessings of the national bank) to hire on wage labor, which is cheaper and can be laid off at will. Besides, the temporary wage workers were assigned the jobs that none of the cooperative members wanted to do, adding another layer to the hierarchical division of labor that characterized the cooperatives' organization.[69]

CONCLUSION

The reform succeeded in fulfilling a narrow version of the second item on its explicit agenda, that is it tackled rental and sharecropping tenures on public lands and absentee-owned private lands. In doing so, both in its written precepts and in the particularistic manner in which it was executed, the reform avoided dismantling the private capitalist and medium commercial farms, and, indeed, may have even encouraged them through opening up access to land and other resources that had been blocked by the pre-capitalist tenures.

Furthermore, the reform eradicated exploitation in its pre-capitalist forms, by abolishing sharecropping and cancelling debts owed by small producers to landlords. However, it did not eradicate exploitation in its capitalist form, for wage labor has by no means been abolished. Indeed, not all former sharecroppers

and small-scale renters who were forced out of
pre-capitalist tenures nor all poor peasants on
fragmented lands could have become beneficiaries of the
reform. Only a minority could. The majority who could
not swelled the ranks of the wage labor force, both
employed and unemployed. Even the reform cooperatives
themselves became employers of wage labor. The hidden
agenda item of converting labor to its commodity form
was also fulfilled.

Finally, the administrative institutions servicing
the reform, such as the national bank and the supply
and marketing cooperatives, encouraged competition and
economic inequality among the production units of the
reform sector as well as in the private sector. The
only allowed path to success was increased
commercialization. The more successful capitalist
farmers, commercial family farms and market-oriented
cooperatives could grow larger and accumulate capital,
while the poor peasants and failing cooperative members
left independent production on the land to go into wage
labor. The reform promoted, rather than curtailed,
class differentiation of agricultural producers into
successful commercial farmers and propertyless wage
workers.

The maintenance, even encouragement, of the
private sector embodied in the reform, the failure to
eradicate exploitation, differentiation within
cooperatives, differentiation among cooperatives, and
now the further development of wage labor employed by
the cooperatives themselves were all bricks in the
construction of capitalist social relations in the
agricultural sector. Whether or not the government
consciously planned the reform to turn out this way is
irrelevant. It was the hidden agenda, implicit in the
very terms with which the reform was set up and
imposed. In this the "agrarian revolution" in Algeria
in the 1970s seems to have completed the historic task
begun by the French intruders in 1830.[76]

NOTES

1. The source cited below as Claudine Chaulet et
al., "Bilan de la révolution agraire" (Algiers: CREA
Equipe de la révolution agraire, 1979), unpublished
manuscript, is an amalgam of the work of a whole team
of people under Chaulet's direction, comprised of a
series of first-hand research projects in various
regions of Algeria (some of which are used in Chapter 4
below), plus published and unpublished reports by
student volunteers who participated in the

82

administration of the land reform, plus analyses of
published and unpublished government reports.
    The research team Chaulet heads is focused
directly on evaluating the "agrarian revolution." They
had been part of the Centre Nationale de Recherche sur
l'Economie et Sociologie Rurale (CNRESR) associated
with the Ministry of Agriculture and the Agrarian
Revolution (MARA). That is how they got access to the
unpublished reports mentioned above.
    When the Ministry of Agriculture abolished the
CNRESR,   the   researchers   regrouped   into   a
quasi-independent institute, the CREA, in order to
continue their work. The CREA is directed by
Abdellatif Benachenhou, whose work has also been useful
to this dissertation (see bibliography).
    2. The terms and goals of the reform are
presented in: République Algérienne Démocratique et
Populaire, Front de Libération Nationale, La charte
nationale (Algiers: Editions Populaires de l'Armée,
1976), pp. 155-166; They are discussed in depth by:
Aït Amara, "Algeria: the Agrarian Revolution,
Reorganization of the Rural World," Ceres 7
(July-August 1974), pp. 41-44; Tony Smith, "Political
and Economic Ambitions of Algerian Land Reform,
1962-1974," Middle East Journal 29 (Summer 1975),
pp. 259-278; and Marc Raffinot and Pierre Jacquemot,
Le capitalisme d'état algérien (Paris: Maspéro, 1977).
    3. Compensation for expropriated lands is made in
the form of registered treasury certificates redeemable
in fifteen years, at a rate of interest of 2.5 percent
per year. Furthermore, the government may purchase
plots of less than five hectares at their full market
value, based on a right of eminent domain.
    4. Based on its 1973 RGA survey, the Ministry of
Agriculture estimated that the economically active
agricultural population in the private sector before
the reform equalled 1.8 million, the equivalent of 454
million workdays per year. However, it found the need
for labor power in private agriculture to be equal to
only 130 million workdays per year, yielding a labor
power utilization rate of only 29 percent for the
country as a whole (with a wide range of variation
among regions, as will be explained below). R.A.D.P.,
Secrétariat d'état au plan, Balances regionales,
Document II: "Elements de synthèse sur les secteurs
agricoles" (Algiers: 1978), no pagination.
    5. This involves fifteen million hectares of
mostly non-agricultural land (part of it near desert),
held by collectivities such as wilayas, communes,
tribes, and religious foundations, and used for herding
sheep and goats. Ownership of the animals themselves
is private and highly concentrated. The reform was
supposed to expropriate herds from absentee owners and

large-scale proprietors, and then redistribute them to
the herdless wage workers and share herders employed by
them.   As of 1979, the latter step had been postponed
indefinitely,   and   substituted   for   it   was   the
establishment   of   state-run   cooperatives   of   herders
managing state-owned animals on the public lands.   This
seems   to   be   the   Algerian version of "enclosures" of
common grazing lands.
    6.   "Association" is a contractual agreement,
usually   of   long   duration,   among a group of families
(often related) to work a parcel of land in common   and
share   the   product   under   a   formula   based   on   the
contributions in labor and means of production of   each
unit.   It was common for some (often urban dwellers) to
contribute only land and tools and no work, while
others contributed only work.
    7.   This was reported to   me   in   interviews   with
Claudine   Chaulet   and   her colleagues at the Centre de
Recherche en Economie Appliquée (CREA) at Algiers.
    Most of the statistics   of   this   chapter,   either
directly   or   via   Chaulet,   come   from the Ministry of
Agriculture (Commission   Nationale   de   la   Révolution
Agraire   data),   the   Banque   Nationale   d'Algérie
(Direction du Financement de l'agriculture),   and   the
reports   of student volunteers (Comité Universitaire du
Volontariat - CUV).   For example, the 1973 agricultural
census   (Recensement   Générale   de l'Agriculture - RGA)
was   actually   conducted   by   soldiers   and   student
volunteers,   most   of   whom had a lot of enthusiasm for
their   task   but   not   much   training.   Mme.   Chaulet
suggested   that the informality of these methods led to
so much confusion   that   no   one   has   enough   reliable
information to challenge the validity of the reform.
    8.   Chaulet et al.,   "Bilan,"   pp. 8-11;   and   Le
Comité   Universitaire   du   Volontariat   (CUV),   La
révolution agraire, bilan et perspectives (Algiers:
1978), p. 29.
    9.   Often officers in the Armée de   la   Liberation
Nationale   (ALN) rewarded themselves and their men with
land.   Kaid   Ahmed,   a   member   of   Boumédienne's
Revolutionary   Council,   Minister of Finance and head of
the FLN   from   1967   to   1972,   owns   more than 3,000
hectares   in   Tiaret,   which   he   did not own prior to
independence   (Raffinot   and   Jacquemot,   Capitalisme
d'état, p. 366).   Boumédienne forced him to resign in
1972 because he openly opposed the agrarian reform.
    10.   About 45 percent of all   proprietors   claimed
to   hold   land   in   indivision, involving about 175,000
units altogether. (Chaulet et al., "Bilan," p. 13.)
    11.   The property limits were set   by   the   income
yielded   from   the land, not the surface area alone.   A
sufficient family income was set equal to   three   times
the income of a full-time self-managed farm worker.   On

84

average, this worked out to a forty-three hectare
private farm unit. The income level was allowed to
rise by one-third for one dependent child, and by 50
percent for two or more dependent children. This farm
income was allowed to be supplemented by an additional
non-farm income of up to 13,500 dinars per year. See
Keith Sutton, "Agrarian Reform in Algeria--the
Conversion of Projects into Action," Afrika Spectrum,
no. 1 (1974), p. 60, for a sample of limits set in
different zones on different types of crops.

    12. The number of proprietors is greater in Table
3.2 than the number of working units in Table 3.1
above, because of the registry of lands in indivision.
The number of hectares is greater in Table 3.2 than in
Table 3.1 because all lands owned, not only the
agriculturally useful, are included.

    13. These results, and the reasons offered for
them are discussed in Chaulet et al., "Bilan,"
pp. 14-15, 18-20; Raffinot and Jacquemot, Capitalisme
d'état, pp. 327, 336-337; and Nourredine Abdi, "La
réforme agraire en Algerie," Maghreb/Machrek, no. 69
(July-September 1975), pp. 35-37. Many anecdotes and
specific examples are offered in the student reports of
1974 and 1975.

    14. Chaulet, et al., "Bilan," p. 44. Different
government agencies have made their own independent
research and estimates. The Secretary of State's
Planning Office claims an SAU (surface agricole utile)
for the reform sector of 963,000 hectares (Balances, no
pagination). A survey based on interviews with the
presidents of the reform cooperatives, finds a total
area of 1,168,555 hectares, of which 896,421 hectares
are usable for agriculture. See R.A.D.P., Ministère
d'Agriculture, Enquête sur les coopératives de la
révolution agraire (Algiers, 1978), p. 116.

    15. Chaulet cites some examples for 1974 in the
wilaya of Saida: commune Sidi Boubekeur--of 22
absentees on List 2, having altogether 200 hectares, 9
were workers on state farms and low-level civil
servants owning 95 hectares. Commune Youb--of 32
absentees on List 2, having 1400 hectares, 120 hectares
belonged to wage workers elsewhere. Commune Sidi
Khaled--of 33 absentees on List 2, having 835 hectares,
14 were workers having 195 hectares (Chaulet et al.,
"Bilan," pp. 20-21).

    16. See Amara, "Algeria Reorganization," p. 44.
As of the end of 1976, the Ministry of Agriculture
reported 203,390 applications to Phase Two of the
reform (CUV, Révolution agraire, p. 67).

    17. These figures are according to R.A.D.P.,
Secrétariat d'état au plan, Balances, no pagination.
The Ministry of Agriculture's own figures are 78,793
cooperateurs as of March 1977 (R.A.D.P., Ministère

d'Agriculture, Enquête sur les coopératives, p. 15).
CUV, Révolution agraire, p. 66, relies on the Ministry
of Agriculture's figures.

18. These lands are unequally distributed, but
there is no control for the quality of the land in the
statistics given: 339 persons (3.5%) hold more than
20 hectares each, 7,078 persons (67.5%) hold 0.5 to 20
hectares each, 2,397 persons (29.0%) hold less than 0.5
hectares each. The group of persons holding less than
0.5 hectares each became beneficiaries mainly by having
their rights recognized on the public lands they worked
as sharecroppers or tenants anyway.

Sixty-six percent of all individual beneficiaries
live in isolated situations (as opposed to 60 percent
of cooperative members), 34 percent live in villages
with services (the same as cooperative members), and
less than 1 percent live in the new "socialist"
villages (as compared to 6 percent of cooperative
members). Of 9,814 individual beneficiaries in
1975-76, 7.9 percent used credit, 21.3 percent used
fertilizer (especially in Blida, Adrar, Bechar,
Tlemcen, and Mascara), 3.6 percent had irrigation
equipment (in Laghouat, Bechar and Blida), and 4.2
percent had work buildings. R.A.D.P., Ministère
d'Agriculture, Enquête sur les coopératives, pp. 23-24,
35-37, 42.

19. Some employment is indirectly created by the
reform, mainly in the service sector. As of 1977, the
643 service cooperatives (CAPCS) surveyed by the
Ministry of Agriculture employed 15,580 permanent
workers. The service cooperatives also employ seasonal
wage labor directly in agricultural production (844,970
days of it in 1975-76) on those lands not allotted by
the reform but held in the land fund (R.A.D.P.,
Ministère d'Agriculture Enquête sur les coopératives,
pp. 71-72).

20. Rachid Benattig, Internal working document on
impact of the agrarian reform on employment, (Algiers:
CREA, 1979), p. 8. Also Raffinot and Jacquemot,
Capitalisme d'état, pp. 351-352, 354.

21. R.A.D.P., Secrétariat d'état au plan,
Balances (no pagination). Examples abound of
disproportionalities in labor markets. The national
bank reports that payments to seasonal wage labor are
double the aggregate value of those to permanent wage
labor in the wilaya of Alger, and are rising each year
due to withdrawals of reform beneficiaries, yet there
is no serious attempt to increase the number of
permanent jobs, and members of the cooperatives
themselves resist increasing the number of
beneficiaries so as not to dilute their incomes. They
prefer to hire seasonal labor. Chaulet, et al.,
"Bilan," p. 114.

In the agriculturally rich wilaya of Constantine, where Phase Two was relatively more successful than elsewhere in the country, there were 66,549 unemployed agricultural workers, but only 1600 beneficiaries had received 26,000 hectares of the 56,000 hectares that had been nationalized. Sutton, "Conversion of Projects," pp. 60-61.

22. The Popular Assembly of the Wilaya (APW), is elected to govern at the province level, while the national popular assembly (APN) performs the same function at the national level. As in other one-party systems, electoral candidates are generally named by the party (in this case, the FLN). Independents have a hard struggle to get elected. The ruling class has been successful, since 1965, in confining the class struggle to contests within the political institutions it controls, the FLN, Army, the industrial labor union (UGTA), the state farm sector, and now the institutions of the reform sector, the peasant union (UNPA) and the cooperatives.

23. That some landholders were truly afraid of an agrarian reform that would objectively benefit them does not contradict the argument that this reform encourages the development of capitalist farming. For one thing, capitalist development is not planned and conscious, and leaves open leeway for error and misinterpretation on the part of individual capitalists. Second, the role of the state under capitalism is to promote the system as a whole, which may often require that some particular privileged segment suffer a loss of some of its privileges.

24. Raffinot and Jacquemot, Capitalisme d'état, pp. 368-369. Ferhat Abbas and Ben Khedda, leaders of the establishment right wing of the Algerian nationalist movement since the 1930s, distributed a press release in Algiers in 1976 attacking the regime and accusing it of fomenting a politics contrary to Koranic Law. They have the support of King Hassan II of Morocco (Marc Ollivier, "Place de la révolution agraire dans la stratégie algérienne de développement," Annuaire de l'Afrique du Nord 1975 (1976), p. 102).

25. Interview with Slimane Bedrani, CREA (Algiers, May 1979). Also Slimane Bedrani, "Elections dans la daira d'Aflou," (Algiers, 1973), unpublished manuscript cited by Raffinot and Jacquemot, Capitalisme d'état, p. 357. Also, Raffinot and Jacquemot, Capitalisme d'état, pp. 332-334; Smith, "Ambitions of Land Reform," pp. 272-273.

26. Raffinot and Jacquemot, Capitalisme d'état, pp. 369-371; Marnia Lazreg, The Emergence of Classes in Algeria (Boulder, Colo.: Westview Press, 1976), p. 107; and Peter Knauss, "Algeria's Agrarian Revolution': Peasant Control or Control of Peasants?"

African Studies Review, no. 20 (December 1977), pp. 76-77.

27. Raffinot and Jacquemot, Capitalisme d'état, pp. 369-372. The students sent their reports back to MARA and President Boumédienne directly, bypassing the local power brokers. Their early reports (1974, 1975) are refreshing in their candor about local conditions (poverty, inequality, corruption within the state and party apparatus) and earnest desire to make the reform a success for the poor and landless peasants. Many of the empirical studies cited in Chap. 4 were done on the inspiration of student volunteers anxious to use their experience to help gut the privileged classes of the countryside and build working cooperatives of producers (a utopian socialist vision). Their Narodnik idealism suffered a heavy bruising when their reports were carefully edited by MARA before publication, when a journal that expressed their viewpoint (Terre et Progrès) was suppressed after publication of material too unfavorable to the national ruling class and its failure to carry through a true agrarian "revolution," and when, as adult professionals, their attempts to make their studies public resulted in their research facilities being closed down.

28. Konrad Schliephake, "Changing the Traditional Sector of Algeria's Agriculture," Land Reform, Land Settlement and Cooperatives, no. 1 (1973), p. 21; Knauss, "Control of Peasants?" pp. 72-73; and Raffinot and Jacquemot, Capitalisme d'état, pp. 332-334.

29. Fatma Diabi, "La décision dans les coopératives de la révolution agraire," (Master's Thesis, University of Algiers, 1977), p. 158.

30. Diabi, "Décision dans les coopératives," pp. 160, 162.

31. Knauss, "Control of Peasants?", p. 72; Smith, "Ambitions of Land Reform," pp. 275-276; and Raffinot and Jacquemot, Capitalisme d'état, p. 358.

32. This entailed employment of 422 wage workers in 1976, and of 211,243 days of seasonal wage labor (R.A.D.P., Ministère d'Agriculture, Enquête sur les coopératives, pp. 71-72). In 1975, in the Mitidja there were 112 production cooperatives on 4,590 hectares of land. But 5,410 more hectares were not allotted due to the lack or withdrawal of candidates. So CAPCS is running these farms with seasonal wage labor. Georges Mutin, "L'agriculture en Mitidja ou les difficultés d'une conversion," Annuaire de l'Afrique du Nord, 1975 (1976), pp. 165-166.

33. Chaulet, et al., "Bilan," pp. 53-57; R.A.D.P., Ministère d'Agriculture, Enquête sur les coopératives, pp. 47-48.

34. CAPAM are Coopératives Agricoles de Production des Anciens Mujahidins. These are farms run

on the same order as the self-managed farms and generally classified with them in government statistics and documents as secteur socialiste (as compared to the secteur privé, and secteur coopératif de la révolution agraire). They were established by the state on abandoned European farms after 1962 to reward some veterans of the war of national liberation with a secure tenure on the land.

35. The proportions among sectors vary greatly among wilayas. Private farmers predominate in CAPCS management in the regions of Adrar, Bechar, Bouira, Tizi Ouzou, Djelfa, Saida, Médéa, and Msila.

36. See Chapter 4 below; also Chaulet et al., "Bilan," p. 60.

37. Stories abound among direct observers of spare parts which never arrive or do not fit when they arrive, of equipment provided by CAPCS that is unsuitable to the task, of provisions arriving too late to be used, of allocating too little seed or fertilizer to possibly meet the communal production plan, of harvests being picked up too late to be successfully marketed. Rachid Benattig and Gauthier de Villers, "Enquête socio-économique sur la situation de l'emploi et des revenus en milieu rural" (Algiers: Ministry of Labor, unpublished manuscript, 1978), p. 16. It is hard to judge whether this inefficiency and irrationality is peculiar to Algerian etatist bureaucratic bungling (as Benattig and de Villers believe) or the predictable unevenness that is typical of a rapidly developing market economy.

38. Chaulet et al., "Bilan," pp. 59-60, 123. After 1967, there was an increase in the national budget appropriations for agricultural education. In 1970-71, agricultural institutes for research and secondary schools for vocational training of agronomists were set up.

39. Knauss, "Control of Peasants?" pp. 75-76; Nico Kielstra, "The Agrarian Revolution and Algerian Socialism," MERIP Reports, no. 67 (1978), pp. 9-10. See Chapter 5 for a fuller analysis.

40. The state also invested directly (not as loans) in rural development. Total direct investment by the state in agriculture and hydraulic works to serve agriculture was 19 percent of the 1970-73 plan, and 15.1 percent of the 1974-77 plan, Jean Claude Karsenty, "Les investissements dans l'agriculture algérienne," Annuaire de l'Afrique du Nord, 1975 (1976), p. 142.

For the four years, 1972 through 1975, for example, a total of 2,038,479,200 dinars was spent for improvement of lands, irrigation, and purchase of animals, and for infrastructure (education, health, housing) in the rural areas, Ahmed Lotfi Boukhari,

"Stratégie de développement et financement de la révolution agraire," (Master's Thesis, University of Algiers, 1976), p. 117.

41. Boukhari, "Financement de la révolution agraire," p. 103. Because the rate of inflation was higher than the rate of interest, BNA loans were a mechanism of indirect subsidy.

42. Boukhari, "Financement de la révolution agraire," pp. 105-108.

43. Abdelmalek Temam, "La contribution de la banque nationale d'Algérie à la révolution agraire," Terre et Progrès (1976), p. 27 (my translation).

44. For example, the 1974-77 four-year plan envisaged an increase of 36 percent in cereal and vegetable production in both the state farm and reform sectors, Omar Bessaoud, "Le mouvement coopératif dans le processus de la revolution agraire en Algérie," (Master's Thesis, University of Algiers, 1976), p. 150.

45. Claudine Chaulet, "Paysans et collectifs de producteurs dans la 'révolution agraire' en Algérie," paper delivered at the Fourth World Congress for Rural Sociology, Torun, Italy, 1976, p. 9. See also Benattig and de Villers, "Emploi en milieu rural," pp. 11-14 of summary.

46. Literally, "pre-cooperative grouping for reclamation (or for putting into valuable use)."

47. Allotments of reform fund land to individuals were usually quite scattered, far from other reform holdings. Individual beneficiaries were expected, but not required, to join cooperatives of the GEP level.

48. See discussions in Kielstra, "Agrarian Revolution," p. 9; Benattig, "Impact of Agrarian Revolution on Employment," p. 20; and Raffinot and Jacquemot, Capitalisme d'état, pp. 353-354.

49. Chaulet et al., "Bilan," pp. 39-42. The Ministry of Agriculture's Enquête sur les coopératives provides us with a distribution of cooperative units, cooperative members, and land as of March 1977. This survey was based on direct inquiries to the presidents and members of the cooperatives (individual beneficiaries were treated separately elsewhere--see note 18). It excluded units that were dissolved or inoperative as of that date.

Type of Coop.	No. Units	% Units	No. of Bene-ficiaries	% of Bene-ficiaries	Agric. Useful Land (ha.) (SAU)	% of Land
CAPRA	4,203	72	51,899	66	735,906	82
CAEC	528	9	5,654	7	56,704	6.5
GMV	930	16	18,401	23	92,013	10
GEP	170	2.9	2,770	3.5	11,798	1.5
GI	10	0.2	69	0.1		
Total	5,841	100	78,793	100	896,421	100

The authors note that the GMV were most common in
Biskra, Tebessa, Msila, and Ouargla. The CAEC
predominated in Tlemcen. The GEP and GI were
significant only in Asnam, Biskra, and Tlemcen.

More than 80 percent of the units had fewer than
twenty beneficiaries each. However seventy-eight units
(1.3 percent), of which forty-seven are GMV, had more
than fifty members each.

Only 307 units (5.2 percent) had an SAU greater
than 500 hectares. The average for all units was 153
hectares of SAU, while the average for CAPRA is 175
hectares of SAU.

50. Beneficiaries assigned to CAPRA in the daïra
of Ain el-Kebira (wilaya of Sétif) themselves requested
conversion to GMV (Chaulet et al., "Bilan," p. 77).

51 Association algérienne pour la recherche
démographique, économique et sociologique (AARDES),
Etude socio-économique sur les attributaires de la
première phase de la révolution agraire (Algiers,
1975). Like the CREA, AARDES is a quasi-independent
research institute that conducts studies from a
critical point of view.

52. Benattig and de Villers, "Emploi en milieu
rural," p. 8.

53. Chaulet et al., "Bilan," pp. 80-81;
Bessaoud, "Mouvement coopératif," p. 174. They came to
dominate units created in those regions in which
self-managed farm workers served as a political
counterweight to the rural gentry in the APCs'
administration of the reform.

54. Chaulet et al., "Bilan," pp. 82-85.

55. Chaulet et al., "Bilan," pp. 85-88. One
observer personally witnessed some rich peasants who
had formerly rented public lands remain on as members
of a cooperative on the very same land, in the
fellowship of their former employees. He says, "This
explains how some reform beneficiaries have important
extra-agricultural incomes. Such is the case for
example of the president of a CAPRA at Sidi-Mebarek who
runs a grocery store and a market in dairy products, or
of a beneficiary who privately owns forty milk cows,
and some tractors, trucks and cars [to rent out]."
Bessaoud, "Mouvement coopératif," pp. 140-141.

56. Chaulet, "Paysans et collectifs," pp. 10-11;
and Chaulet et al., "Bilan," pp. 89-91, 113, 115.

57. Chaulet et al., "Bilan," pp. 49-51, 67-68,
76-77, 113, based on student volunteer reports.

58. AARDES, Attributaires de la première phase,
pp. 39, 42. Ninety-six to 98 percent of all
beneficiaries are men. The rate of illiteracy for
women is 71.8 percent.

See also Chaulet et al., "Bilan," pp. 102-103,
108-109. It is difficult in Arab Muslim society, where

the wisdom of the elderly is highly respected, to
retrain older beneficiaries. They also cannot work as
hard. Another problem is that young trained
beneficiaries are more likely to withdraw in favor of
wage labor. Forty-eight percent of individual
beneficiaries (as opposed to 30 percent of cooperative
members) are fifty years old or more. Ministry of
Agriculture, Enquête sur les coopératives, p. 40.
 59. Ministry of Agriculture, Enquête sur les
coopératives, pp. 31-32.
 60. Payments of these subsidies by the state
amounted to:

1972	8,668,340 dinars
1973	69,036,795
1974	80,322,382
1975	67,448,271
1976	63,849,284 (through October 30

only).

 The drop from 1974 to 1975 is due to some
cooperatives from Phase One of the reform becoming
self-supporting (Chaulet et al., "Bilan," p. 125, based
on BNA figures).
 61. Chaulet, "Paysans et collectifs," p. 8. The
target revenue set by the reform authorities for
1975-76 was 3,825 dinars per year per beneficiary to
support a rural family (up from 3,000 due to
inflation). Self-managed farm workers generally get
higher than this, and urban industrial workers higher
still, while reform beneficiaries get less. Benattig
and de Villers, "Emploi en milieu rural," pp. 19-20.
 62. See discussions in Benattig and de Villers,
"Emploi en milieu rural," p. 25-26; Benattig, "Impact
of agrarian revolution on employment," p. 20; and
Chaulet et al., "Bilan," pp. 93-98.
 Prior to 1974, when the government's development
plan was to rapidly industrialize, farm prices were
held down, so that the wage rate in industry would not
have to rise while the total wage bill climbed as the
industrial workforce was rapidly expanded. But prices
of inputs, both those produced by Algerian industry and
those imported from other countries undergoing rapid
price increases, were allowed to rise. Here are some
examples:

Agricultural input prices (in dinars)

	1969	1973
Medium wheeled tractor (45 hp.)	15,900	28,300
Heavy wheeled tractor (65 hp.)	20,600	37,000
Thresher-harvester	45,600	61,700
Fertilizer spreader - 300 liters	1,700	2,300
Sowing machine - 3 meters	3,800	7,700
Sowing machine - 5-6 meters	6,500	13,370
	1970	1973
Nitrate or phosphate fertilizer per kilogram	.28	.34
Ammonitrate or superphosphate fertilizer, per quintal	9.38	15.30

(Source: Bessaoud, "Mouvement coopératif," p. 182.)

63. The data are not controlled for longevity of the cooperatives. Presumably those in place earlier would be more likely to be showing a profit. There are no controls for land quality or irrigation either.

64. Chaulet et al., "Bilan," pp. 130, 132.

65. Raffinot and Jacquemot, Capitalisme d'état, pp. 342-344; Abdi, "Réforme agraire en Algérie," pp. 34-38. Abdi suggests that there was "brutal integration" of former operatives into the CAPRA, and that it was "necessary to use coercion to keep the beneficiaries on the reform lands," but he does not give statistics or examples. He also argues that the relative increase in CAPRA vis-à-vis the CAEC and the relative increase in individual attributions in Phase Two are due to the authorities' need to control the beneficiaries and to keep them from leaving the land.

66. CUV, Révolution agraire, pp. 71 and 77.

67. Knauss, "Control of Peasants?" p. 73, cites El-Jarida, no. 17, for the following rates of withdrawal (Phase One only): Aurès-10 percent; Oran, Constantine-20 percent; Cheraga-50 percent; and Ain Benian, Mahelma, Staoueli-75 percent.

68. Raffinot and Jacquemot, Capitalisme d'état, pp. 335-336; Ollivier, "Révolution agraire dans la stratégie algérienne," p. 110; and CUV, Révolution agraire, pp. 77 and 81.

69. So much for the substance of the reform's motto: "la terre a ceux qui la travaillent." Benattig, "Impact of the agrarian reform on employment," p. 19; Raffinot and Jacquemot, Capitalisme d'état, p. 353; Chaulet, "Paysans et collectifs," p. 16; Benattig and de Villers, "Emploi en milieu rural," pp. 18-19.

70. Three works have recently become available in the Algerian literature that confirm the analysis made here. They are Slimane Bedrani, L'agriculture

algérienne depuis 1966, étatisation ou privatisation?
(Algiers: Office des Publications Universitaires,
1981); Fadela Haider, Les attributaires de la
révolution agraire, IV, emplois et revenus des
populations candidates à la révolution agraire (Algiers:
Institut National d'Etudes et d'Analyses pour la
Planification, 1980); and Ammar Touat, Villages
socialistes et révolution agraire, les problèmes de
l'emploi et des revenus (Algiers: Institut National
d'Etudes et d'Analyses pour la Planification, 1981).

4
The Impact of the Agrarian
Reform on Local Communities

This chapter reviews a set of studies based on first hand investigations of the changes wrought by the agrarian reform on the socio-economic structure of particular localities. The focus will be on the private agricultural sector and the new cooperative sector. The self-managed farms will be mentioned only in passing, since their status remained pretty much the same in the 1970s except for the changes in the pricing and marketing system described in Chapter 5 below. The reform of the 1970s did not create new state, or "self-managed," farms, but it left the existing ones unchanged.

At the most general level, we are looking for pressures emanating out of the reform toward increased commercialization, or the production of commodities for sale in the market, in the private and cooperative sectors of agriculture. This can, of course, take the form of encouraging both private family farms and the new production cooperatives to convert from subsistence agriculture to cash cropping. If this took place without other shifts in the socio-economic structure, then the reform would have created, or at least enlarged, the category of yeomen farmers, or simple commodity producers.

However, it is also possible that the reform could, at least tacitly, encourage the development of capitalist agriculture, both in the private sector and in the cooperative sector. In this analysis the "development of capitalism" is used as defined in Chapter 1 above. Commodity production for market exchange is a necessary, but not a sufficient, condition. What distinguishes capitalism from simple commodity production is (1) the consistent employment of wage labor by the owners of capital and their concomitant appropriation of surplus labor and (2) investment in capital, often embodying new technology, in order to raise labor productivity and thus to raise the profitability of the farm unit.

Because the latter process implies the accumulation of capital, as a capitalist system develops it is characterized by class differentiation over the long run. That is, competition among production units results in the success of the more profitable ones, which grow larger, while the less profitable tend to go into debt and fold. Among simple commodity producing farmers ("yeomen") this results in a bifurcation between a class of employer farmers ("gentry") on the one hand and a class of dispossessed wage laborers on the other hand, many of whom leave agriculture altogether.

Family farming does not necessarily disappear entirely, as mechanization displaces wage labor and the unit running the enlarged farming enterprise remains in family (as opposed to corporate) hands. This was the pattern that prevailed in the United States until the 1980s in grain production. It can also happen that the expansion in urban demand for certain types of labor-intensive crops, such as market garden vegetables and dairy products, may encourage the maintenance of family farms. But this can take place side-by-side with the capitalization of agriculture, and puts only the tiniest damper on the secular tendency for surplus labor to be shifted out of agricultural employment altogether.

Comment on Sources. In this chapter, reform-induced changes in the socio-economic organization of various communities has been inferred from an accumulation of several types of information.[1] The primary investigations were carried out with both survey-questionnaire and participant-observation techniques, which gives them a certain uniformity of approach. However, they were not all done under the auspices of a single research program, so there is a great deal of variation in the depth and quality of the data they provide, ranging from highly polished works by seasoned professionals to pilot studies at research institutes and unpublished master's-degree theses by Algerian students. The presentation of each study will be accompanied by a brief evaluation of its reliability and methodological sophistication.

These studies are the ultimate base for understanding the real impact of the reform, and thus their weaknesses and strengths underpin the weaknesses and strengths of this book. The weakness of the overall argument made in this chapter is that it ultimately relies on individual sources which are often individually unvalidated and unvalidatable. But the strength of the argument rests on the fact that these are all of the sources available--none was left out and none was pruned in any way that would prejudice the results derived from it. This strength is reinforced

by the fact that these studies, undertaken by
individuals without a coordinated tendency to pre-judge
the evidence (indeed many expressed surprise at what
they found), tend to confirm one another. The
conclusions emerge fairly consistently from one to the
next, and breed confidence as they accumulate.

The empirical studies follow one of two possible
methodologies. In some the researchers provide
numerical data on socio-economic class differentiation
for particular localities by comparing the size
distribution of land holdings, as correlated with other
forces of production (employment of wage labor, use of
machinery, technological innovation), before the land
reform and after.² In several cases, they explicitly
also compare the private sector to the
newly-established reform sector, and describe the
institutions and social relations of the latter. This
set of studies is the more reliable.

In the other studies, based mainly on participant
observation and questionnaires in the anthropological
style, the researchers provide descriptive data on
social and production relations in the private sector
in comparison with the reform sector. These studies
thus offer only indirect, circumstantial evidence.

Nature of Data Examined. One crucial type of data
examined is the distribution of land and other means of
production in the private sector. What lands, public
or private or both, and in what amounts, were converted
to cooperative production? In those communities where
evidence of the presence of capitalism before the
reform is provided, how is that presence affected by
the reform? Is there continued inequality in land
distribution and access to other resources such as
water? Is there continued employment of wage labor,
and is there continued inequality in levels of
productivity and profitability within the private
sector. Are there tendencies for these measured
inequalities to widen under the pressures of
commercialization and competition?

Related questions revolve around data indicating
whether the new institutions created by the reform have
affected the private sector through the markets for
land, inputs and credit. Has the elimination of urban
absenteeism in the private sector in those regions
where the reform was most successful in its own terms,
such as Constantine, freed the land to go to private
capitalist farmers as well as to the reform
cooperatives? Have the capitalist farmers obtained
increased access to inputs, credit, and marketing
facilities, as a result of the reform, because the
monopoly power of the old landlord-merchant-usurer
class was curtailed by the reform service cooperatives?
Which farmers are favored by credits awarded by the

national bank?

Another type of data to be examined is the effect of the reform on the transfer of the small producers from independent work on the land into wage labor in both agriculture and industry, or into unemployment. Has the pace of this transfer been accelerated or decelerated? Did most of the renters and sharecroppers who were dispossessed from the nationalized lands become beneficiaries who received land under the reform? What happened to those who did not receive land? How has the encouragement of productivity-increasing mechanization in all agricultural sectors by the relative price structure and credit allocation policies accompanying the reform affected employment in agriculture and the pre-existing pattern of migration to the cities? Do the reform cooperatives differ from the private farms in this regard? If surplus labor is being forced to leave the land, has provision been made to absorb these workers into alternative employment or to provide them with a minimum standard of living during the transition?

A third type of data comes from examination of the dynamics of the cooperative sector itself. What is the distribution of endowments among the cooperatives? Are they expected to specialize along lines governed by their franchise from the communal authority that set them up? Do they operate in a centrally planned or a competitive market environment? What is the criterion of success for the production unit: profit-maximization, output maximization, or employment maximization? Do the cooperatives have differential access to bank credit, based on the bank's estimation of their prospects for success? Do they have differential capacities for investment and accumulation? What happens to the members of a failed cooperative?

Related questions revolve around relations among members within a cooperative. Are they equally endowed, in terms of access to land and other means of production, the maintenance of previous social and economic status, income distribution, and in possibilities for employment of or search for wage labor? What happens to the less well-endowed members of a cooperative?

Organization of Data. The presentation of the data is organized in this chapter by region of the country. This method has a historical as well as a geographical dimension. Table 4.1 shows the distribution of the communities studied by geo-economic zone and the type of evidence offered by those who studied them.[3]

There are five geo-economic zones. Zone I is made
up of the rich coastal plains around the urban
industrial centers, Alger in the center (the plain of
Mitidja), Oran in the west, and Annaba in the east.
These were the regions in which the Europeans exercised
their most penetrating influence, both in terms of the
establishment of their own capitalist farms and the
encouragement of land concentration and class
differentiation among the Algerian population. The
colonial farms with their advanced techniques became
mostly self-managed in the aftermath of the war of
national liberation, so the self-managed farms tend to
predominate here today.

It is no accident that the process of
socio-economic transformation was most advanced in this
region of Algeria at the time of the reform. It was
the region most heavily penetrated by colonialism prior
to independence, and had undergone rapid
industrialization since then. It is the area in which
agricultural capitalism has the longest history and in
which the demand for wage labor was growing in the
1960s and 1970s. The first factor pushes the small
producers off the land by undermining their
self-sufficiency, while the second factor pulls them
off by offering the only available alternative to slow
starvation.

By 1971, when the reform was declared, there were
no real "peasants" left here, either in the sense of
self-sufficient domestic producers or in the sense of
simple commodity producers. While the majority of
private farms are owned and run by families, and are in

TABLE 4.1--Communities Studied, by Geo-Economic Zone and Type
of Evidence

Zone	Type of Evidence		
	Statistical	Mixed	Descriptive
I. Coastal plains	Besbès	Zemmouri	Cheraga, Thénia
II. Foothills up to Tellian Atlas	Souagui Merad	El-Arrouche	Berroughia
III. High plains	F'kirina	Ain Djasser El-Khroub	Ain Nehala Ras el-Oued Sour el-Ghozlane
IV. High interior mountains; Kabylia	Bousselam	Arris Collo	Salah Bey Guenzat Babor
V. Desert oases	Touggourt M'ghaier Djemaâ	Oumache	

that sense family farms, they engage in
truck-gardening, using wage labor, irrigation and
intensive methods to produce fruit, vegetables and
dairy and poultry products for the urban markets and
for export. The rest of the population are wage and
salary workers, in industry, in offices, commerce and
services, and on the self-managed and private farms.

Zone II includes the river valleys (for example,
Chelif and Soummam) and foothills leading up to the
Tellian Atlas mountains (coastal range). This zone,
not as naturally rich as Zone I and harder to farm, is
not as far along in the development of the modern forms
of agricultural production. Class differentiation is
ongoing, with some large-scale private production of
cereals, but also with some small and middle peasants
still producing cereals for subsistence and selling
their labor power seasonally to local self-managed and
private farms. The most rapid growth for intensive
private farming is occurring in tree fruits,
vegetables, and grapes for sale at nearby urban
markets. The self-managed sector is moderately
important.

Zone III includes the high plains, areas
penetrated to a lesser degree than Zones I and II by
the colonizers but still influenced heavily by colonial
capitalist market and land policies. These plains,
punctuated by inland urban enclaves (such as
Constantine, Saida, Tlemcen) which house both large
markets and absentee landowners, naturally lend
themselves to highly mechanized extensive
cereal-culture and animal grazing. Class
differentiation is well developed here, with a long
history of land concentration and the rural-to-urban
migration of small and landless peasants seeking wage
employment. The self-managed farms are important, but
not predominant, in this zone. Cereal production and
now beef cattle, as well as sheep rearing, are the
agricultural growth sectors.

Zone IV is the region of high mountains,
especially of the inland Saharan Atlas range and the
Kabylia range, which remain remote and underdeveloped
in both the economic and social senses. The colonial
power sorely neglected the needs of this zone, since
the European colonizers did not find any profitable
activity to pursue here, and, through their land
expropriation policies elsewhere, forced these regions
to become overpopulated, over farmed and eroded. These
inaccessible areas were where the native population
retreated in seeking to defend itself against the
French armies. These regions have a long history of
having the poorest and most backward agriculture, a
poor peasantry scratching a meager existence from the
land and the highest rates of outmigration, especially

to France, to find work. Class differentiation has occurred, but within a narrower range than elsewhere. The market-oriented private farmers are cultivating fruit trees. These seem to be mainly family farms, supplemented by seasonal wage labor.

Zone V is a chain of oases extending from Biskra (at the base of the southern face of the Saharan Atlas) into the Saharan desert. This zone, like Zone III, was heavily influenced by the colonizers (although not as thoroughly as Zone I) who learned by the end of the nineteenth century that date-palm production could be highly profitable. Some of the finest dates in the world, highly prized in the markets of Europe, are grown here. Class differentiation is well developed here too, with a high degree of palm concentration and the extensive employment of palm-less sharecroppers and, increasingly, wage labor on large plantations. Self-managed plantations exist here in significant numbers, but the private plantations are much more important.

Three of the sets of studies used here attempt to provide systematic comparisons among localities and regions.[4] Their cross-sectional comparative approach is based on the reasoning that the historic process of capitalist development in Algeria took place at different rates in different regions, paced by the penetration of French colonialism and the institutional changes made in response to it. Because the qualitative description provided by many of the community studies substantiates the validity of the cross-sectional comparative approach, it will be used again in this chapter, accompanied whenever possible by time-series data as well.

ZONE I. THE COASTAL PLAINS

There are six Zone I communities for which information is available, one in the plain of Annaba near the coastal industrial town of Annaba, and five in the plain of Mitidja surrounding the national capital Algiers (Alger). While the analysis of Besbès (Annaba) is more complete and relies more on numerical data, the others are brief and descriptive. Besbès was analyzed by a Ministry of Labor - International Labor Organization team, as part of a comparative study of four communes in four different zones (Besbès in Zone I, Souagui in Zone II, F'kirina in Zone III and Bousselam in Zone IV). The methodology applied to these four, then, is strictly symmetrical and of great value to a broader analysis.[5]

Plain of Annaba: Besbès

The commune of Besbès, in the daïra Dréan, wilaya
of Annaba, is typical of the coastal plain wherein
industrialization is combined with large-scale modern
agriculture. It therefore has a very high proportion
of people living outside agriculture and a very high
proportion of wage workers. In 1973, out of a total
population of 25,435 only 32 percent were dependent on
the private agricultural sector for their livelihood.
Fifty-nine percent of the economically active
population (23 percent of all adults) were wage
workers, including those employed on the self-managed
farms.

Because this region was historically overrun by
European settlers, the self-managed farms (former
colonial estates) are extensive. They occupied 13,830
hectares (78 percent of the area's total usable
agricultural land) in 1975-76, and employed 1,793
permanent workers.

Except for interviews conducted by the researchers
concerning economic activity, the only data used in the
Benattig-de Villers study come from the 1973
Recensement Générale d'Agriculture (RGA) survey,
hereafter to be referred to as the agricultural census,
by the Ministry of Agriculture, and are thus subject to
some stringent qualifications. The usefulness of these
data is limited in three regards. First, the 1973
agricultural census gives statistics only on land
owners resident in the commune--the inclusion of
absentee-owners would probably raise the land
concentration ratio significantly. The exclusion of
absentee-owners distorts results by hiding a major form
of pre-capitalist tenure. Second, the agricultural
census does not distinguish land owned from land
rented, the latter being much less evenly distributed
than the former, nor does it distinguish irrigated from
non-irrigated land. Third, the census data were
collected on the eve of the second phase of the reform,
and do not take account of all the evasions and
distortions landholders used to avoid being
expropriated. The best that these data provide, then,
is a lower limit of the extent of class differentiation
(in itself marked) and numerous, often inadvertent, but
scattered pieces of evidence that capitalist production
was developing prior to the reform and continues today.

Table 4.2 (agricultural census, 1973, for
residents only) shows a marked level of inequality in
land distribution. Because of the relatively rich
quality of the soil at Besbès, the reform agents set
five hectares of dry land as the amount needed to
support a family, with the ceiling for private holdings
set at twelve hectares (for a family with dependent

children). The top 10 percent of farm units (those
having five hectares or more) hold 85 percent of the
usable agricultural land. Those units having fifty
hectares or more (only 1 percent of all units) alone
control 32 percent of the usable agricultural land,
according to this survey.

There is a positive association between size of
land holdings and the pursuit of modern cultivation.
Those units having between one and ten hectares have
one-fourth to one-third of their land fallow, much more
than those having more than ten hectares (large
proprietors with extensive market-oriented cereal
production) or those having less than one hectare, most
of whom are involved in intensive, irrigated production
of vegetables for market. The latter have almost half
their lands in market gardens. The one to ten hectare
group have only about one quarter of their lands in
market gardens. The ten-hectare-and-up group have 42
percent of their lands in market gardens, and, within
that, the fifty-hectare-and-up group have over half in
market gardens and a greater amount than any other
group in other uses.

The authors also report an association between the
extensive production of marketable cereals by the
larger units (ten hectares and up) and the production
of leguminous vegetables and animal fodder, which are
both market crops and serve to replenish the nutrients
in the soil in a three-field system of crop rotation.
Eighty-five percent of these units use mechanical
traction, most of which is owned by them (it appears in
Table 4.2 that cattle are not highly concentrated,
perhaps because the larger units have little use for
animal traction).[6] Furthermore, half of those units use
chemical fertilizer. As we shall demonstrate below,
the employment of wage labor by these units is also
extensive.

The agrarian reform had a minimal impact on this
structure. The first phase nationalized 148 hectares
of communal lands. The second phase nationalized 2,364
hectares (which was 60 percent of the total usable
agricultural land of the private sector prior to the
reform), however it was mostly the property of
absentees holding more than twelve hectares each,[7] and
therefore was largely outside the agricultural census
data reported in Table 4.2 above. After the second
phase of the reform, the registered agricultural land
was divided among the sectors thus: 78 percent to
self-managed farms, 14 percent to the reform, and 8
percent to the private sector.

The researchers report that it is common knowledge
in the communes that large-scale resident proprietors
escaped expropriation by registering the land in the
names of many family members who are in principle, but

104

TABLE 4.2--Distribution of Private Agricultural Land Holdings, Animals, and Crops, Besbès 1973, by Size Category of Farm Unit

| Size Category of Farm Unit (hectares) | Farm Units | | Total Land Area | | Distribution of Total | | | |
| | | | | | Cereals | | Fallow | |
	No.	%	No.	%	Ha.	%	Ha.	%
Less than 1	519	81	34	3	4	1	7	7
1-4.99	62	10	144	12	55	11	26	25
5-9.99	34	5	170	15	77	15	38	36
10-19.99	11	2	139	12	58	11	16	15
20-49.99	11	2	301	26	182	36	10	9
50 and more	5	1	371	32	132	26	9	8
Subtotal of landed units	642	100	1,159	100	508	100	106	100
Landless units	545	...	...	...	...	...	...	...
Total of all units	1,187	...	...	...	...	...	...	...

SOURCE: Benattig and de Villers,"Emploi en milieu rural,""Besbès," pp. 8 and 40, based on RGA 1973 data (adapted).

[a]Includes vineyards, orchards, olive groves.

TABLE 4.3--Distribution of Adult Population Living on Farms, Besbès 1973, by Size Category of Farm Unit and Economic Activity

| Size Category of Farm Unit (hectares) (1) | Economic Activity of Farmers | | | Family Aids Who Work Solely on Own Farm (5) |
	No. of Farmers[a] (Col. 3 + 4) (2)	Farmers Who Work Solely On Own Farm (3)	Farmers With Other Activity Part-time (4)	
Less than 1	526	79	447	313
1-<5	62	24	38	41
5-<10	26	17	9	35
10-<20	10	7	3	17
20-<50	11	8	3	28
50 and up	4	4	0	10
Subtotal landed farmers	639	139	500	444
Landless farmers	487	77	410	540
Total all farmers	1,126	216	910	984

SOURCE: Benattig and de Villers,"Emploi en milieu rural,""Besbès," p. 3 (adapted).

[a]The number of farmers in Tables 43 and 44 is slightly different from the number of farm units in Table 42 because of leasing and indivision.

TABLE 4.2--Continued

Land Area by Crop Type				Distribution of Animals					
Market-Garden		Other Uses[a]		Cattle		Sheep		Goats	
Ha.	%	Ha.	%	No.	%	No.	%	No.	%
15	3	8	7	361	23	229	20	72	31
49	11	14	13	103	7	32	3		
35	8	20	19	45	3	81	7	13	6
47	11	18	17	67	4	56	5		
103	24	6	6	50	3	13	1		
190	43	40	38	29	2	53	5		
439	100	106	100	655	41	464	40	85	37
...	...	...	...	929	59	698	60	145	63
...	...	...	...	1,584	100	1,162	100	230	100

TABLE 4.3--Continued

Economic Activity of Farm Family Members

Family Aids With Other Activity Part-Time (6)	Wage Workers, Off Own Farm (7)	Non-Agric. Non-Wage Workers, Off Own Farm (8)	Econ. Active Adult Pop. (Col. 2 + 5 + 6 + 7 + 8) (9)	Housewives and Inactive (10)	Total Adult Pop. (Col. 9 + 10) (11)
2	217	11	1,069	1,311	2,380
0	32	2	137	152	289
0	13	0	74	72	146
0	8	1	36	28	64
0	3	0	42	32	74
0	0	0	14	12	26
2	273	14	1,372	1,607	2,979
7	198	23	1,255	1,034	2,289
9	471	37	2,627	2,641	5,268

not in practice, expected to work the land themselves. Proper reporting of their holdings would certainly raise the concentration level in the above tables. Even those proprietors who were limited under the land reform have maintained their superior economic status, because the lands they kept they have since brought under irrigation (a form of capital investment only the gentry can afford to make). The large-scale capitalist farmers are not dependent on the service cooperative for farm equipment or inputs, as they have their own sources and as they market their output through private merchants. For example, they have their tomatoes delivered directly to two privately-owned canning factories in the town of Besbès. Their most serious constraint is the scarcity of spare parts for machinery and the lack of repair facilities.

Of the simple commodity producers and smaller-scale capitalist farmers, the five to twenty hectare group, fifty-one benefited directly from communal-sponsored projects in 1976-77 to intensify irrigated vegetable production using new seeds, motorized pumps, and cultivators. They are marketing their increased output through private channels, however, abnegating their contractual obligation to market through the state service cooperative (CAPCS).

The authors describe actual cases of the three classes of farm units, cases which they define as representative of their direct field observations. These observations were made after the reform.

Type I is a large-scale capitalist farm. The farmer owns 21.5 hectares (and is associated with a brother who also has 21.5 hectares);[8] he owns a tractor, two cows and twenty sheep, rents other machinery as he needs it, and hired 3,500 days of wage labor in 1976-77. One half of his gross product is in wheat and one half in tomatoes. In a good tomato year, such as 1976-77, this farmer (alone, not counting his brother's income) nets 98,024 dinars; a bad year might yield only 60,000 dinars. This is a very profitable operation.

Type II is a middle "peasant," or simple commodity producer. The farmer owns 3.5 hectares, part in cereal for family consumption, part in tomatoes for sale to the cannery. He owns no animals and no machinery. He himself does not work outside the farm, but his son does (as a day worker on a self-managed farm). He does not hire wage labor. He must borrow money at planting time to purchase seed. His net revenue is three thousand dinars, exactly what a reform beneficiary is supposed to earn (and what is considered necessary to support a rural family).

Type III is a "poor peasant." The farmer and his brother together own 1.5 irrigated hectares and two

cows. They produce vegetables for family consumption
and tomatoes for sale to the cannery. They must rent a
tractor, purchase fodder for the cows, and borrow to
purchase seeds and fertilizer at planting time. Their
joint net agricultural revenue is 2,215 dinars per year
(which is the equivalent of one-fourth of the yearly
salary of a full-time wage laborer). They are both
permanent full-time wage workers on a neighboring
self-managed farm.[9]

Besbès shows the most developed form of class
differentiation of the four regions studied by Benattig
and de Villers. In fact one can hardly speak of "rich
peasants" and "poor peasants" here, for these have
already evolved into capitalist farmers and wage
workers, respectively--the vast gap in income is only
the most obvious sign. The relative decline of the
self-sufficient middle peasant class (which bifurcates
into a few successful rich peasants and many poor
peasants as capitalist development proceeds) is the
linch pin in the process. The necessity for the son of
the simple commodity producing farmer to do wage labor
denies true self-sufficiency.

In order to examine the impact of the reform on
the deployment of wage labor, the researchers conducted
a survey of farm households. The results for 1973 for
Besbès, prior to the second phase of the reform, are
shown in Table 4.3. In this table, the distribution of
the total adult population living on farms in Besbès is
shown by size category of farm unit and type of
economic activity. There seems to be an association
between the size of the farm unit and the outside
employment of farmers (male heads of farm family
households): 84 percent of the landless farmers work
outside the farm units on which they live as renters or
leasers, as compared to 85 percent of those having less
than one hectare, 6 percent of the 1-5 hectare group,
35 percent of the 5-10 hectare group, 30 percent of the
10-50 hectare group, and none of the 50-hectare-and-up
group. Altogether, 55 percent of the economically
active population work outside (columns 4, 6, 7, 8),
and the rate falls as the size class goes up.
Sixty-six percent of economically active males are
employed outside their farms, and fully two-thirds of
wage workers living on farms have regular full-time
jobs off the farm.

The larger units have higher revenues and can
support a larger number of non-workers. Table 4.4
shows that the average size of the farm household tends
to increase along with the size of the farm unit, while
the average number of economically active persons
living on farms who work outside the farm decreases.
The importance of outside economic activity in
agriculture is greatest for the landless group, and

TABLE 4.4 --Size of Household and Number of Economically Active Persons outside of Farm Unit, Besbès 1973, by Size Category of Farm Unit

Size Category of Farm Unit (hectares) (1)	No. of Farmers (2)	Total Farm Population (3)	Avg. Size of Household/Farmer (Col. 3 ÷ 2) (4)	No. of Persons Working in Agric. Off Own Farm (5)	No. of Persons Working Outside of Agric. Off Own Farm (6)	Ttl. No. of Persons Working Off Own Farm (Col. 5 + 6)[a] (7) No.	%[b]	Avg. No. of Persons Working Off Own Farm Per Farmer (Col. 7 ÷ 2) (8)
Less than 1	526	3,769	7.2	379	298	677	63	1.3
1-<5	62	466	7.5	28	44	72	53	1.2
5-<10	26	184	7.1	11	11	22	30	0.8
10-<20	10	80	8.0	1	11	12	33	1.2
20-<50	11	104	9.5	2	4	6	14	0.5
50 and up	4	37	9.3	0	0	0	0	0
Subtotal landed Farmers	639	4,640	7.3	421	368	789	58	1.2
Landless Farmers	487	3,552	7.3	429	209	638	51	1.3
Total all Farmers	1,126	8,192	7.3	850	577	1,427	54	1.3

SOURCE: Benattig and de Villers, "Emploi en milieu rural," "Besbès," pp. 4 and 5 (adapted).

[a]These totals for each size category are equal to the addition of columns 4, 6, 7, and 8 in Table 4.3. Column 9 in Table 4.3 gives Economically Active Population.

[b]Percentage of Economically Active Population.

non-agricultural outside employment is relatively more important as the size of unit increases. The exception is the five-to-ten hectare group, the simple producers, who work their own land more intensively.

While 87 percent of salaried (full-time) agricultural wage workers are employed on the self-managed farms, there is demand for wage labor in the private agricultural sector as well. As Table 4.5 shows, farm units having ten or more hectares provide the equivalent of 208 full-time jobs, but can fill only forty-two of them from their own family members. Because many of the larger families registered as working their own land in order to avoid expropriation when they actually do no labor themselves, this figure of 208 is a minimum. Column 7 of Table 4.5 gives a maximum estimate of the rate of disguised unemployment.

The reform has had only a marginal impact on the distribution of the labor force. At first there were 784 candidates who presented themselves for allotments of lands. However, about half of those eventually opted for non-agricultural jobs as wage laborers, so that beneficiaries had to be recruited from outside the region. The reform set up twenty-five production cooperatives on 2,158 hectares of land,[10] with between 331 and 378 cooperative members, sixty of whom were immigrants.[11] With planned irrigation, the number of beneficiaries on these lands was supposed to double. However, by 1978, one-third of the cooperative members sampled by the researchers had withdrawn, in order to go into higher-paying wage labor, and not all had been replaced.

The production cooperatives are generally either well-endowed with good land and equipment or their lands are potentially irrigable and they have access to good equipment through the service cooperative. There are constraints on their success however: they must compete with the private sector for the service cooperative's equipment. The beneficiaries illegally plant for domestic consumption and try to avoid following the communal plan. They must hire scarce and expensive part-time wage labor to fulfill their work plans. And their internal structure is authoritarian rather than democratic, with power concentrated in the president's hands. Although all six production cooperatives studied made profits in 1974-75, and three made profits in 1975-76,[12] the beneficiaries' personal income (3,000 to 9,200 dinars/year) is generally inferior to that of the self-managed farm workers. The self-managed workers were earning 6,000 to 13,500 dinars per year in Besbès at this time, while the average wage of the reform candidates who were not awarded land allotments and went into other employment was 7,800 dinars per year.

TABLE 4.5--Employment Furnished by Farm Units and Estimated Rates of Disguised Unemployment, Besbès 1973, by Size Category of Farm Unit

Size Category of Farm Unit (hectares) (1)	Equiv. of No. of Persons Available for Full-time Work (2)	Equiv. of No. of Active Persons Working Full-time Off Own Farm (3)	Equiv. of No. of Active Persons Full-time on Farm (Col. 2-3) (4)	Ttl. Employment (No. of Full-time Jobs) Furnished on Farm (5)	Employment Shortage (+) or Surplus (-) (Col. 4-5) (6)	Rate of Disguised Unemployment (Col. 6÷2) (7)
Less than 1	1,007	452.5	554.5	49	505.5	50%
1-<5	123	53	70	43	27	22%
5-<10	74	17.5	56.5	44	12.5	17%
10-<20	22	10.5	11.5	61	-49.5[a]	...
20-<50	29	4.5	24.5	65	-40.5[a]	...
50 and up	6	0	6	82	-76[a]	...
Subtotal landed units	1,261	538	723	343	380	30%
Landless units	890	429.5	460.5	107	353.5	40%
Total all units	2,151	967.5	1,183.5	450	733.5	34%

SOURCE: Original data from Benattig and de Villers,"Emploi en milieu rural," "Besbès," p. 8. See Appendix C for methodology.

[a]The "surplus" of jobs on the larger-scale farm units implies the employment of wage labor there, and reduces the overall rate of disguised unemployment.

TABLE 4.6--Distribution of Private Agricultural Land, the Mitidja, 1973, by Size Category of Property

Size Category of Property (in hectares)	No. of Proprietors	% of Proprietors	Land Area (hectares)	% of Land Area
0-1	2,150	49	689.1	4
>1-5	1,484	34	3,319.9	18
>5-10	326	8	2,269.5	12
>10-20	246	6	3,768.0	20
>20-50	88	2	2,874.5	16
More than 50	57	1	5,493.4	30
Total	4,351	100	18,414.4	100

SOURCE: Georges Mutin, "L'agriculture en la Mitidja ou les difficultés d'une reconversion," Annuaire de l'Afrique du Nord, 1975 (1976), p. 153.

In summary, in the case of Besbès, we see that capitalist agriculture was ongoing prior to the reform within the confines set by the relative importance of the self-managed sector in this region. The reform nationalized only the absentee-owned lands and left the capitalist sector described here largely undisturbed in terms of the land distribution, means of production it holds, and wage labor it employs. The reform did not give land to the majority of the landless farmers, and did not solve the rural underemployment problem. But it has contributed to moving the small producers both in Besbès and from elsewhere into wage labor in local agriculture and industry.

Furthermore, the reform has improved the prospects for private agriculture by freeing up employable labor from the absentee-held lands that were nationalized, and by providing the social overhead capital investment required for irrigation, machinery embodying new technology and seed selection.

The Plain of Mitidja

The Mitidja, the rich plain surrounding Algiers, was the heart of the French colonial project.[13] Before the reform, the private sector held only 18,414 hectares, 15 percent of all agricultural lands, most of which were specialized in intensive cultivation of crops such as fruits and vegetables for sale to the urban market. Despite the small size of the private sector, commercial agriculture, especially based on irrigation of the market-garden farms, is well-developed. The rest of the land is held by self-managed farms inherited from the former European farmers, except for 4,669 hectares of public lands, which were controlled by rich native Algerian farmers.

The distribution of the private lands is shown in Table 4.6. Nine percent of proprietors have ten hectares or more, for a total of 12,135.87 hectares (about two-thirds of the land). The author of this table tells us that the holdings of less than one hectare are rarely worked as distinct units, and that leasing is rare, but he does not tell us what does happen to these lands. In any event, the reform nationalized 3,468 hectares of the public lands and 6,578 hectares of private lands, significant amounts which must have some effect on the social structure. Unfortunately, we do not have a distribution of lands by size category of holdings after the reform. We are only told that only small and medium farms (size category not specified) are left, and that private farms that existed as enclaves inside the boundaries of the self-managed farms have been eliminated.[14]

To get a fuller picture, one must turn to investigations of particular communities. For the plain of Mitidja, there are three separate studies involving five communes, two east of Algiers (Zemmouri and Thénia) where the reform seems to have been insignificant, and three west of Algiers (Douera, Staoueli and Zeralda, all in the daïra of Cheraga) where its impact is important but not overwhelming.

Zemmouri. The community of Zemmouri, county Boudouaou, province of Alger, is only sixty-eight kilometers east of the city of Algiers. It is like Besbès in both its natural endowments and its history of intense colonial penetration. It is comprised mainly of fertile plains, with some forests and eroded foothills on its boundary. In winter, the river Isser floods the plains, making them suitable for wet lands crops. Orchards and animal fodder production are common in the areas above the flood plain. Its richness attracted European settlers in the nineteenth century, and continues to attract migrant Algerians today; it is therefore well supplied with routes of transportation and commerce. Its population in 1974 was 17,307, up an impressive 22 percent from 1966. About 88 percent of the male active workforce are employed in agriculture, most on self-managed farms.

Our only information on this commune comes from a thesis written by a student interested in a related topic, the impact of the reform on the income of beneficiaries.[15] His study was based on first-hand interviews and survey research. However, because his focus is different from ours, he provides only a limited amount of data for our use. Furthermore, he relies entirely on local government data for the distribution of land in the private sector, and makes no attempt to offer an independent evaluation of its validity. All we can say about it is to remember its general limitations. The first limitation is that it was gathered under the duress of the impending reform and thus encouraged large landholders to obscure their holdings in order to avoid expropriation. The second limitation is that it was gathered by the same agency responsible for enforcing the reform, which in most cases was a local government controlled by the very landholders who were officially supposed to be the objects of the reform.

The richness of the land in Zemmouri and its historic attraction to European settlers led to the cultivation of predominantly cereals and wine grapes for sale to market. When the Europeans left in 1962, most of their estates were converted to self-managed farms by the Algerian workers employed there. The relative importance of these types of crops and of the self-managed farms in Zemmouri agriculture in 1970 can be seen in Table 4.7. The "socialist sector" (self-managed farms) held 58 percent of total usable agricultural land, and 61 percent of all usable agricultural land actually under cultivation. Of its cultivated lands, the self-managed sector had 64 percent in cereals and wine grape production. Although the private sector had 64 percent of its cultivated lands in cereals alone and none in wine grapes, and had a higher percentage of its total usable land uncultivated, 40 percent for the private sector (as opposed to 26 percent for the self-managed sector), it also showed a respectable number of productive hectares in fruit and vegetable production for market, 36 percent, much of which is irrigated (760 hectares).

The author does not provide a distribution of private lands by size category prior to the reform. He does define, however, what the reform's exact impact was. First, it transferred part of the communal lands that had been rented out to the control of newly created production cooperatives (between 352 and 372 hectares out of the 517--and only fifty-eight hectares are irrigated--presumably the balance was retained by private lease holders). Second, it nationalized sixty-three hectares of private absentee-owned lands. The distribution of registered lands after the reform is given in Table 4.8. In the case of Zemmouri, the reform had the effect of increasing the amount of land cultivated by the private farmers (from 2,464 hectares in 1970 to 3,257 hectares in 1975), as the owners put unused land to use in order to avoid expropriation.[16]

The reform awarded allotments to twenty-nine cooperative members organized into five production cooperatives. The author says withdrawal from the cooperatives has been high, especially with the growth of local industries, such as quarrying and fish processing. The production cooperatives compensate by themselves hiring wage labor.

In the case of Zemmouri, the reform's impact seems to have been negligible. The private sector was registered as holding about one-third of the agricultural land prior to the reform and held that same share after the reform. Within the private sector, after the reform, owners of five hectares or more (5 percent of all private owners) were registered as holding 31 percent of the privately held land. Owners of ten hectares or more (1 percent of all private owners) still held 15 percent. As in Besbès, only public lands and absentee-owned lands were nationalized, and their absolute size remains small (only 5 percent of all lands after the reform). Also, as in Besbès, the transfer of producers into the wage labor force has not been altered. For Zemmouri, one can say that the reform preserved the private sector and wage labor flow, but we have no evidence that it either slowed down or sped up their further development.

Thénia. Thénia is a coastal community in the province of Algiers, next door to Zemmouri. It is distinct in that, while it has rich agricultural lands and an important self-managed farm sector created out of former colonial estates, the private sector is very strong. Like other communities around Algiers, it is relatively industrialized: there are two state-owned factories producing explosives, which employ 750 people, and two more were in the process of being built in 1978. Many industrial workers commute to work in factories at nearby Rouiba, Reghaia and Boumerdes.[17] Thénia has a well-developed infrastructure, for example, adequate schools and medical facilities, and a

TABLE 4.7--Distribution of Agricultural Land, Zemmouri 1970, by Sector and Type of Crop

Type of Crop	Socialist Sector[a]	(%)	No. of Hectares Private Sector	(%)	Communal Sector[c]	(%)	Total All Sectors
Cereals	1,472		1,580		52		3,104
Market garden	447		290		37		774
Animal fodder	462		134		6		602
Pulse	165		100		65		330
Fruit orchards	148		100		248		496
Olive trees	112		90		8		210
Table grapes	127		90		30		247
Citrus groves	186		80		66		332
Wine grapes	1,557		0		5		1,562
Tobacco	30		0		0		30
Subtotal all productive lands	4,706	(61%)	2,464	(32%)	517	(7%)	7,687
Unproductive lands[b]	1,671		1,642		0		3,313
Total all lands	6,377	(58%)	4,106	(37%)	517	(5%)	11,000

SOURCE: Arbadji, "Revenu des attributaires," p. 21.

[a]"Socialist sector" means "self-managed" farms.

[b]"Unproductive lands" include those left fallow.

[c]"Communal sector" are all those publically or collectively held lands that were to be nationalized in the first phase of the reform.

TABLE 4.8--Distribution of Productive Agricultural Land[a], Zemmouri 1975, by Size Category of Farm Unit and Sector

Size Category of Farm Unit (ha.)	Sector of Farm Units	No. of Farm Units	Land Area (ha.)	% of Total Land Area	Average Size of Farm Unit (ha.)
Less than 5	private	2,190	2,240	24	1.02
5-10	private	90	533	6	5.92
10-20	private	19	256	3	13.47
20-50	private	7	228	2	32.57
Subtotal	all private	2,306	3,257	35	1.41
50-100	CARRA	5	352	4	70.40
More than 100	CARRA[b]	1	137	1	137.00
Subtotal	all CAPRA	6	489	5	81.50
	state farms	10	5,483	59	548.30
Total		2,322	9,229	100	3.97

SOURCE: Arbadji, "Revenu des attributaires," p. 23.

[a]Figures do not include unproductive or fallow agricultural land.

[b]This "CAPRA" is actually a converted former CAPAM, a state farm run by veterans of the war of national liberation. This explains its unusually large size.

standard of living twice as high as the national
average (measured as purchasing power of average money
income).

The study described here was conducted by a
student as part of the CREA survey of the impact of the
reform on various communities.[18] It is based on
administered questionnaires, interviews, and
participant observation. The author is self-conscious
about her critical theoretical outlook, which allows
her to offer valuable insights into the social
relations of the community. Her basic themes are that
the reform is a state-administered enterprise, that the
real decisions made by the production cooperatives are
minimal, that when the state falters the gap is filled
by the private sector, and that the reform cooperatives
themselves are tightly tied to the private sector and
reflect the inequalities of the private sector in their
own internal organization. The author challenges the
official reform ideology that the interests of the
state and poor peasants coincide, expressing the
disillusionment she shares with the other CREA
researchers with the reform's failure to achieve its
"socialist" goals.

In Thénia, the reform eliminated the last remnants
of pre-capitalist agriculture in the communal tenures
and the absentee landlord tenures. According to the
agricultural census, out of a total usable agricultural
land area of 5,500 hectares, prior to the reform 37
percent was held by three self-managed farms and 63
percent was held by 2,500 private farmers (a tiny
fraction of the latter as renters on communal lands).
Within the private sector, one-fourth of the land was
held by farmers having more than fifty hectares each.
As this is some of the most fertile land in Algeria,
these are rather rich holdings.[19] The reform
nationalized only the communal lands and the private
land of one absentee landlord, so that the reform
sector now holds only 4 percent of the total usable
agricultural land. Therefore, land distribution in the
private sector was left almost wholly intact after the
reform.

The private sector, both before and after the
reform, seems to have a thoroughly market-oriented
organization. All of the farms produce specialized
crops solely for market. The larger ones and
capital-intensive ones seem to be clearly capitalist,
as they employ wage labor systematically. The crops
produced include poultry,[20] vegetables, fruits, cereals
and animal fodder, table grapes and raisins, dairy
products and cattle for meat production.

In several ways, the private agricultural sector
has benefited from the reform. First, a more extensive
rental market in land and means of production has

emerged.   Financially strapped reform cooperatives
lease out their land to private farmers.   This is
technically   illegal,   but   Diabi   found that one
production cooperative earned more than half of its
revenue this way.   Sometimes the cooperatives also rent
out their unused equipment to the private farmers.   On
the other hand, when the service cooperative fails
them, the production cooperatives often turn to renting
equipment   from the large-scale private farmers or from
the self-managed farms.
      Another way   in which   the   private agricultural
sector benefited from the reform is through development
of specialization.   For example, the 1977 communal plan
had specified that the Thénia reform cooperatives were
to introduce cattle raising and to vertically integrate
that   activity   with   fodder   production.   The
cattle-raising part of the project never succeeded,
although the fodder supply was appropriately increased.
The result is that the private cattle producers already
linked to profitable urban meat markets now have a
reliable source of inexpensive fodder.[21]
      In some ways, the non-agricultural private sector
has also benefited from the reform.   State agencies are
delegated   the   responsibility   of   supplying   farm
equipment to the cooperatives (when the latter are able
to get credit approval from the bank;   see below).
However, these agencies do not provide spare parts or
after-sales service.   Therefore, these services are now
provided   by   local   private   firms.   Marketing of
agricultural output by the reform cooperatives through
private   channels   still   remains widespread.   In 1977,
all olives, wood, animal fodder and reeds were marketed
this way.   While all fresh fruits and vegetables
produced by the cooperatives are officially required to
be marketed through the state agencies, often these
agencies cannot handle all of the supply, or they fail
to pick them up and pay for them on schedule.   The
reform cooperative members then rely on   private
merchants to pick up the sometimes substantial slack.
      One of the reasons that the capitalist private
sector   seems to have retained, and even enhanced, its
role after the reform is that it remains in control of
the   critical   political institutions that administered
the reform.   In the communal assembly that made the
first set of decisions regarding land nationalizations,
for example, no poor farmers or self-managed farm
workers were represented;   the assembly was composed of
merchants, teachers, government functionaries, and big
landholders.   Land-holding members of the assembly made
a symbolic gesture of donating some tiny fraction of
their   poorer quality lands to the reform, in exchange
for a commitment in the communal budget for 1976 for
development of local industry, services and transport.

Their friends and allies outside of the assembly, the
rich farmers whose lands were supposed to be limited by
the reform, were allowed to declare their own holdings
without official corroboration.

The story of the peasant association (UNPA) in
Thénia is similar to that of the communal assembly.
The catch here is that this "peasant" organization in
Thénia functions to protect the private farmers'
interests, arranging credits from the national bank,
for example, to buy pumps for wells or henhouses for
private chicken farmers. In spite of the 1973 reform,
the UNPA at Thénia is still composed totally of
property owners, two of whom have four to five hectares
of irrigated lands, and many of whom have been to
Mecca.[22] One, a president of a production cooperative,
is reputed to be "rich": all of his children have been
to school, one son is a local central bank functionary,
and another is an Air Algérie (national airline) pilot.
Most of the reform beneficiaries interviewed do not
perceive the UNPA as "their" organization.

The way the reform was administered seems to have
created as many problems for the cooperative members as
it solved. The allotment of the lands, the
organization of the three production cooperatives, and
even the choice of crops to produce were decided
without the participation of the beneficiaries
themselves. The lands initially assigned by the
communal assembly were fragmented, needed intensive
work to become productive and were relatively poor
quality compared to other sectors in Thénia. They did
not even provide the minimum land necessary to support
a family. There were eighteen withdrawals immediately
after the assignments were made.

When a newly elected enlarged communal assembly
tried to improve on these assignments (for example, to
give cooperative Number One seven hectares of irrigated
lands, to build a henhouse for cooperative Number Two,
and give out an additional two hundred hectares of
nationalized land), it was prevented from doing so by
two state enterprises with interests in the area, one
of which distributes animal feed and the other of which
produces and distributes hydrocarbon products.[23]

Access to means of production other than land
depends on the cooperatives being able to get credit
from the national bank to purchase it. The grants are
made solely on the basis of financial solvency and
potential profitability (rentabilité financière),
although interest rates are low enough to constitute
indirect subsidies to those cooperatives that do get
the credit.[24] Because of the unequal initial
endowments, these credits tend to favor the already
relatively privileged cooperatives which can more
easily show actual or potential profitability. Only

one of the three production cooperatives in Thénia, based on mainly irrigated lands, earns a regular profit. The other two are continually in deficit and not expected to survive as ongoing enterprises.

There is stratification of authority within the production cooperatives that reflects the outside social structure. Whereas 86 percent of beneficiaries were formerly wage workers and most are illiterate, the presidents of the three production cooperatives are educated (at the elementary-school level) and serve as representatives to the outside world-- they construct the production plans (including amount of domestic consumption and the division of labor) and make applications for credit. The beneficiaries' assembly elects a governing council, but its function is merely to do the day-to-day work while the president makes the decisions. Furthermore, there is a status distinction within the assembly between the tractoristes, who do no direct manual labor, and the unskilled workers. Below the unskilled members are the non-member seasonal workers, mostly sixteen to twenty-year-olds who are paid low wages and do not have a right to share profits. In the reform cooperatives at Thénia almost half of all workdays are filled by seasonal labor: there are 1.6 non-member seasonal workers to each member beneficiary. There have been many interpersonal tensions within the cooperatives (for example, accusations of stealing and nepotism) arising from these inequalities, which have inhibited their smooth operation.[25]

The beneficiaries' income is unevenly distributed and many are forced to turn to other economic activities. Each beneficiary receives 175 dinars per month from the state as an advance on revenue through the year. Any profits at the end of the growing year are then shared according to the number of days worked. If the harvest is bad, or if the state marketing agencies fail to collect their output or provide too low a price, the beneficiaries expect to go into deficit and turn instead to consuming their own product. Many beneficiaries resist the state's urgings to increase output because these agencies do not take their product at a profitable enough price when market supply as a whole goes up.

Beneficiaries also turn to individual methods of earning extra money income from sales on the private markets of the produce from their private plots, and from their animal herds. As these lands and animals are unevenly distributed, such extra-cooperative activities exacerbate the inequalities among members.[26] Other sources of money income arise from renting more private land to work (one beneficiary does this), permanent agricultural employment on others' land

(three beneficiaries do this), season agricultural
employment on others' land (nine beneficiaries do
this), and non-agricultural wage labor (four
beneficiaries do this).

Many poorer cooperative members cannot take
advantage of what services the reform does provide
them. While all use the service cooperative's souk
(market for consumer goods) and dispensary, only eight
beneficiary families have children in school. Those
eight are the families with significant
extra-cooperative earnings. The others say that they
are ashamed to send their children to school barefoot
and in rags. Others complain that their housing is so
far from their land parcels and from the service
centers that they cannot possibly work their lands,
take care of their families and obtain the services
they need in the framework of their daily round of
tasks.

The rate of withdrawal from the reform is very
high here. Of the forty-nine original beneficiaries
(whose age range, forty-one to fifty years old, was
elderly by Algerian standards), only eighteen remained
in February 1977. Most of those who withdrew went into
wage labor elsewhere. The communal assembly cannot
find local replacements and claims that the reform
cooperatives have become merely a stepping stone on the
path followed by the agricultural wage worker, rather
than the way of life envisioned by the reform ideology.
The newest reform beneficiaries here are all from the
south, the sons of "rock breakers" (quarry workers?),
for whom the reform in Thénia represents an escape from
the poverty of the less well-endowed regions of the
country.

In Thénia, then, we have seen that the reform has
eliminated the last vestiges of pre-capitalist
structures, maintained and perhaps even benefited the
capitalist structures, created a tendency toward
capitalist relations within the cooperative sector, and
served as a channel for the flow of small agricultural
producers in both this region and from elsewhere into
wage labor.

Cheraga. Cheraga is a daïra (county) in the
western section of the wilaya of Alger. Lands here,
relatively rich and productive and close to the capital
city, were mainly taken over by Europeans during the
colonial period, and are now mainly run as self-managed
farms. The private agricultural sector and the reform
sector are thus proportionally small here.
Furthermore, industrial growth and an industrial
wage-labor force are increasingly important.

The study of Cheraga was done by an
inter-disciplinary research team through interviews and
participant observation in two communities, Douera and

Staoueli. A brief overview was done of a third
community, Zeralda, by another part of the team.   It is
good-quality   anthropology,   yielding   descriptive
insights, but without hard statistics.[27]

   The self-managed farm   sector   is   predominant   in
terms of both landholdings and proportion of the labor
force employed.   Of a total agriculturally useful   land
of   20,483   hectares in Cheraga, the self-managed farms
had 83 percent, the war veterans' farm and public lands
had   8.8 percent, and the pre-reform registered private
lands were only   8.2   percent.   However,   the   private
lands are mainly in the littoral and are specialized in
irrigated crops (fruits and vegetables) for   the   urban
market.   There   is no "self-sufficient" class of small
or middle peasants, producing either for   domestic
consumption   or   as simple commodity producers, in this
region.

   Of   a   total   economically   active   population   of
28,800   in   1966,   slightly less than half were in the
agricultural sector, and most of those were on   the
self-managed   farms   (5,000   as   permanent   workers and
7,660 as seasonal workers).   The   rest   were   employed
outside   of   agriculture   although   many still lived on
farms.[28]   Staoueli has a   dozen   industrial   units
(textiles,   wood processing, construction materials and
quarrying), and Douera has five (textiles,   plastics,
and   packaging).   The   nearby   towns of Ain Benian and
Cheraga   have   fifty-one   factories   between   them
(textiles, sweets, furniture, poultry processing, shoes
and chemicals).   Up to 12 percent of the labor force is
employed directly in industry.

   On   the   one   hand,   the   greater   power   of   the
self-managed   farm workforce in this region relative to
the lesser strength of   the   private   landowners   made
expropriation for   the reform easier to carry out.   On
the   other   hand,   the   availability   of   alternative
employment has allowed reform beneficiaries to withdraw
when the reform cooperatives have not worked out.

   Douera and Staoueli.   Before the reform,   communal
lands   had   been   rented   out   to   private   farmers,
categorized below by the amount of annual rent:

No. of Renters	Annual Rent Paid (in dinars)[29]	
37	less than 500	
23	501 - 1000	
12	1001 - 1500	Douera
10	1501 - 2000	
9	2001 - 2400	
3	4500 - 10,000	
8	10,001 - 20,000	
1	20,001 - 30,000	Staoueli
1	more than 30,000	

At Douera, 77 percent of the renters owned no land and worked their rented lands with family labor and wage labor--they were eligible to become beneficiaries of the first phase of the reform. Some of them were successful employer farmers, though they did not own the land themselves. The other 23 percent, having outside employment, but not themselves employing wage labor, were disqualified because they would be away too much. The land reform effectively benefited the haves more than the have-nots here.

At Staoueli, out of thirteen renters, seven were rich farmers employing four to five permanent workers and three to five seasonal workers each. The other six renters had outside employment and did not themselves work their lots. None of these renters was eligible to become a beneficiary of the first phase of the reform, although the workers they employed were.

The first phase of the reform expropriated 930 hectares of communal lands (of which 854 hectares were usable agricultural land) and organized them into twenty-eight production cooperatives with seven marketing cooperatives. Eight-hundred sixty-four candidates presented themselves in 1972 for the 678 places available. At Douera there were more candidates than places, while at Staoueli there were more places than candidates. The communal assembly rejected 380 of the local candidates, for unspecified reasons, and therefore had to transfer candidates in from other regions and then shift them around in order to correct disproportionalities. The rate of withdrawal went up to 40 percent by 1974 and the communal assembly turned to employment of seasonal workers, who in turn moved on to better paying wage labor elsewhere.[30] By the end of 1974, twenty-five of the twenty-eight units formed in the first phase of the reform were still in operation, the unused lands of the three disbanded units having been entrusted to the self-managed farms. The service cooperative took over another one of these units in 1974 and now runs it with hired wage labor.

The second phase of the reform has not fared much better. It nationalized 407 hectares of non-irrigated private lands and 96.16 irrigated hectares in the whole county. These were turned over to one individual beneficiary, one production cooperative, and the local marketing cooperative.

The production cooperatives, set up under both phases of the reform, are facing problems that lead to continued bankruptcy of some operations and flow of members into wage labor. First, within each cooperative, former small-scale farmers resent their inability to continue herding their own animals, and conflicts of interest arise between the privileged former renters and struggling former workers. Second, the poorer beneficiaries lack skill at wet lands cultivation, live far from their plots, have no transportation, and feel that decisions are made bureaucratically, relegating them to the role of badly paid indentured workers. Third, the national bank's provision of short-term credit is insufficient--it systematically underestimates costs of inputs and the rate of inflation, and the beneficiaries do not trust the marketing cooperative to market their output. Consequently, many beneficiaries do not choose to "maximize money profit" because of the insecurity and risk of market-oriented farming. The four production cooperatives which were studied intensively all showed rising indebtedness in the 1972-73 and 1973-74 seasons. Due to their low income, the beneficiaries resort to moonlighting, sending their children to work as seasonal wage laborers, consuming their output instead of delivering it to the cooperative, and, finally withdrawing from the cooperative.

Zeralda. As in Douera and Staoueli, the reform has had a heavier impact here (west of Alger) than in the eastern part of the Mitidja where Zemmouri and Thénia are found. In Zeralda, the reform now has 7.4 percent of the usable agricultural land. The amount of land nationalized in both phases of the reform was equal to about 39 percent of the total private sector holdings reported in the 1973 census. That is to say, the private sector is still two and one half times as large as the reform sector. This would be higher if large-scale leaseholders on rich irrigable public lands, dispossessed in the first phase of the reform, were also counted. It is the opinion of the researchers, however, that large-scale properties have only been reduced, without eliminating their proprietors as a class. The ten expropriated large-scale owners have gone into transport, commerce and service enterprises, and three of them still have extensive agricultural operations. The class of middle-sized proprietors producing fruits and vegetables for the urban market has not been touched by the reform at all.

The reform has also had some impact on employment in Zeralda. While only 4.6 percent of the active workforce are reform beneficiaries, the cooperatives employ 2.2 seasonal workers for every beneficiary. The land needs of the local landless are surpassed by the lands available for allotment (189 percent) so that either beneficiaries must be brought in from elsewhere or wage-labor employment must be increased.

For Cheraga as a whole, then, self-managed farms have the heaviest weight in the agricultural economy. The small private sector is organized around irrigated market gardening, using intensive techniques and

employing wage labor. The reform has touched the
private sector here more than in Zemmouri or Thénia,
but the market garden farms seem to be basically
intact. There is no evidence that the reform has
either impeded or sped up the development of private
capitalist farming. However the same set of problems
in cooperative organization as outlined for Zemmouri
and Thénia exist here. As in Besbès, Zemmouri, and
Thénia, the reform cooperatives have a high rate of
withdrawal and have become a conduit for the flow of
wage labor into both local agriculture and nearby
industry.

ZONE II. FOOTHILLS

There are four Zone II communes for which
information is available. Three (Souagui, Merad and
Berrouaghia) are located in the foothills adjacent to
the plain of Mitidja, forming an arc around the Algiers
region. There is relatively complete "hard"
statistical data for Souagui and Merad, but only a
brief description for Berrouaghia. The fourth Zone II
commune, El-Arrouche, is located in the foothills
adjacent to the plain around Constantine, in the
eastern part of the country, about equidistant from the
industrial urban agglomerations of Constantine and
Skikda. Data for El-Arrouche are skimpy.

Foothills above the Mitidja

Souagui. The community of Souagui (daïra
Beni-Slimane, wilaya of Médéa) is representative of the
cereal-growing piedmont area, much less agriculturally
productive than the plains regions of Zone I, operating
more on the margin of subsistence and with a history of
producing seasonal migrant wage labor for the Mitidja.
This region is also generally poorer than that of the
High Plains (Zone III).
Two studies are available on Souagui. One was
done by the same team that produced the Besbès study
described above. The second was a pilot study done by
the same research team that studied Cheraga, calling
into question the validity of the data gathered by the
Ministry of Agriculture's 1973 agricultural census.[31]
It appears that class differentiation and capitalist
agriculture were much more advanced in Souagui than
those census data showed.
Souagui registered a total population of 19,630 in
1973, of whom 17,138 were dependent upon agriculture
for a living. Of the total usable agricultural land of
17,000 hectares, 16,000 hectares were privately owned,
640 hectares were self-managed and 140 hectares were

TABLE 4.9--Distribution of Private Agricultural Land, Animals and Crops, Souagui 1973, by Size Category of Farm Unit

Size Category of Farm Unit (ha.)	Farm Units		Total Land Area		Distribution of Land by Crop Type						Distribution of Animals					
					Cereals		Fallow		Other Uses[a]		Cattle		Sheep		Goats	
	No.	%	Ha.	%	Ha.	%	Ha.	%	Ha.	%	No.	%	No.	%	No.	%
less than 5	1,305	60	3,133	24	2,522	24	584	21	29	43	544	44	1,991	43	1,283	55
5-<10	539	25	3,619	27	2,905	28	705	26	9	13	357	29	1,329	29	520	22
10-<20	230	11	3,049	23	2,326	22	713	26	10	15	178	14	554	12	228	10
20-<50	96	4.4	2,765	21	2,096	20	650	24	19	28	115	9	361	8	148	6
50 and up	10	0.5	671	5	569	5	102	4	0	0	20	2	55	1	8	0.3
Subtotal of landed units	2,180	100	13,237	100	10,418	100	2,754	100	67	100	1,214	97	4,290	93	2,187	95
Landless units	140		...	...	...	...	...	...	...	...	33	3	339	7	127	5
Total all units	2,320		...	...	...	...	...	...	...	...	1,247	100	4,629	100	2,314	100

SOURCE: Benattig and de Villers, "Emploi en milieu rural" "Souagui," p. 30, based on RGA 1973.

[a]Includes vineyards, orchards, olive groves, gardens.

communal. Table 4.9 shows the distribution of farm
units by size category, according to the census (RGA
1973) data. The Ministry of Agriculture considered ten
to twenty hectares (non-irrigated) to be sufficient to
support a family in this region. This category can be
considered as "middle peasants," because they have
sufficient lands and other means of production to be
self-supporting from their own labor, either directly
by producing for home consumption or indirectly by
producing an income from crop sales. In this table, 11
percent of farm units, having 23 percent of the land,
fall in this class. "Rich peasants" would be those
having more land than they need to support a family and
can work themselves. Five percent of farm units,
having 26 percent of the land, fall in this category.
On the other end of the spectrum, "poor peasants" would
be those having too little land to support a family.
Eighty five percent of farm units, having 51 percent of
the land, plus 140 landless units, fall in this class.

However, as we saw in the discussion of Besbès
above, the 1973 census systematically underestimates
the differences among the classes. First, the data in
this table are solely for residents of Souagui;
non-residents own another two thousand to three
thousand hectares of usable agricultural land that are
not counted and which the researchers suspect to be
more highly concentrated. Second, no distinction is
made in the census data between owned and rented lands.
Third, the census was taken just prior to the reform,
when rich peasants and capitalist farmers, as well as
pre-capitalist landlords, would not be likely to
divulge their true economic strength.

For all these reasons, the census data on
distribution of land by crop type and of animals, as
well as of land by size category, must be interpreted
with caution. These data tell us that most land was
either in cereals or lying fallow, that holdings were
less concentrated than in Besbès, and that animal
herding was more important. Almost no one admitted to
the use of chemical fertilizer. Seventy percent of the
units of more than twenty hectares claimed to use
animal traction while a measly 3.4 percent of all units
with land reported using mechanical traction. Only
five units reported employing permanent wage labor in
1973, while thirty employed temporary wage labor.

However, the CNRESR survey, which included
absentee-owned lands, found a different system in
operation. First, it found a much higher proportion of
land lying fallow, especially in large-size holdings
(50 percent in units with more than fifty hectares, 30
percent in units with more than five hectares).[32] Such
a high proportion of fallow land in large units sounds
suspiciously like a traditional absentee

landlord/sharecropper system. But the CNRESR survey also found large capitalist units that engage in intensive production of cash crops: out of six units of more than fifty hectares studied intensively by the authors, four were planted in market gardens or arboriculture (that is, specialized production of fruits and vegetables, not cereals) on irrigated lands. On big units, crop rotation (alternation of human food crop with animal fodder crop), use of fertilizer and selected seeds, and soil preparation by mechanical traction were common.

The CNRESR survey found that a majority of units with more then twenty hectares employed day workers (often paid in kind), who frequently did all the work on the unit. Intensification of land use was also common on smaller units using irrigation, that had purchased motorized pumps on credit from the bank. The CNRESR researchers found that five out of six units with more than fifty hectares had their own tractors, while medium-sized farms had good animal traction, and small farms had to rent either tractors or animal traction.

A related CNRESR survey of 1,123 farms in the neighboring commune of Beni Slimane (which is similar to Souagui and representative of the daïra as a whole) also showed a distinct association between the possession of means of production (land, machines, and work animals) and the employment of wage labor, production of marketable surplus product and high monetary income from its sale, and the reinvestment of income in the unit. Benattig and de Villers, aware of the CNRESR results, believe this pattern to be true of Souagui as well, though it does not appear in the official census data.

Three types of farm units were distinguished by the independent researchers at Souagui. Type I, "rich peasants," constitute about 16 percent of all units. The typical farm unit holds more than twenty-five hectares, is mechanized and systematically employs wage labor. Each unit produces its own cereal needs, and sells its surplus from animal production or other food production in the market, earning an average annual revenue from sales of about 7,200 dinars. The authors estimate for 1975-1976 that this unit would have a net profit (after deducting costs of production and household consumption) of five thousand dinars from sales and another two thousand dinars from renting out machinery. The larger units, especially those producing tree-crops and poultry products, earn much more.

Type II, "middle peasants," constitute about 20 percent of all units. They are a simple commodity producing yeomanry, because their farms are self-reproducing and self-sufficient. A typical unit holds seven to twenty-five hectares, possesses good draft animals, and uses only family labor. Between the production of cereals and animal products, the unit covers household needs, and sells about 30 percent of output to earn money to pay for other expenses. With a revenue of only three thousand dinars per year, it cannot afford to mechanize. There are more middle peasant units here than in either the Zone I or Zone III communities, for example, in the high plains like F'kirina.

Type III, "poor peasants," constitute 64 percent of all units. The typical unit possesses less than seven hectares, has no other means of production, and no animals, and must have members work outside the unit (either in Souagui or elsewhere) in order to cover household needs.

The reform had a minimal impact on this structure. The reform sector wound up with less than one thousand hectares (out of a total usable agricultural land area of seventeen thousand hectares) of which 140 came from communal holdings and the remainder from the private sector (although as of late 1978, 289 of those hectares had yet to be physically taken over and redistributed). Since the upper limit to private holdings was set at forty hectares for an individual and seventy-five hectares for a family with at least two children, only

TABLE 4.10--Distribution of Adult Population, Souagui 1973, by Size Category of Farm Unit and Economic Activity

	Economic Activity of Farmers			
Size Category of Farm Unit (ha.) (1)	No. of Farmers[a] (Col. 3 & 4) (2)	Farmers who Work Solely On Own Farm (3)	Farmers with Other Activity Part-Time (4)	Fam. Helpers Who Work Solely on Own Farm (5)
Less than 5	1,302	994	308	497
5-<10	529	457	72	303
10-<20	234	204	30	191
10-<50	99	87	12	72
50 and up	10	9	1	6
Subtotal Landed farmers	2,174	1,751	423	1,069
Landless farmers	111	41	70	6
Total all farmers	2,285	1,792	493	1,075

SOURCE: Benattig and de Villers,"Emploi en milieu rural," "Souagui," p. 5.

[a]The number of farmers in Tables 4.10 and 4.11 is slightly different from the number of farm units in Table 4.9 because of leasing and indivision.

six resident proprietors (out of those declared to the agricultural census in 1973) had some land expropriated. Of 180 registered absentee owners, only thirty-eight had their lands expropriated. Furthermore, in some ways the reform has been beneficial (not merely neutral) in its effect on the private sector: the service cooperative, while it is inefficient in providing needed inputs of seed and fertilizer, is oversupplied with machinery and rents it out to the private farmers at moderate rates. Fifty percent of credits to the private sector in 1976-77, both for short-term and equipment loans, were to units having more than twenty hectares.

The relationship between size category of farm unit and the economic activity of the labor force can be seen from Benattig and de Villers' survey data (which includes landless units, that is, tenants, sharecroppers). Table 4.10 shows that landless units are the only class in which the farmers who work outside their own farms are more numerous than those who do not. For the less-than-five-hectare group, the ratio is 3.2 (of those who do not over those who do);[33] for the 5 to 10 hectare class, it is 6.3; for the 10 to 20 hectare class it is 6.8; for the 20 to 50 hectare class it is 7.2; and for the 50 to 100 hectare class it is 9. That is to say, there is an inverse association between the size of land holding and

TABLE4.10--Continued

Economic Activity of Farm Family Members					
Fam. Helpers With Other Activity Part-Time (6)	Wage Workers, Off Own Farm (7)	Non-Agric. Non-Wage Workers, Off Own Farm (8)	Econ. Active Adult Pop. (Col. 2, 5 6, 7 & 8) (9)	Housewives and Inactive (10)	Total Adult Pop. (Col. 9 & 10) (11)
77	331	34	2,241	3,372	5,613
50	167	20	1,069	1,672	2,741
30	65	15	535	810	1,345
16	27	6	220	424	644
0	4	1	21	62	83
173	594	76	4,086	6,340	10,426
1	35	2	155	297	452
174	629	78	4,241	6,637	10,878

employment outside the farm. On the other hand, Table
4.11 shows that the average size of the household
increases with the size of the holding-- larger units
can support more unproductive persons, presumably
because they have either a higher output or a higher
income per head (or both).

An examination of the estimates of employment
generated by each size category (Table 4.12) can give
an idea of the use of wage labor on the larger units:
the 20 to 50 hectare units provide slightly fewer jobs
than working members (204 and 216 respectively). The
50 to 100 hectare units have only 20.5 economically
active family members but require 48--so they must hire
on the equivalent of 27.5 full-time workers. All
classes below twenty hectares have more economically
active members than jobs--and this is what pushes the
unemployment and subemployment rates up so high (over
40 percent) here.[34]

The reform has made only a small dent in the
volume of unemployment. Out of a population of 1,850
peasants with less than ten hectares of land and more
than one thousand landless peasants and agricultural
workers, 750 applied to the reform agency.[35] Six-hundred
eighty-nine were considered acceptable. However, of
these, only thirty-seven received allotments in Souagui
(twenty-eight organized into six production
cooperatives, plus nine individual lots), of whom three
had withdrawn by 1978, and thirty more were sent to
take up allotments in the Mitidja (the traditional
recipient of surplus labor from Souagui).

Furthermore, the production cooperatives that have
been set up are not doing well. The service
cooperative gives them little in the way of inputs and
technical advice. Since they were unable to repay
credits awarded in 1974-75 and 1975-76, only minor new
credits were awarded by the service cooperative and the
bank in 1977-78.[36] The quality of their land and
animals is very poor, and there has been little motion
out of the archaic cereal-fallow (two-field) rotation.
Thirteen out of eighteen beneficiaries interviewed said
their incomes are now lower than before the reform;
only one said his had improved. The beneficiaries, on
average, received only 2,100 dinars in 1975-76, while
the state farm worker got 9,500 to 17,500 dinars;
candidates to the reform who were not given allotments
but went into wage labor were averaging six thousand
dinars.

As production cooperative members work only ninety
days out of the year, there is continual outmigration
to take up seasonal wage employment on the self-managed
farms in the Mitidja. The state has plans to expand
the local lumber and construction materials industries
at Souagui, but as of 1978 no new jobs had been created

TABLE 4.11--Size of Household and Number of Economically Active Persons Outside of Farm Unit, Souagui 1973, by Size Category of Farm Unit

Size Category of Farm Unit (ha.) (1)	No. of Farmers (2)	Total Farm Population (3)	Avg. Size of Household, per Farmer (Col. 3 ÷ 2) (4)	Ttl. No. of Persons Working Off Own Farm[a] No.	Ttl. No. of Persons Working Off Own Farm[a] (as % of Econ. Active Pop.)
Less than 5	1,302	8,842	7	750	33
5-<10	529	4,211	8	309	30
10-<20	234	2,139	9	140	26
10-<50	99	1,074	11	61	28
50 and up	10	138	14	6	29
Subtotal Landed farmers	2,180	16,404	8	1,266	31
Landless farmers	140	734	7	108	70
Total all farmers	2,320	17,138	8	1,374	32

SOURCE: Benattig and de Villers, "Emploi en milieu rural," "Souagui," pp. 7 and 9.

[a]Equal to the addition of columns 4, 6, 7 and 8 in Table 4.10. Column 9 in Table 4.10 gives Economically Active Population.

TABLE 4.12.--Employment Furnished by Farm Units and Estimated Rates of Disguised Unemployment, Souaguí, 1973, by Size Category of Farm Unit

Size Category of Farm Unit (ha.) (1)	Equiv. of No. of Persons Available for Full-time Work (2)	Equiv. of No. of Active Persons Working full-time Off Own Farm (3)	Equiv. of No. of Active Persons Working full-time On Own Farm (Col. 2 − 3) (4)	Ttl. Employment (No. of full-time jobs) Furnished on Farm (5)	Employment Shortage (+) or Surplus (−) (Col. 4 − 5) (6)	Rate of Disguised Unemployment (Col. 6 ÷ 2) (7)
Less than 5	2,352	557.5	1,794.5	313	1,481.5	63
5-<10	1,151	248	903	308	595	52
10-<20	577	110	467	234	233	41
20-<50	263	47	216	204	12	5
50 and up	26	5.5	20.5	48	−27.5[a]	...
Subtotal landed units	4,369	968	3,401	1,107	229.4	53
Landless units	198	72.5	125.5	11	114.5	58
Total all units	4,567	1,040.5	3,526.5	1,118	2,408.5	53

SOURCE: Original data from Benattig and de Villers,"Emploi en milieu rural,""Souaguí," p. 10. See Appendix C for methodology.

[a]The "surplus" of jobs on the largest-scale farm units implies the employment of wage labor, and reduces the overall rate of disguised unemployment.

this way. Once again, the reform has not stemmed the flow out of petty agricultural production into wage labor.

In sum, for Souagui we have clear evidence that the Ministry of Agriculture census data greatly obscured the concentration of economic power by capitalist farmers who use advanced techniques and employ wage labor. The independent researchers have also made a substantial case that only the pre-capitalist sector, the absentee owners, were really affected by the reform. In some ways, it appears that the capitalist sector has benefited from the reform, in that credit and machinery are now more accessible than before and in that the supply of wage labor is now enlarged.

Merad. The commune of Merad, daïra of Blida, wilaya of Alger, is located in the western reaches of the Mitidja, ranging upward from the plain through the foothills into the Atlas mountains. It is a relatively poor region, growing cereals and raising animals, lacking in industry, with only a small amount of petty commerce. People must travel to Hadjout (three kilometers away) to do serious shopping. It had become a commune mixte in 1875, when the Muslim population of five thousand found itself in the company of twenty-five European concessionaires who established commercial cereal production on their lands. The latter were supplemented by another influx of colonizers in 1888, this time to implant commercial production of wine grapes. The establishment of colonial capitalist agriculture was based on widespread land expropriations and enclosures of common pasturelands.

As happened throughout Algeria, this process had a twofold effect on the native population. On one hand, the old Muslim grandes familles based on tribal organization were eliminated.[37] On the other hand, many of the small subsistence producers were displaced, first from the better lands of the plains up into the poorer mountain lands, then from subsistence farming altogether into the wage-labor force. Government documents record the presence of Muslim wage labor on colonial vineyard farms from about 1903. Thirty-two of the persons who became reform beneficiaries in Merad had been employed as seasonal workers on the colonial farms prior to independence. These colonial farms were mainly converted to self-managed farms right after independence, which accounts for the relatively large share of agricultural land (58 percent or 75 percent depending on source below) held by these farms.

The source of information on Merad is a master's thesis, based on a series of interviews administered in 1975 and 1976, along with participant observation of cooperatives and research of local archives and documents.[38] The interviews were done with forty-three beneficiaries of the reform in Merad, and with officials of the local chapter of the peasants' union, the service cooperative, communal assembly and production cooperative management councils. The virtue of the study is the author's meticulous care in comparing her own survey results on land tenure with those offered by the local government officials who administered the reform-- the difference is striking. Its limitation, however, is that she does not offer any systematic study of the relation between land tenure and other means of production such as machinery, irrigation, and modern techniques. But there are a few hints about the employment of wage labor in her discussion of the personal history of the reform beneficiaries.

The commune's population can be estimated at between 10,000 and 11,000.[39] According to the local government, of a total area of 14,310 hectares, only 4,293 (about 30 percent) is usable for agriculture.

TABLE 4.13--Distribution of Land Before the Reform according to APC Records, Merad 1970, by Sector and Type of Land

Type of Land	Private Sector	No. of Hectares Self-Managed Farms	Communal	Total All Sectors
Agricultural land				
Plains				
Irrigated	31	64	0	95
Non-irrigated	169	1,941	120	2,230
Foothills				
(All non-irrigated)	600	1,200	118	1,918
Mountains				
(All non-irrigated)	50	0	0	50
Subtotal all agricultural lands	850	3,205	238	4,293
Non-Agricultural land				
Plains	50	241	0	291
Foothills	2,000	944	0	2,944
Mountains	1,782	0	5,000	6,782
Subtotal all non-agric. lands	3,832	1,185	5,000	10,017
Total all lands	4,682	4,390	5,238	14,310

SOURCE: Benbarkat, "Merad en mutation," pp. 34-35 (adapted).

The local government (APC) furnished Benbarkat with
Table 4.13, showing how self-managed farms reportedly
have 75 percent of the agricultural land. Three
aspects of this table with regard to the private sector
are noteworthy. First, the total agricultural land
reported here is rather small, only 850 hectares.
Second, most of that total is in the foothills where
the land is of poorer quality than in the plains. And
third, although the private sector reports having less
than one-third of the total agricultural land that the
self-managed sector has, it has fully one-half as much
irrigated land. Irrigated land is usually associated
with rich peasants or capitalist farmers producing cash
crops.

Benbarkat's own survey data, presented in Table
4.14, provides an illuminating contrast. First, she
discovers a total of currently cultivated land of
2,084.56 hectares in the private sector, more than
twice the government's total. This would lower the
share of the self-managed farms to about 58 percent of
agricultural lands. Furthermore, the category of total
lands includes "non-cultivated land," that is, forests
and agricultural land temporarily left fallow, as well
as agricultural land that has been abandoned, the
latter equal to 1,002.25 hectares. It is unfortunate
that there is no breakdown for irrigated as opposed to
non-irrigated land, nor of rented as opposed to owned
land. She also reports that 85 percent of the
proprietors who claimed to hold one hectare or less
held it in "undivided" form, that is, work it in common
with other family members. Such claims are frequently
used by rich peasant families as a ruse to prevent
expropriation.

Taking Benbarkat's data on face value (it provides
a lower limit estimation of concentration of land
holdings), proprietors having more than twenty-five
hectares (3 percent of all proprietors, 2 percent of
all farmers) control 42 percent of the total land in
the private sector. Using fifteen hectares as the size
of a holding of non-irrigated land that would support a
family (the figure of ten hectares is usual for other
poor cereal-producing regions, so we err on the side of
caution), proprietors of more than fifteen hectares (4
percent of all proprietors, 3 percent of all farmers)
control 46 percent of the total land. Eight hundred
seventy-seven small and parcellized peasants (96
percent of all proprietors or 68 percent of all
farmers) control 53.5 percent of the total land. Three
hundred eighty-two farmers have no land.

The data for "cultivated land" show less
concentration than those for "all lands." Only one
proprietor of more than twenty-five hectares reports
cultivating his own land of seventy-five hectares (that

TABLE 4.14--Distribution of Private Agricultural Land before the Reform, Merad 1970, by Size Category of Farm Unit, according to Benbarkat Survey

Size Category of Farm Unit[a] (ha.)	Cultivated Lands				All Lands			
	No. of Proprietors	% of all Proprietors	Land Area (ha.)	% of all Land Area	No. of Proprietors	% of all Proprietors	Land Area (ha.)	% of all Land Area
Up to 5	805	88	1,076	52	717	78	1,200	24
>5-15	101	11	787	38	160	18	1,436	29
>15-25	7	1	146	7	12	1	227	5
>25	1	0.1	75	4	25	3	2,059	42
Subtotal all landed units	914	100	2,084	...	914	100	4,922	100
Landless units	382	...	...	...	382	...	...	...
Total all units	1,296	...	...	...	1,296	...	...	...

SOURCE: Benbarkat, "Merad en mutation," pp. 43 and 46 (adapted).

aBenbarkat labels these as: gros propriétaires >25 ha.
paysans moyens >15-25 ha.
petits paysans > 5-15 ha.
paysans parcellaires 5 ha. and less

is, 0.1 percent of proprietors or 0.08 percent of all
farmers cultivate 3.5 percent of the land). Only eight
proprietors of more than fifteen hectares report
cultivating their own land (0.9 percent of proprietors
or 0.8 percent of all farmers cultivate 11 percent of
the land). Nine hundred six small and parcellized
peasants (99 percent of all proprietors, 70 percent of
all farmers) report cultivating their land (1,863.6
hectares, or 89 percent of the land).

However, the number of parcellized peasants
cultivating land is greater than the number reporting
ownership of land, and the author does not tell us what
holdings the landless peasants work. A suggested
explanation is that the poor and landless peasants work
the lands of the proprietors having more than fifteen
hectares, especially of those having more than
twenty-five hectares. Two ways in which this is done
are through renting (which she mentions occurs, but
without providing data) and through the employment of
wage labor. Benbarkat reports that 312 of the 914
proprietors had employment outside their own farm; of
these 312, 280 were proprietors of five hectares or
less, and 32 were proprietors of more than five
hectares. Of the 312, 221 were employed as seasonal
wage workers, 86 were permanent wage workers, and 5
were in commerce. More than half of the 312 were in
France. Benbarkat's interviews with the reform
beneficiaries also revealed employment of wage labor in

TABLE 4.15--Distribution of Agricultural Land[a] after the Reform, Merad
1973, by Sector and Type of Land, according to APC Records

Type of Land (Agricultural Only)	No. of Hectares			
	Private Sector	State Farms	Agrarian Reform	Total All Sectors
Plains				
Irrigated	31	64	0	95
Non-irrigated	144	1,941	140	2,225
Foothills (all non-irrigated)	445	1,200	235	1,880
Mountains (all non-irrigated)	50	0	0	50
Total all lands	670	3,205	375	4,250

SOURCE: Benbarkat, "Merad en mutation," p. 36 (adapted).

[a]Non-agricultural lands were not included in the original source.

the private sector: four had been permanent workers and two had been temporary workers on private lands.

Land tenure in Merad was only feebly affected by the reform. Table 4.15 presents the government data given to Benbarkat. First, the grand total of agricultural land is somewhat less than before the reform (see tables 4.13 and 4.14 above); somehow some land always "disappears" in a land reform, without official explanation. Second, almost two-thirds of the land rendered over to the reform came from public lands; only 36 percent came from private lands. Third, of the private lands turned over to the reform, most (117 hectares out of 136) were in the hills; only nineteen hectares were in the richer plains. Fourth, no irrigated land was nationalized. Fifth, only absentee proprietors had their lands expropriated, and Benbarkat reports that these were only small holders residing outside the commune (167 of the 914 proprietors resided outside the commune). Adding to all this Benbarkat's discovery that less than half of private land holdings were recorded by the local government, it appears that the larger proprietors' economic base must remain intact.

Within the agricultural population, 1,099 persons (717 parcellized peasants plus 382 landless peasants) would have been potential reform beneficiaries in the sense that they could not make a living from their land alone. (Benbarkat does not provide separate data for the non-agricultural workforce.) As of the end of 1976, 646 persons had applied to become beneficiaries; of these, 443 were accepted by the local government. However, by 1977, only fifty-seven had been assigned land, grouped in six cooperatives, and the government had no plans to extend the reform further. The relief offered by the reform for landlessness and pressure on poor peasants to become wage laborers was thus minimal. In fact, the reform cooperatives employ seasonal wage labor themselves--they could not harvest their crops without it.[40]

The decline of the small independent producers as a class has been ongoing since the colonial era. Of the forty-three beneficiaries interviewed by Benbarkat, thirty-seven were able to define the economic status of their fathers: 16 of the fathers had been agricultural workers, 5 had been sharecroppers, 4 had been renters, 3 had been charcoal-makers, 8 had been landowners (4 of whom had been "economically independent") and 1 had been an artisan. Less than half (16 out of 37), then, had been wage workers. In contrast, all of the 43 beneficiaries had worked for wages, 18 as permanent workers and 25 as temporaries (who also worked either rented lands or a small family plot). None of the latter generation was able to maintain himself as a small independent producer.

The process of expulsion of the small producers from the land was sped up during the war of national liberation. Twenty-six of the beneficiaries interviewed were placed in regroupement centers (barbed wire enclosures) in the late 1950s by the French army.[41] The other seventeen were full wage laborers and already living in the zones where regroupement was established. After the war, only three of the twenty-six were able to return to the lands they had worked; one was able to buy out the colonial owner from whom he had been renting.

The reform seems not to have put a stop to the pace of dispossession, but has created an annex to the yeomanry (or middle peasantry producing market crops at a level which provides an income sufficient to live on). Indeed, Benbarkat is hopeful that the cooperatives will succeed in Merad. As compared to richer, more industrialized regions, the beneficiaries in Merad are not older than the base population. There had been only eight withdrawals out of fifty-two beneficiaries (15 percent) as compared to 112 out of 312 (36 percent) at Mouzaia (a central Mitidja commune), and seven were quickly replaced. Thirty-four out of the forty-three beneficiaries interviewed felt that their lives were better after the reform than before. Benbarkat reports that, within each cooperative, the sharing of the product is equitable, plans of cultivation are collectively decided, and the division-of-labor is smooth.

On the other hand, Benbarkat points out, the cooperatives are subject to internal and external pressures that tend to generate inequality and uneven development both within and among them. For one thing, the literacy criterion for production cooperative (CAPRA) presidents severely constrains the number of eligible candidates; only seven of the forty-three beneficiaries Benbarkat interviewed were literate. Second, while twenty-one of the beneficiaries have no other source of income, twenty-two have access to small private agricultural plots and small herds of animals, from which they can independently produce marketed products. These twenty-two are concentrated in those cooperatives in which members did not have to move their residence or agree to travel long distances daily in order to join. Furthermore, the beneficiaries of the second phase of the reform received a lower installment subsidy than those of the first phase, and get no payment in kind. Their lands are also more dispersed and of poorer quality than the Phase One lands. Therefore revenues vary widely from one cooperative to another, the more profitable ones being able to purchase sheep and goats to enlarge their herds. Finally, the service cooperative is again inetficient, demanding high rental fees for equipment, failing to deliver inputs on time, or delivering the wrong material.

Perhaps because of the strong presence of the self-managed farms (whose workers were often allies and supporters in the execution of the reform), the cooperative members at Merad seem to have more political influence than elsewhere. Benbarkat observed that the reform beneficiaries appear to exercise power through the peasant union (its elected officers are mostly production cooperative presidents who were also liberation front activists during the war), and in the local government (half of whose representatives are from the peasant union leadership)--tor example, this bloc had the local national bank agent replaced because he refused to distribute their salary advances. In contrast, the small private peasants and landless peasants and herders exercise very little power in any of these institutions, and are at an economic disadvantage vis-à-vis the cooperative members because of the higher prices they must pay for seeds, use of machinery, and other inputs. Benbarkat fails to discuss the role of the rich peasants or other privileged strata in these political and economic institutions.

In sum, the evidence on Merad is mixed. If Benbarkat's data on land tenure are more correct than the government's, then the private sector and its attendant inequalities remain significant after the reform, with about 40 percent of the land. Only the pre-capitalist absentee lands and public lands were affected. Second, the pace of movement of the small producers into wage labor in both agriculture and industry seems not to have been altered at all by the reform. Third, while the reform cooperatives seem to be more successful here than elsewhere in terms of establishing a small but locally influential yeomanry, they still face the same competitive pressures as elsewhere.

Berrouaghia. Berrouaghia is a commune in the wilaya of Médéa, 75 kilometers south of the city of Alger, and 20 kilometers from the city of Médéa. Information on this commune comes mainly from anthropological description and contains insights scattered among very disorganized data.[42] The region has a mixed agricultural system, about half self-managed farms and half private, combining cereal cultivation with fruit orchards and vineyards. Of a total usable agricultural land area of 9,993.48 hectares, 4,228.15 were self-managed farm held, 125.33 were communal, and 5,580 were reported to be privately held before the reform.

In the private sector, of a total of 1,702 proprietors reporting to the Ministry of Agriculture's census in 1973, 1,290 claimed to hold less than five hectares each--and were obliged to use association, renting, sharecropping or the sale of wage labor in order to make a living. The larger-scale capitalist farmers (the twenty largest have 1,861 hectares among them) use mechanical traction and fertilizer (with reputedly good returns of eight quintals to the hectare),[43] employ wage labor systematically, and often supervise the work themselves. Absenteeism is common, however, with 1,378 to 2,121 hectares belonging to absentees (size categories are not specified). The biggest absentee-rentier family, Tabti, purchased its lands from colonizers during the war, and employs a manager and permanent wage-labor force to work them.

The miniscule communal (public) lands were nationalized in the first phase of the reform and the first cooperative of nine beneficiaries was established on them. However, this entailed the eviction of the fifteen families who had been working them, and who bitterly resisted when only seven of their ranks became beneficiaries. Unfortunately, their current economic status is not examined in the study. The second phase of the reform in 1975 nationalized the following privately held lands, mainly from absentees: 1,523 hectares of non-irrigated land, 19 hectares of vineyards, and 25 hectares of orchards.

Serious problems with the new production cooperatives (number unspecified) have prevented success. First, those who own private lands and herds take time off from the cooperative to work them. Second, those who do not own private lands and herds still sell their labor power on the side. And, third, the local peasant association is still run by bigger farmers whose lands were barely touched by the reform.

For Berrouaghia, then, while rigorous quantitative data are lacking, qualitative data indicate that mainly absentee held lands and public lands were nationalized, that capitalist farmers retain their economic base and their influence in local politics, that more small producers may have been dispossessed during the reform than received land as a consequence of the reform, and that economic inequalities between employer farmers and wage laborers have been maintained within the reform cooperatives.

Foothills above Constantine

El-Arrouche. The commune of El-Arrouche, wilaya of Constantine, is tucked in among the hills which comprise the eastern extension of the Kabyle mountains.

It is halfway between the industrial coastal city of Skikda (to the north) and the rich commercial city of Constantine (in the plain to the south).

The brief description available on El-Arrouche comes from a secondary source who offers a comparative sketch of six communes in the eastern part of Algeria in which he argues that the variable impact of the reform is a function of the type of socio-economic structure found in the diverse localities.[44]

In the first half of the nineteenth century, El-Arrouche was part of the pastoral nomadic complex (combining sheep and goat herding with seasonal cerealculture), in which tribes collectively "owned" and used the territory (the arch system of ownership, common throughout the Arab world). With the penetration of the region by the colonial armies in the 1850s,[45] part of the tribal lands were expropriated and turned over to Europeans to farm. These later became the basis for the self-managed farms that today occupy 31 percent of the agriculturally useful land. The tribal lands that were left over were then converted to private property through their official registration under the names of the tribal leaders, thus automatically creating a number of very large, concentrated holdings. The "private" "Muslim" sector then came to hold 65 percent of the agriculturally useful land.

Under the stimulus of the development of urban markets, some of these large-scale property owners invested in improving their lands and intensifying their techniques, developed into capitalist farmers employing wage labor. While Cote brackets El-Arrouche with Ain Djasser (see Zone III below) as former arch (tribal) societies influenced by colonialism in the same general way, he provides a size distribution of holdings for only Ain Djasser.

The reform had a small, but significant, impact in El-Arrouche. It has absorbed 15 percent of the total reported agriculturally useful land (4 percent from the public lands nationalized in Phase One and 11 percent from the private lands nationalized in Phase Two), most of it expropriated from absentees.[46] Only about one-third of the candidates to the reform were awarded land allotments, while land distribution in the rest of the private sector, untouched by the reform, remains highly unequal. The private sector retains 54 percent of the land.

ZONE III. HIGH PLAINS

Information is available for six communities in Zone III, the high plains which traverse the country from east to west between the two major mountain ranges. Of the three communes of the east, F'kirina, Ain Djasser and El-Khroub, the best, most complete, and most critical analysis is for F'kirina; data for the other two, provided by the same author[47] as for El-Arrouche in Zone II, are scanty but instructive. For the one community in the west, Ain Nehala, and the two in the center, Ras el-Oued and Sour el-Ghozlane, more descriptive anthropological work is available.

Eastern plains

F'kirina. The commune F'kirina (daïra Ain Beida, wilaya of Constantine, located 130 kilometers southwest of the city of Constantine) is representative of the inland high plains region in which extensive, mechanized cereal cultivation predominates, a region which has historically produced masses of out-migrating landless peasants.

In pre-colonial times, semi-nomadic tribes made their living here by combining cultivation of winter wheat with sheep and goat herding on collectively-held land. With the French intrusion, tribal lands were broken up and converted to private property in lots either purchased by the European settlers or granted to them by the colonial government. The settlers introduced soft wheat as a cash crop for export to Europe and expanded the acreage used for cereal production. This (along with epidemics) forced the contraction of the animal herds and of the native human population, pushing the remaining peasants into the adjacent mountains and forest regions. Subsequent erosion and deforestation of the mountains then drove part of the native population again into migration, this time to Tunisia and Syria.

The number of hectares in cereals rose from 10,000 in 1845 to 75,000 in 1854,[48] while the number of hectares in pasture declined from 1,490,000 to 175,000 and the native population dipped from 56,000 to 28,000 in the same period. However, by the first part of the twentieth century, the colonizers turned their agricultural investment to the more lucrative vineyard production in Zone I, and this region reverted to native Algerian control. This explains why the self-managed farm sector is so small here now, only one farm having 2,365 hectares, 4 percent of the agriculturally useful land. Production of cereals for market by native Algerians has a decades-long history in this region.

There are available two studies of private agriculture in F'kirina, one by the same team that did Besbès and Souagui, based partly, albeit critically, on the 1973 census by the Ministry of Agriculture (just

before the second phase of the reform), and one by a
student based on an independent survey.[49] The census
data at best provide a lower limit on the extent of
land holding concentration before the reform, and do
not include some critical pieces of information (for
example, on land distribution among absentee owners).
But Benattig and de Villers' study does include other
useful information on the labor force, which, in
combination with Ait-el-Hadj's research on the impact
of the reform on the structure of property holding and
production, gives a more complete picture. The
comparison of these works, like that for Souagui above
and for Oued Rhir below, provides the means to
critically evaluate the uses and limits of the Ministry
of Agriculture statistics. These critical evaluations
help to more accurately delineate the extent of the
reform which was executed using their statistics. (See
comparison of F'kirina with neighboring communes
below.)

The agricultural census reported a total
population of 11,498 in 1973. However, this was only
for people actually living in F'kirina at the time.
Ait-el-Hadj got a total of 13,851 in 1974. Part of
this difference is accounted for by absentees (15.3
percent of the employed part of the population), and
the rest appears to be due to the failure to register.
The census reported 16,000 hectares of agriculturally
usable land belonging to residents at F'kirina, whereas
Ait-el-Hadj reports 30,894 hectares of agriculturally
useful land total, most of the difference belonging to
absentees. Based on their own investigation, Benattig
and de Villers estimate that the whole private sector
(resident and absentee) held up to 40,000 hectares of
agriculturally usable land prior to the reform. The
census reported 1,352 working private farm units (891
with land and 461 landless), whereas Ait-el-Hadj found
2,175 working units. This difference again is due to
absenteeism which the census failed to capture
(Ait-el-Hadj found that absenteeism was 13 percent for
proprietors having greater than seventy hectares) and
due to the failure of land owners to register in order
to avoid the impending reform.

A comparison of the distribution of privately held
land by size holdings offered by the two studies is
instructive (Tables 4.16 and 4.17), although the size
classes do not have the same boundaries. The
inequality among properties owned appears to be
similar, but Ait-el-Hadj stresses that, even for her
independent survey which was taken at about the same
time as the census, the large number of small
properties owned is an artifact of land owners trying
to avoid the reform by registering land in small
parcels under the names of individual family members.

TABLE 4.16--Distribution of Private Agricultural Land, Animals and Crops, F'kirina 1973, by Size Category of Farm Unit

Size Category of Farm Unit (ha.)	Farm Units		Total Land Area		Distribution of Land by Crop Type						Distribution of Animals					
					Cereals		Fallow		Other Uses[a]		Cattle		Sheep		Goats	
	No.	%	Ha.	%	Ha.	%	Ha.	%	Ha.	%	No.	%	No.	%	No.	%
Less than 5	220	25	604	4	425	4	175	4	4	6	124	9	1,117	10	422	13
5 - < 20	444	50	4,038	25	2,957	25	1,066	27	15	23	361	26	3,677	34	1,047	32
20 - < 50	156	18	4,935	31	3,825	32	1,090	28	20	30	263	19	2,024	19	444	13
50 - < 100	54	6	3,543	22	2,697	23	829	21	17	26	141	10	1,020	9	186	6
100 and up	17	2	2,796	18	2,020	17	766	20	10	15	74	5	190	2	43	1
Subtotal of landed units	891	100	15,916	100	11,924	100	3,926	100	66	100	963	70	8,028	74	2,142	65
Landless units	461		...	...	...	...	...	...	...	...	418	30	2,828	26	1,148	35
Total all units	1,352		...	...	...	...	...	...	...	...	1,381	100	10,856	100	3,290	100

SOURCE: Benattig and de Villers, "Emploi en milieu rural," "F'kirina," p. 62 (based on agricultural census).

[a]Includes orchards, olive groves, vegetable gardens.

TABLE 4.17—Distribution of Private Agricultural Land before the Reform, F'kirina (Independent Survey) 1974,[a] by Size Category of Farm Unit

Size Category of Farm Units (ha.) (1)	Farm Properties Owned No. (2)	%	Farm Units Being Worked[b] No. (3)	%	% of Farm Units Being Worked Owned By Farmers who Work Them (4)
0- <10	1,120	59	105	5	6.4
10-< 25	410	22	830	38	49.0
25-70	240	13	980	45	24.4
>70	120	6	260	12	46.0
Total	1,890	100	2,175	100	...

SOURCE: Ait-el-Hadj, "Restructuration: F'kirina," pp. 30-31.

[a]The total land area in the private sector was 30,894 hectares, but the author did not show the raw data of its breakdown by size category.

[b]The differences between columns 2 and 3 are due to abandonment of very small holdings or their being rented out to larger farmers to work, and to the renting in of communal lands to augment the size of working units. The large number of small properties "owned" may also be an artifact of the attempt by large-scale owners to avoid expropriation.

She offers a corrective for this by comparing the distribution of working units she observed. Once this is done, the proportion of small units becomes much lower and the proportion of large units becomes much greater. This is explained, first, by the fact that parcels registered in the names of many related persons are often worked together as large units, and, second, by the fact that 93.6 percent of small properties owned (those under ten hectares) are not economically viable. Many have simply been abandoned, and many others have been leased out to be worked as part of larger units. This factor plus the leasing in of communal lands by the owners of larger units explains the greater number of working units than of properties owned,[50] and the greater total area of working units (a minimum of 41,105 hectares) than of units owned (between 30,894 and 40,000 hectares).[51] There appears to be a lively rental market for agricultural land in F'kirina.

Both studies point out that the smaller working units (less than twenty-five hectares) generally plant for subsistence consumption, but that the larger units (more than twenty-five hectares) plant at least part in soft wheat for sale to urban markets and in barley for sale to animal herders. This makes even more sense when an examination of "distribution of animals" in Table 4.16 shows that 39 percent of cows, 36 percent of sheep, and 48 percent of goats are raised by landless units having less than five hectares. These are units that specialize in meat and milk products and must purchase their animal feed.

Ai-el-Hadj argues that there are two groups of animal raisers: those who do so on a small scale for their own consumption (the owners of five to ten hectares, line two of Table 4.16) and those who are employed as herders (bergers, line seven of Table 4.16) by large-scale commercial ranch owners who produce wool and meat for sale to urban wholesalers.[52] In addition, she reports that there are about forty irrigated vegetable farms (with a total of twenty hectares) owned by propriétaires aisés (rich peasants) who produce for local market. Although the village of F'kirina is not yet well supplied with transport and commerce facilities, it exports wheat to the south in exchange for fruits and vegetables. A poultry farmer in the nearby commune of Berriche has acquired ten thousand egg-laying chickens, on which he did successful crossbreeding experiments to increase output, and he now sells his eggs to the Constantine market. These pieces of evidence create a strong impression that specialized production for market by profit-oriented private farmers was growing before the reform.

But commodity production for market does not necessarily indicate a capitalist socio-economic

structure. The manner in which production is organized
is also critical. Ait-el-Hadj offers some descriptive,
circumstantial evidence on the nature of production:
the poultry farmer, for example, became so successful
because he did crossbreeding experiments on his
chickens that led to increased output. There were
reports from as early as 1971 that private farmers from
F'kirina went to Annaba to buy fertilizer and to Skikda
to buy selected grains. The vegetable farmers own
their own irrigation pumps and have built canals and
dikes to control the water supply, a capital-intensive
operation. Ait-el-Hadj directly observed the
large-scale farmers using modern crop rotation and
soil-replenishment techniques instead of fallowing.
Most critical of all, she reports that the employment
of permanent wage labor varies directly with the size
of the farm[53] and the size of the herd, and that
seasonal day labor is widespread on the mechanized
farms.

Benattig and de Villers provide harder data, based
on the 1973 agricultural census, but these data require
very delicate interpretation. First, the census survey
reports only three working units using fertilizer.
This is contradicted out-of-hand by Ait-el-Hadj's
informal but direct observation of working units (she
provides no numbers). Second, the census reported
widespread use of mechanization, varying from 77
percent of owned units under 5 hectares, to 89 percent
of owned units having 5 to 20 hectares, to 99 percent
of those having 20 to 50 hectares, and 94 percent for
those having over 50 hectares.[54] The explanation for
this pattern comes from Ait-el-Hadj's observation that
working units are much larger than owned units, because
of land leasing arrangements. It is hard to imagine
how small units could independently afford to use
machines.[55] Since the reform did not threaten private
ownership of means of production other than land,
Benattig and de Villers offer their representative
sample showing the distribution of animal and
mechanical traction (Table 4.18) as an accurate
reflection of the population as a whole. There is a
direct association between size of unit and possession
of farm machinery. Those who rent equipment must of
course do so from those who own, giving the latter a
double economic advantage over the former (scale
economies yielding higher average profits, plus the
transfer of profits through rent).

The reform had a significant but not overwhelming
impact on this social structure. All in all, the
reform absorbed 35 percent of the registered usable
agricultural land, leaving 61 percent to the private
sector. The first phase of the reform (1972) gave
11,929 hectares of public lands to 358 beneficiaries

TABLE 4.18—Ownership and Renting of Animal and Mechanical Traction, F'kirina (Independent Survey) 1974, by Size Category of Farm Unit

Size Category of Farm Unit[a] (1)	No. Farmers in Survey (2)	Animal Traction		Mechanical Traction		Combine-Harvesters; Reapers-Binders	
		No. Farmers Renting (3)	No. Farmers Owning (4)	No. Farmers Renting (5)	No. Farmers Owning (6)	No. Farmers Renting (7)	No. Farmers Owning (8)
< 25 ha.	17	10	2	13	0	13	0
25-< 70 ha.	7	3	0	4	1	2	2
70 and up	6	1	1	1	4	1	5
Total	30	14	3	18	5	16	7

SOURCE: Benattig and de Villers, "Emploi en milieu rural," "F'kirina," p. 65.

[a]"Owned" vs. "rented" farm land is not distinguished.

organized into twenty cooperatives on cultivated land,
and to 300 beneficiaries organized into a work team to
bring uncultivated land under the hoe. It is not clear
what happened to the 850 working units who had leased
and cultivated these public lands prior to the reform.
Obviously, not all became beneficiaries. Furthermore,
when we consider that the uncultivated parts of these
lands were forests, scrub and steppes used as common
pastures and sources of wood for heat and for making
marketable charcoal, the closing off of these lands
must make it harder for the small independent producers
to make a living. Those who were not lucky enough to
become beneficiaries or who did not have other
resources to fall back on must have been forced into
wage labor.

The second phase of the reform (1974) nationalized
only 2,755 hectares of privately-held agriculturally
useful land.[56] This is only a small proportion of the
estimated 16,000 to 26,000 hectares held by absentees
before the reform or of officially registered
large-scale holdings. Furthermore, the allowed maximum
area set by the second phase of the reform for this
locality was seventy hectares for an individual and 105
hectares for a family with two children, which would
leave all medium-sized and the majority of large-sized
units intact anyway. Ait-el-Hadj reports that the
actual numbers of proprietors affected were: 24 having
0 to 25 hectares; 13 having 25 to 100 hectares; and
25 having more than 100 hectares. Therefore the impact
on the land tenure structure of the private sector was
not great, and seems to have been confined to absentee
owners.

Virtually no changes were effected for the other
means of production. As elsewhere, farm equipment was
not nationalized.[57] The only constraints placed on its
use by the institutionalization of the reform were a
reduction in the price for which private owners can
lend out their equipment and the potential refusal of
the local service cooperative, which has its own
machinery, to either lend to the private, small-scale
farmers at low rates or borrow from the private
large-scale farmers at high rates.

Private farmers continue to market their product
through the marché parallèle, the private wholesalers'
network which functions alongside the state marketing
agency. They continue to complain about the inadequate
supply of wage labor, which forces them to import
workers from Biskra (in the south). In its role as
creditor to the agricultural sector since the land
reform, the national bank has not neglected the private
sector. It does not appear to favor the largest-scale
farmers in terms of the absolute numbers of loans made.
Of BNA credits to 267 private farmers in F'kirina in

1977-78, 67 percent of farmers were holders of less than 25 hectares, 32 percent were holders of 25 to 70 hectares, and only 1 percent were holders of more than 70 hectares. These credits seem to favor the yeomen, rich peasants and smaller-scale commercial farmers over the larger-scale capitalist farmers and traditional landlords. However, it is noteworthy that there is no control here for the size or type of the loans, for their purposes (irrigation, type of crop), or for the terms of the loans (duration, interest rate).

Benattig and de Villers deduce an evolving capitalist social structure from their evidence. They draw up composite pictures of the three social class situations they observed to exist in the private sector at F'kirina in the immediate post-reform period, and compare them to the situations of the self-managed farm worker and the reform beneficiary.

Type I is a "rich peasant" evolving into a capitalist farmer. The farmer has a working unit of 72 hectares, of which he owns 42 (well under the reform ceiling), rents 10, and has access to 20 more through "association."[58] He owns a tractor and a thresher-harvester with another farmer (usually a relative like a brother or cousin). He personally owns smaller equipment and a herd of farm animals (4 cows, 4 calves, 1 bull and 25 sheep). He works his land with his sons and hired day laborers and earns the major portion of his income in money from the sale of cereals and meat. His income is generally more than that of a full-time self-managed farm worker. He would be a full-fledged capitalist farmer if his farm were worked mainly by wage laborers.[59]

Type II is a "middle peasant." The farmer holds twenty-one hectares of agriculturally useful land (owned and/or rented). He owns no equipment of his own, and must therefore rent it. He owns two cows and ten sheep, which provide barely enough for own-family consumption. If he produces a surplus, he will sell it for money income. His income is about the same as that of a reform beneficiary. The authors conclude that this class is still important but in decline.

Type III is a "poor peasant." The farmer works nineteen hectares of agriculturally usable land or less, owns no equipment and cannot afford to rent it, and has no animals. If he produces any surplus, he will try to market it. But he will generally lose or abandon his land after two consecutive years of harvest failure and become a berger, wage worker in herding, or agricultural laborer, or migrate looking for work.

It seems, then, that the private commercial agriculutral sector, including an important capitalist component, is still alive in F'kirina, and that the pressures driving the small subsistence and

market-oriented agricultural producers into wage labor
have not been eliminated by the reform. We can pursue
this proposition further by examining the structure of
the labor force and the nature of the reform
cooperatives themselves.

For 1974, Ait-el-Hadj found a total population
(resident and absent) of 13,851. Of the active
masculine population, 62.6 percent were in agriculture,
and one-third of those could be classified as
"independent" in the sense that they produce enough
output either for family consumption or for sale to
market to support the family. Three percent were in
industry, crafts and construction, and 4.5 percent were
in services, public employment, and trade. The
remainder, almost 30 percent, were full-time
unemployed--about 1,100 men. The broader problem of
underemployment becomes more obvious when we realize
that less than one-third of the active labor force is
in permanent wage employment, while more than one-third
is seasonal day labor (the remainder being
"self-employed," mainly in agriculture). Most wage
labor at F'kirina goes into local agriculture, as
opposed to urban or overseas migration.

Table 4.19 shows the distribution of the labor
force by size category of farm unit. As in Besbès,
there is an inverse relation between the size category
of farm unit and the farmer's employment off his own
farm. While 33 percent of landless farmers work off

TABLE4.19--Distribution of Adult Population, F'kirina 1973, by Size Category
of Private Farm Unit and Economic Activity

Size Category of Farm Unit (ha.) (1)	Economic Activity of Farmers			Family Aids Who Work Solely on Own Farm (5)
	No. of Farmers[a] (Col. 3 & 4) (2)	Farmers Who Work Solely On Own Farm (3)	Farmers With Other Activity Part-time (4)	
Less than 5	220	157	63	225
5- < 20	450	404	46	594
20-< 50	156	144	12	271
50-< 100	53	52	1	125
100 and up	16	16	0	47
Subtotal landed farmers	895	773	122	1,262
Landless farmers	401	269	132	316
Total all farmers	1,296	1,042	254	1,578

SOURCE: Benattig and de Villers, "Emploi en milieu rural," "F'kirina," p. 5.

[a]The number of "farmers" in Tables 4.19 and 4.20 is slightly different from
the number of farm units in Table 4.16 due to leasing and indivision.

the farms they rent, 29 percent of the less-than-five hectare farmers work off their own farms, as compared to 10 percent of the five-to-twenty hectare farmers, 8 percent of the twenty-to-fifty hectare farmers, 2 percent of the fifty-to-one hundred hectare farmers, and none of the one-hundred-hectare-and-up farmers.

Table 4.20 (based in part on Table 4.19) shows the relationship between size category of farm unit, on the one hand, and size of household and type of economic activity off the farm unit, on the other hand. There are two important features of differentiation among the size categories of farm units. First, the average size of household increases directly with the size of the farm: larger farms have higher total income and can support more people. Second, the average number of workers per farm employed outside the farm is inversely related to the size of the farm: larger farms have a higher income per head from the farm itself, while smaller farms sell wage labor to supplement farm income. It is only in the "landless" class that more workers are employed off their own farms in agricultural jobs than in non-agricultural jobs; this is because of the high proportion of this class employed as herders and day laborers on the large mechanized farms. For all other classes, non-agricultural employment outside the farm is more important.

Table 4.21 shows the relation between the size

TABLE 4.19--Continued

Economic Activity of Farm Family Members					
Family Aids With Other Activity Part-Time (6)	Wage Workers, Off Own Farm (7)	Non-Agric. Non-Wage Workers, Off Own Farm (8)	Econ. Active Adult Pop. (Col. 2 & 5 & 6 & 7 & 8) (9)	Housewives and Inactive (10)	Total Adult Pop. (Col. 9 & 10) (11)
6	34	1	486	412	898
13	81	3	1,141	934	2,075
9	35	4	475	360	835
0	13	1	192	131	323
0	3	1	67	54	121
28	166	10	2,361	1,891	4,252
12	93	5	827	779	1,606
40	259	15	3,188	2,670	5,858

TABLE 4.20--Size of Household and Number of Economically Active Persons Outside of Farm Unit, F'kirina 1973, by Size Category of Farm Unit

Size Category of Farm Unit (hectares) (1)	No. of Farmers (2)	Total Farm Population (3)	Avg. Size of Household/Farmer (Col. 3 ÷ 2) (4)	No. of Persons Working in Agric. Off Own Farm (5)	No. of Persons Working Outside of Agric. Off Own Farm (6)	Ttl. No. of Persons Working Off Own Farm (Col. 5 & 6)[a] (7) No.	Ttl. No. of Persons Working Off Own Farm (Col. 5 & 6)[a] (7) %[b]	No. of Persons Working Abroad (from among those off own farm) (8)	Avg. No. of Persons Working Off Own Farm Per Farmer (Col. 7 ÷ 2) (9)
Less than 5	220	1,358	6	48	56	104	21	25	0.47
5-< 20	450	3,168	7	58	85	143	13	57	0.31
20-<50	156	1,252	8	21	39	60	13	25	0.38
50-<100	53	491	9	3	12	15	8	5	0.28
100 and up	16	174	11	1	3	4	6	1	0.25
Subtotal landed farmers	895	6,443	7	131	195	326	14	113	0.36
Landless farmers	401	2,537	6	131	101	242	29	29	0.60
Total all farmers	1,296	8,980	7	262	296	568	18	142	0.44

SOURCE: Benattig and de Villers, "Emploi en milieu rural," "F'kirina," pp. 6, 7, and 8 (adapted).

[a]These totals for each size category are equal to the addition of columns 4, 6, 7 and 8 in Table 4.19.

[b]Percentage of Economically Active Population.

TABLE 4.21--Employment Furnished by Farm Units and Estimated Rates of Disguised Unemployment, F'kirina 1973, by Size Category of Private Farm Unit

Size Category of Farm Unit (hectares) (1)	Equiv. of No. of Persons Available for Full-time Work (2)	Equiv. of No. of Active Persons Working Full-time Off Own Farm (3)	Equiv. of No. of Active Persons Full-time on Farm (Col. 2-3) (4)	Ttl. Employment (No. of Full-time Jobs) Furnished on Farm (5)	Employment Shortage (+) or Surplus (-) (Col. 4-5) (6)	Rate of Disguised Unemployment (Col. 6÷2) (7)
Less than 5	380	69.5	310.5	52	258.5	68%
5-<20	862	113.5	748.5	251	497.5	58%
20-<50	340	49.5	290.5	256	34.5	10%
50-<100	141	14.5	126.5	174	-47.5	...
100 and up	46	4	42	126	-84	...
Subtotal landed units	1,769	251	1,518	859	659	37%
Landless units	656	170	486	81	405	62%
Total all units	2,425	421	2,004	940	1,064	44%

SOURCE: Original data from Benattig and de Villers, "Emploi en milieu rural," "F'kirina," p. 14. See Appendix C for methodology.

[a]The "surplus" of jobs on the larger scale farm units implies the employment of wage labor there, and reduces the overall rate of disguised unemployment.

categories of farm units and the amount of employment furnished by each. It allows an estimate of the amount of total employment and unemployment within the wage labor force in private agriculture in F'kirina. The 50-to-100 hectare class is lacking 47.5 workers and that of the more-than-100 hectare class is lacking 84 workers. The larger size farms (more than 50 hectares) must then employ labor, 131.5 jobs worth, while the smaller size farms (less than 20 hectares) sell their labor power. This brings the overall estimated rate of full-time equivalent disguised unemployment to 44 percent.[60] If the reform were to totally eliminate unemployment, then, it would have to replace all these jobs, and create new jobs in addition, when it nationalized private sector land.

Ait-el-Hadj reports that the reform reduced the absolute level of full-time unemployed workers from 1,100 to 943. Why was the impact so small? One-thousand six-hundred two workers applied to become reform beneficiaries,[61] of whom 1,300 were accepted as eligible but, by the end of 1977, only 954 finally were chosen to receive allotments.[62] Of these, 136 withdrew, three-fourths of them from the reclamation cooperative alone.

Several factors were found to exert pressure to keep the reform cooperatives small and to lead the members of the poorer cooperatives to seek outside employment. In contrast to the cooperatives formed in the first phase of the reform, for example, those formed in the second phase do not have a common place to meet to plan each day's work together; they did not have storage facilities or equipment; and their parcels of land were small, of poor quality, and dispersed at great distances from one another.

The consequence of this is that, while many cooperatives are showing a "profit,"[63] the rate varies widely among them. In only one case in F'kirina in 1975-76 did the cooperative's profit yield an income to the beneficiaries equal to the standard set by the reform guidelines (that is, equal to the base pay of a full-time self-managed farm worker).

A second factor influencing the decision of the cooperative members to seek outside employment is that they work an average of only 130 days per year in the cooperative. (They do not have recourse to hiring wage labor in the cooperatives at F'kirina because the members themselves are underemployed.) While they do get free medical services, they do not receive family allowances or pensions, so they must purchase everything they need out of their income from the cooperative. According to Benattig and de Villers' interviews, the cooperative members feel themselves to be financially insecure. Forty-nine percent report that their income after the reform is less than it was before, while 42 percent report that it is more.[64]

The cooperative members' response to this situation takes two forms. First, they hold onto part of their output for domestic consumption and use part of their land allotment for family gardens and family herds. Both of these activities are illegal under the reform franchise. Second, again illegally, they supplement their income as cooperative members by working as part-time agricultural laborers on private farms, and, in the extreme, abandon their cooperatives altogether for wage employment elsewhere.

Ait-el-Hadj reports that the local service cooperatives intend to set up a series of ateliers (workshops) to process agricultural and animal products, which would provide employment to the "surplus" labor. But as of 1978, no new jobs had yet been created by these means.[65]

In F'kirina, then, the reform's major impact on land tenure was to nationalize the communal lands and lands belonging to absentee owners. Private commercial farms, even capitalist ones, remain unscathed. The local service cooperative does seem to have put a crimp in the private market for rented farm equipment, and the national bank has been shown to have favored small farmers in the private sector over large ones in terms of the number of credits it granted, but neither of these pieces of evidence indicates a serious attack on the capitalist sector. The reform absorbed only a small part of the large number of unemployed and sub-employed here, and seems to have increased the flow of labor into wage employment through the closing off of the communal lands and the low success rate of the cooperatives.

TABLE 4.22--Distribution of Private Agricultural Lands in the Region of Ain Beida 1973, by Size Category of Farm Unit (in percent)

Size Category of Farm Unit (hectares)	% of Farm Units	% of Usable Agricultural Land
Less than 10	35	6
10-20	26	12
20-50	24	24
50-100	9	19
100 and up	6	39

SOURCE: de Villers, Pouvoir politique, p. 311.

   <u>Comparison of F'kirina with neighboring communes</u>.
Another survey of the Ain Beida region (of which
F'kirina is part) at the time of the reform also found
a much higher level of land concentration than showed
up in the agricultural census, as illustrated in Table
4.22.[66] This is included just to give an indication of
how far off the mark the agricultural census data may
be. The author gives no other information and
apparently did not do a follow-up study of the reform's
impact on this distribution.
   Another independent research project on the
neighboring commune of Oum el-Bouaghi, also in the Ain
Beida region, provides further illustration of the
concentration of landholdings and other means of
production (see Table 4.23). Though based on the
agricultural census, these data give what the
researchers believe to be a more accurate picture of
the extent of wage employment and modern techniques,
especially on the middle and large farms, than had
previously been known. The Ministry of Agriculture did
not publish these data itself.[67]
   If Oum el-Bouaghi is similar to F'kirina, as it is
alleged to be, then these data provide an interesting
qualification on the agricultural census data presented
for F'kirina in Table 4.16, and fit comfortably with
the independent researchers' data for F'kirina in
Tables 4.18 through 4.21 and with those researchers'
own on-the-spot observations.
   One thing that is striking about these data is the
economic strength of the 20-to-50 hectare category of
holders. While these are 21 percent of all farm units,
holding only 29 percent of all dry farm land, they use
mechanical traction almost universally, use more than
one-third of all fertilizer (which is admittedly small
in absolute terms), have about one-quarter of all
permanent cultures, employ <u>one-third</u> of all permanent
wage laborers, and have more than <u>one-half</u> of all
irrigated land. Many of these farms are clearly
intensive capitalist enterprises, which would have been
untouched by the reform because of medium land size.
There is no more information on them, and there was no
post-reform study of this commune available for
comparative purposes. It does seem reasonable to
suggest that if they are present here, they are
probably present in other Zone III communes in this
region, such as F'kirina, El-Khroub, and Ain Djasser.
   <u>Ain Djasser</u>. Ain Djasser is similar in history
and socio-economic development to El-Arrouche (Zone
II), except that its lands are richer and more
productive, being in the plains instead of the hills,
and that the public holding of lands remained more
important. European farms were not extensive here. At
the time of the reform, the self-managed farms occupied

only 10 percent of the reported usable agricultural land, while large-scale private farms were relatively concentrated. As Table 4.24 shows, about 6 percent of farm units, each holding fifty hectares or more, held almost half of the agricultural land in 1973.

The reform has taken over 29 percent of the usable land (one of the higher figures), but mainly from public lands (24 percent public, 5 percent private), so that the private sector continues to hold 61 percent of the usable agricultural land, still inequitably distributed. Only about half of the candidates to the reform received land allotments.

Despite the paucity of data here, given that this region has a long history of developing capitalist farming, with increasing mechanization and the expulsion of the small producers from agriculture as holdings became more concentrated (see discussion of El-Arrouche above), it is reasonable to surmise that the reform did not disturb these trends for Ain Djasser.[68]

El-Khroub. El-Khroub is a very rich agricultural area in the plain of Constantine which serves the large urban market in the city of Constantine. As compared to El-Arrouche in Zone II and Ain-Djasser in Zone III, which are protected by hilly terrain, El-Khroub was very attractive to European wheat farmers and relatively easy for the colonial armies to control because of its openness. In this it is similar to Zone I, the coastal plains. However, it had the peculiar characteristic of being a center for the simultaneous growth of European farms and of large-scale Algerian private agriculture, side by side. The European farms produced wheat for export, while the Algerian farms produced wheat for the growing domestic market. As in Ain-Djasser, the Algerian capitalist farms here introduced mechanization and became more concentrated, in terms of the size of landholdings, up to the time of the liberation war. Many employed wage labor systematically, just like the European farms did. As a consequence, at the time of the reform, very few small holdings were left here; there was no real "peasant" class in the sense of self-sufficient simple commodity producers or subsistence farms.[69]

At the time of the reform, the self-managed farms held a large portion of the agriculturally usable land, 45 percent, taken over as part of the movement that came in the wake of independence. Fifteen percent of the land was in communal or public ownership, and 40 percent was privately held in highly concentrated units. As Table 4.25 shows, more than three-fourths of the properties (representing 98 percent of the privately held land) were greater than twenty hectares each. More than one-third of the properties (holding

160

TABLE 4.23--Distribution of Private Agricultural Land, Animals and Crops,
Oum el-Bouaghi 1973, by Size Category of Farm Unit

Size Category of Farm Unit (ha.)	Farm Units		Dry Farm Land Area		Irrigated Lands		Permanent Cultures	
	No.	%	Ha.	%	Ha.	%	Ha.	%
Less than 5	386	21	1,001	3	0.89	2	5.25	27
5-<20	927	50	9,417	24	4.11	8	7.50	38
20-<50	386	21	11,265	29	28.34	55	5.00	25
50-<100	94	5	6,314	16	1.51	3	0	0
100 and up	60	3	10,703	28	17.01	33	2.00	10
Subtotal landed units	1,853	100	38,700	100	51.86	100	19.75	100
Landless units	882		0		0		0	
Total all units	2,735		. . .		. . .		. . .	

SOURCE: C.U.R.E.R., "Structures foncières de Oum el-Bouaghi," no pagination (adapted).

TABLE 4.24--Distribution of Private Agricultural Land, Ain Djasser 1973,
by Size Category of Farm Unit (in percent)

Size Category of Farm Unit (hectares)	% of Farm Units	% of Land Area
Less than 5	31	5
5-<20	47	22
10-<50	16	24
50-<100	4	17
100 and up	2	32
Total	100	100

SOURCE: Cote, "Le cas de l'est," p. 177.

NOTE: Percentages are approximate, as data were culled from a bar graph.

TABLE 4.23--Continued

| No. of Permanent Wage Workers Employed | | Farms Using Mech. Traction | | Farms Using Fertilizer | | Distribution of Animals | | | | | |
| | | | | | | Cattle | | Sheep | | Goats | |
No.	%	No.	%	No.	%	No.	%	No.	%	No.	%
2	3	326	19	2	14	222	8	1,517	7	823	10
19	25	857	50	0	0	764	27	5,780	25	2,236	28
25	33	360	21	5	36	639	23	6,043	26	1,587	20
5	7	93	5	1	7	236	8	1,190	5	302	4
24	32	59	3	6	43	267	9	2,950	13	297	4
75	100	1,695	99	14	100	2,128	75	17,480	76	5,245	66
0		6	1	0		706	25	5,401	24	2,662	34
. . .		1,701	100	. . .		2,834	100	22,881	100	7,907	100

TABLE 4.25--Distribution of Private Agricultural Land, El-Khroub 1973, by Size Category of Farm Unit (in percent)

Size Category of Farm Unit (hectares)	% of Farm Units	% of Land Area
Less than 5	7	0
5- < 20	15	2
20- < 50	21	5
50- < 100	20	13
100 and up	37	80
Total	100	100

SOURCE: Cote, "Le cas de l'est," p. 177.

NOTE: Percentages are approximate as data were culled from a bar graph.

about 80 percent of the privately held land) were greater than one hundred hectares each. However, most of the big proprietors lived in the city of Constantine; in the wilaya as a whole, 95,000 hectares were registered as owned by absentees.

The reform had a greater impact here than anywhere else in the country, taking over 35 percent of the reported agriculturally useful land (15 percent from the public lands and 20 percent from private lands), reducing the private sector's holdings to only 20 percent of the total. While all of the qualifications about the Ministry of Agriculture land registry, on which basis the reform was carried out, apply here as elsewhere, there is no doubt that the reform made a relatively clean sweep of the urban absentee owners in El-Khroub.

This success seems to have been due to the particular confluence of social forces in this region. The absentee landowners apparently were unable to control the local political structures responsible for administering the reform. Instead, because of the heightened state of wage worker consciousness here on the large-scale private farms (because of the long history of land concentration and push of the petty producers into wage labor), and because of rigorous support from the self-managed farmworkers, the landless agricultural workers were able to force through the expropriation of 14,000 out of the 17,000 hectares registered as owned by large-scale proprietors in El-Khroub. Ninety percent of the eligible candidates who applied for allotments became beneficiaries of the reform here, a total of nine hundred people. They were organized into thirty-eight production cooperatives, which are given a better-than-average chance of success because of the relatively good quality of the lands expropriated.

The author of the study (Cote) is completely uncritical of the reform and accepts official government data at face value. Interviews with researchers at CREA revealed that they agree that the reform was most sweeping in the area around Constantine, that is they agree that the reform succeeded here in its own terms better than anywhere else. However, they point out that research is needed on the local level to evaluate what actually happened against what the Ministry of Agriculture official data say. The elimination of urban absenteeism does not necessarily mean the elimination of capitalism, but, on the contrary, may mean its unfettering to the extent that urban absentee landholding inhibited further investment in agricultural development at El-Khroub. The question remains unresolved in this case because of the lack of direct field research.

TABLE 4.26--Properties Belonging to Urban Residents of Constantine,
El-Khroub 1973, by Size Category of Farm Unit

Size Category of Farm Unit (ha.)	No. of Proprietors	% of Proprietors	Land Area (hectares)	% of Land Area
0-1	0		0	
1-10	17	12	63.5	0.4
10-50	47	34	1,255.4	7
50-100	27	20	1,870.6	11
100 and up[a]	46	34	14,259.0	82
Total	137	100	17,448.5	100

SOURCE: C.U.R.E.R., "Propriété foncière de Constantine," no pagination.

[a]Of these, two hold properties between 500 and 1,000 hectares and three hold properties between 1,000 and 2,000 hectares.

TABLE 4.27--Distribution of Agricultural Workforce at Ain Nehala
(Ain Tellout) 1973

Occupational Status	Permanent	Seasonal	Total
Workers			
Self-managed farms	373	286	659
CAPAM, reform cooperatives (phase one)	20	40	60
Private farms	412	0	412
Subtotal	805	326	1,131
Private farmers	...	...	1,341
Total[a]	...	...	2,472

SOURCE: Benguergoura, "Ain Nehala," p. 28.

[a]This is a total agricultural workforce, out of a total active population of 2,784. Of the other 312 persons, 90 are unemployed, 147 were emigré workers, and the rest were in non-agricultural occupations.

Another source,[70] whose work the CREA researchers respect, presents elaborate data on the Constantine region as a whole for the period just prior to the reform. Their figures on concentration of holdings by absentee owners are similar to those provided by Cote, as Table 4.26 shows. But they hasten to point out the limitations of the census in which these data were gathered,[71] and estimate the margin for error in the data as between 10 percent and 20 percent at a minimum. They also point out that, although some of these properties belonged to traditional "great families" that antedate the arrival of the French, many other properties being worked today are composed of purchases made from the Europeans at the time of independence, and that they are often worked under the direct supervision of their owners. If this is correct, and if mainly absentee owners were affected by the reform, then the estimated margin for error leaves room for the maintenance of owner-operated capitalist farms after the reform even in this region most heavily affected by the reform.

Western plains

Ain Nehala (commune of Ain Tellout). Ain Nehala is the first "new village" of the reform to be opened. It is located in the high plains commune of Ain-Tellout in the wilaya of Tlemcen. This cereal-growing region experienced the familiar pattern under colonialism: the native population was pushed off the better lands, with the majority going into sharecropping on poor lands or into wage labor on the European estates and eventually overseas. During the war of national liberation, the population was "regrouped" again by the French Army for "security" purposes. After the war, the population was again reorganized by the new government into cités (residential hamlets). This was a period of confusion, with fierce competition between native rich farmers trying to engross their holdings by buying colonial lands, khammes (sharecroppers) and poor peasants returning from the regroupment centers and cités trying to reoccupy lands they had worked, and the self-management movement surging among wage workers on former colonial estates. Due to the confusion, there was a great deal of parcellization of holdings and the scrambling of residences among the holdings.

As of the 1973 Ministry of Agriculture survey, registered agriculturally usable landholdings at Ain Tellout were organized thus: 8,090 hectares for self-managed farms, 5,536 hectares for private farms, 4,390.85 hectares for communal lands (which were to go to the new cooperative sector), and 111.5 hectares for

TABLE 4.28--Distribution of Private Agricultural Land, Wilaya of
Tlemcen 1968, by Size Category of Farm Unit

Size Category of Farm Unit (hectares)	Farm Units		Land Area	
	No.	%	Ha.	%
10-19.9	3,160	55	41,505	29
20-49.9	1,950	34	54,235	38
50-99.9	510	9	34,155	24
100-199.9	85	1	11,340	8
Total	5,705	100	141,235	100

SOURCE: Benguergoura, "Ain Nehala," p. 138.

TABLE 4.29--Previous Economic Status of Beneficiaries, Ain
Nehala (Ain Tellout) 1973

	No.	%
Proprietors	15	27
Renters	21	39
Associators	4	7
Sharecroppers	3	6
Workers	11	21
Total	54	100

But of the total 54, 16 had a double status:

Proprietor/renter	8
Proprietor/associator	2
Proprietor/worker	1
Renter/associator	3
Renter/worker	3

SOURCE: Benguergoura, "Ain Nehala," pp. 71-72.

NOTE: Table based on interviews with all 54 beneficiaries
(out of a total of 111 beneficiaries resident at Ain Nehala).

a CAPAM.[72]

The study of this commune is more anthropological description than a consistent statistical survey, but it gives insight in many places about the village social/political dynamics. The author is a believer in the official policy of the reform, that it should restructure rural agriculture along egalitarian producer-cooperative lines. He is disappointed first in the state's failure to carry through a true agrarian reform and second in the resurgence of inequalities in the social relations of production in the reform cooperatives.[73]

The study is the result of detailed questionnaires given to fifty-five out of 111 beneficiaries (who with their families constitute the 607 inhabitants of this first new reform village), and of interviews with other persons affiliated with the reform and the cooperatives. The great value of this particular study is its investigation of the previous and current economic status of the beneficiaries and of differentiation both within and among reform cooperatives.

The author reports contradictory information on the private sector agriculture. On one hand, he says that in 1973 two-thirds of officially registered private lands were in fallow, and the rest in cereals, with less than 1 percent in commercial crops (such as vegetables, fruits, fodder, and industrial crops).[74] On the other hand, he presents a table (Table 4.27) which has 1,341 private farmers and 412 permanent agricultural workers in the private sector, which implies a definite class of rich farmers employing wage labor.

The author also offers evidence of differentiation in the size distribution of private landholding for the wilaya as a whole (Table 4.28), which can be used to evaluate the impact of the reform. Holdings below ten hectares are not given in the original table. The top 10 percent of farm units, holding fifty or more hectares each, hold 32 percent of all land in this survey, based on official government data. This can be considered a minimum estimate of land concentration.

It is not clear that the reform had a great impact on this distribution in the wilaya of Tlemcen. The second phase of the reform nationalized a total of 20,041 hectares belonging to 1,102 proprietors in the wilaya as a whole, which is 14 percent of the total in Table 4.28. However, the size distribution of the expropriated lands is not presented. As has been demonstrated in other communities, it is typical of this reform that the small-scale absentee-held properties constitute the majority of the lands expropriated. Holding that reservation aside, even if

all of the expropriated lands came from the top three
categories of holdings in Table 4.28 (an assumption
yielding a maximum estimate of the reform's impact),
there still would be a good many large landholders left
in the twenty to 49.9 hectare group, and concentration
would have been reduced but not eliminated. As it is,
as of the time of the Ain Nehala study (1975), only 57
percent of the nationalized lands had actually been
redistributed from their holders to the reform
beneficiaries.

In Ain Nehala specifically, Benguergoura found
that the second phase of the reform was to nationalize
a maximum of 1,139 hectares of private lands, mostly
from absentees, with only 373 hectares taken from six
limitable local residents; so the vast majority of
private farmers would be untouched by the reform and
the social structure would remain intact except for the
removal of the absentees. As of the time of this study
(1975), not even these minimal expropriations had been
carried out.

The reform seemed to create, and even enhance,
inequality among the production cooperatives at Ain
Nehala. At the time this investigation was made, only
1,090.5 hectares of the Phase One reform lands were in
use by the beneficiaries, 80 percent in cereals, 20
percent in cash crops (fruit trees, grape arbors and
vegetables), plus 540 additional hectares in
newly-planted fruit trees. The plots were demarcated
to individual beneficiaries, but organized into
thirteen geographically contiguous production
cooperatives. The space was well-organized for the use
of machinery and other facilities in common (such as
storage, stables, tools), with the newly-built
residential zone in the middle, complete with plumbing,
electricity, sewage disposal and a marketing center.

In contrast to the relatively good organization
and endowments of the Phase One cooperatives, the
proposed Phase Two lands were scattered at quite a
distance from one another and the construction of
housing for the expected forty Phase Two beneficiaries
had not yet been begun. Benguergoura opined that this
did not bode well for the potential success of the
Phase Two cooperatives. Furthermore, the
specialization pattern among the cooperatives, based on
differences in land endowments and access to
irrigation, was already leading to differences in
profitability and indebtedness.

The inequality of initial endowments interacts
with unequal access to other means of production to
generate income differentials. The State has not
provided necessary new irrigation works, heavy
equipment and storage facilities (which would raise
productivity and reduce waste). These are considered

to be investments that the cooperatives must obtain for themselves. They can either purchase these capital goods or rent them. In order to purchase them,[75] they can borrow long-term from the national bank. Even the purchase of seeds and fertilizer has to be financed through short-term (one year) loans from the national bank, and these must be repaid from the proceeds of next harvest. The bank's decision to award loans is based on the cooperatives' ability to repay. Of the six cooperatives whose internal finances were studied intensively by Benguergoura, all had borrowed amounts equal to or greater than their expenses for 1972-1973, and all but one had receipts less than expenses for that year. Only one was making a profit after paying the bank, and that was the only one in the whole community. If this be a common pattern, only the luckiest, best endowed cooperatives will be able to survive and succeed.

Units which cannot afford to buy equipment must have recourse to renting it. Officially the state service cooperative is to have equipment and tools on hand to rent at reasonable rates. However, the availability so far is limited, and the cooperatives are forced to rent from the private or self-managed farm sectors, at rates much higher than the finance charges they would pay to purchase the same materials. Again, only the luckiest cooperatives will succeed, and the private sector owners and self-managed farms will benefit in the meantime.

Another factor which enhances inequality among them is that the production cooperatives are at the mercy of the marketing institutions. They are allowed to keep 25 to 30 percent of their output as payment in kind, and obliged to turn over the rest to the marketing cooperative (CAPCS), which gives them credit, not cash, payment; this creates a cash-flow problem for the poorer cooperatives. In order to raise their money income, many cooperatives illegally sell their output to private wholesalers--at lower than official prices, but in return for hard cash. The cooperatives also raise cash by renting out their equipment to the private sector. Once again, only the most well-endowed cooperatives will be able to hold out from year to year, and the private sector wholesale merchants will benefit.

The reform did not eliminate, and may even have exacerbated, inequalities among the beneficiaries within the cooperatives. First, there is presently a predominance of landed proprietors and renters (sometimes the same persons) over sharecroppers and agricultural workers among the beneficiaries (Table 4.29). That the former were economically better off than the latter is shown by their tendency to have

TABLE 4.30--Previous Economic Status and Household Size of Beneficiaries
Ain Nehala 1973

No. of Household Members	Proprietor	Renter	Associator	Sharecropper	Worker	Total
1	0	0	0	0	0	0
2	0	0	0	0	1	1
3	1	3	1	1	0	6
4	0	4	0	0	2	6
5	0	2	0	1	1	4
6	1	5	0	2	4	12
7	8	5	0	0	0	13
8	0	4	1	0	1	6
9 and up	4	0	2	0	0	6
Total	14	23	4	4	9	54

SOURCE: Benguergoura, "Ain Nehala," pp. 76-77.

NOTE: Table based on interviews with the 54 beneficiaries (out of
a total of 111 beneficiaries resident at Ain Nehala).

TABLE 4.31--Previous Economic Status and Current Income of Beneficiaries,
Ain Nehala 1973

Level of Income (dinars per year)	Proprietor	Renter	Associator	Share-Cropper	Worker	Total
0-3,000	0	0	2	4	4	10
3,000-5,000	4	14	2	0	5	25
5,000-10,000	9	9	0	0	0	18
10,000 and up	1	0	0	0	0	1
Total	14	23	4	4	9	54

SOURCE: Benguergoura, "Ain Nehala," p. 92.

NOTE: Table based on interviews with all 54 beneficiaries (out of a
total of 111 beneficiaries resident at Ain Nehala).

larger households (see Table 4.30).[76] Furthermore,
Benguergoura observed that the former proprietors and
renters generally inhabit larger and better houses than
the former sharecroppers and workers within the new
reform village, and that their income level currently
tends to be higher (see Table 4.31).

Second, the reform has made it less possible for
the poorer beneficiaries to provide for their own
subsistence, and has forced them to become more
dependent on the market for their basic needs. The
reform village organization provides little space for
familial animal herds (sheep, goats) and no space for
chicken raising, which had traditionally been important
sources of non-marketed foodstuffs. The new village
organization also mixes together families who are
complete strangers, and, because all beneficiaries are
men, and women who are strangers are not allowed to mix
freely, the traditional neighborly cooperation among
women to produce non-marketed subsistence needs (for
example, food processing, cloth and blanket weaving) is
undermined. On the other hand, there is no provision
for the reform cooperatives to offer subsistence goods
or services through the cooperative. This has resulted
in an increased demand for marketed wage goods (canned
foods, factory-made clothing and household objects),
and an increased supply of them through private sector
entrepreneurs.

However, the cooperatives generally do not provide
a money income large enough for the beneficiaries to be
able to make all these purchases. Each beneficiary
received a starter subsidy from the state of 150 dinars
per month (which was to end after the cooperatives
became established), and a twice-yearly loan of 175
dinars from the state. The cooperatives themselves
were to pay wages to the beneficiaries to bring their
total minimum yearly income up to 2,600 dinars,
considered the minimum to support a family in this
region before the reform. However, many families have
found that their need to buy subsistence goods has
increased faster than their money income (because of
the reform's reorganization of physical and social
relations), and that their standard of living is
actually falling.

Those beneficiaries who own private resources
outside of the cooperative, such as land, have an
advantage within the cooperative. They can make up the
needed income from those resources and are thus under
less pressure to withdraw. Those beneficiaries who do
not own other resources can have recourse to only one
other method of earning an income, wage labor. Many of
the beneficiaries work outside the cooperative as
seasonal agricultural laborers on nearby self-managed
and private farms. Their women are also being drawn

into paid employment: many beneficiaries' wives make clothing at home on a putting-out basis for private merchant-entrepreneurs, and eighteen of their daughters work at privately-owned local rug-weaving shops.

At Ain Nehala, then, proclaimed as one of the new "socialist villages" created whole by the land reform project, private agriculture appears to remain intact, employing wage labor just as it did before. Private marketing of output and rental markets in equipment remain extensive, and private production of wage goods seems to be an important local cottage industry. Inequalities prevail both among cooperatives and among beneficiaries within cooperatives, such that economic pressures continually drive the less well-endowed and more indebted into wage labor. Finally, a self-sufficient mode of production is less viable now in agriculture than it was prior to the reform.

Center plains

Ras el-Oued. Ras el-Oued is located in the fertile high plain near the inland city of Sétif. Besides cereal production, it specialized in fodder crops and in wetlands cultivation of vegetables. Like El-Khroub, Ras el-Oued experienced the growth of large-scale private farms employing wage labor. Many of these farms were purchased from the Europeans before they left on the eve of independence, a factor which prevented as extensive a development of the self-managed sector here as elsewhere. Some of these farms were greater than one hundred hectares each, that category comprising 14 percent of private lands officially registered in the Ministry of Agriculture's 1973 survey. Very few real "peasants" were left here at the time of the reform, as witnessed by the fact that 90 percent of the beneficiaries of the reform had been wage workers.[77]

As in El-Khroub, the predominance of large-scale farms employing wage labor, with a high degree of class-consciousness among the agricultural workers, resulted in the reform having a significant impact. The reform took over 11.5 percent of the useful agricultural land and 3.4 percent of the workforce. The private lands have been reduced to only twice the useful agricultural land area of the reform lands,[78] and the class of big properties has been reduced, but not eliminated, while middle properties are left intact. As only one-half of a hectare of irrigated land is needed to support a family here, and wetlands vegetable production for urban markets is done with intensive cultivation on small and medium farms, the latter employing wage labor, there is ample scope remaining for continued private capitalist agriculture.

Sour el-Ghozlane. Sour el-Ghozlane is a daïra (county) in the wilaya of Médéa, in the plains south and east of the hills where Souagui and Berrouaghia are located. Information comes from two studies done by one person at different times, one after the first phase of the reform and one after the second phase. The direct impact of the reform on the private sector was not the focus of these studies, but the anthropological descriptions of the operations and problems of the cooperatives provide insights into the social relations of production in the reform sector.[79]

As elsewhere, the major impact of the reform here was to nationalize the communal lands, on which four of the production cooperatives studied by Jazra were set up. Privately held lands were much less affected, the expropriations yielding enough land for just one more cooperative to be set up in Phase Two of the reform. The author used participant observation to study these five cooperatives intensively.

Inequality among the cooperatives in endowments is perceived as a serious problem here. As on the nearby self-managed and private farms, these cooperatives are specializing in the production of particular crops for market, cereals, leguminous fodder crops, vegetables and melons. Subsistence farming is virtually nonexistent in this region. However, Jazra reports that this division of labor leads to a wide disparity in revenues to the various cooperatives, and that some are under much more pressure than others to disband operations due to indebtedness. The problem of mismatches in equipment provision by the marketing cooperative has led here, as elsewhere, to a widening rental market in means of production involving the reform and private sectors. Here too, as elsewhere, the cooperatives have taken up marketing their produce through private channels and renting out some of their lands to private farmers in order to get cash.

Inequalities among beneficiaries are reported to have led to conflict within the cooperatives. Of a sample of thirty-six beneficiaries in the Phase One cooperatives, twenty-three had been small farmers and twenty-six had been leasers of communal lands before the reform. Among the latter subset, eleven were specialized wetlands farmers, producing vegetables for market. The other fifteen were specialized in cereal production, of whom five held twenty to fifty hectares and two held more than fifty hectares. As these were much larger than a family needed for subsistence, they must at least have been rich farmers producing a surplus for market. This is confirmed by the fact that mechanization and the employment of wage labor were ongoing before the reform on holdings greater than thirty hectares.[80] The mixing of rich farmers who employed wage labor prior to the reform with poor farmers creates a conflict of interest within the cooperative.

Furthermore, these divisions are perpetuated within the cooperative's social relations. No production cooperative president is himself a worker; all are either rich or middle-scale farmers with continued outside ties who tend to run the cooperative in an authoritarian manner. There is an unequal division of labor and a hierarchization of functions within the cooperative. Conflict occurs over how to spend time and use common means of production between those who still possess their own private lands and herds and those who do not. Conflicts also occur among beneficiaries from different regions of the country. Some poorer cooperative members resent having to walk long distances from their residences to their work assignments.

Another source of internal conflict arises because the smaller farmers fear to specialize too intensively in one crop that might fail. As they are forbidden to plant their own gardens, failure would mean that they have no recourse but to go into wage labor, while the larger-scale employer farmers with other resources could wait out a failure. They also lack experience with intensive techniques and collective work and so make costly errors with seed planting, application of fertilizer and herbicides, and use of machinery. They thus have to work under the direction of the rich farmers if the cooperative is to be a success.

According to Jazra's survey, the income of the cooperatives was being equitably distributed among their members, due to the state accounting agency taking responsibility for keeping the cooperatives' accounts. Two-thirds of the beneficiaries surveyed said that their money income had increased since the reform. This income is still lower than that of the self-managed farm worker or other wage laborer, and does not make up for the loss of home production. The consumption standards of most have therefore gone down since the reform. As a direct result, some beneficiaries have withdrawn and gone into wage labor elsewhere. The remaining members of the cooperatives have not requested new members to replace those who withdrew, but instead hired on seasonal labor in order not to dilute their individual profit shares.

ZONE IV.   HIGH MOUNTAINS

The higher reaches of the Atlas and Kabyle mountains historically served as both a refuge and a

dumping ground for the Algerian population pressed by
colonial expansion and land expropriation. Like Zone
II, only more so, these areas were not inhabited
directly by the Europeans because of their
inaccessibility and lack of opportunity for profitable
export crops. They are thus not subject to significant
self-managed farm influence today.

In the nineteenth century, these areas were the
retreat of native Algerians pushed off the better
lands, the only area where simple small-scale
subsistence agriculture was still practiced. The land
consequently became overpopulated, fragmented and badly
eroded. Over the course of the twentieth century, the
"solution" to this problem became the outmigration of
adult men, many to France, to become wage laborers on
the bottom rung of the French industrial and service
job ladders. To this day, remittances from such
workers form a crucial part of income in the mountains
and a source of foreign exchange for the country as a
whole.

Market-oriented agriculture exists in these areas
on a small scale. A minority of commercial farms
employs wage labor here, while the vast majority of the
population is dependent on wage labor outside the
community, combined with some subsistence agriculture
(home gardening and sheep rearing) by the women,
children and elderly left behind, in order to make a
living. An important aspect of capitalist growth is
its unevenness, and these mountains have simply been
left behind in the development race.

A survey reported by de Villers for the Hodna
mountain region (wilayas of Sétif and Médéa) typifies
the scale of this combination of economic activities
(see Table 4.32). The number of larger units (greater
than twenty hectares) is greater than the number of
smaller units (up to twenty hectares), because of the
difficulty a family has in making a living here.
According to the researcher only the larger farm units
are economically viable. More than half of the larger
units received overseas remittances and they tend to be
richer in tractors and animals than the smaller units;
their relative wealth is as much a reflection of the
flow of income from outside as of internal class
differentiation.[81]

There are six Zone IV communities for which
information is available, but only one for which data
is relatively ample. The pattern is the same for all:
the reform has had virtually no impact in Zone IV, and
the neglect of these areas and the process of
outmigration continue unabated.

Bousselam. The commune Bousselam (daïra Bougao,
wilaya of Sétif) is typical of the mountainous regions.
In 1973, the total population of Bousselam was 19,814,

of whom 16,577 were at least partly dependent on agriculture for a living. Of a total adult population of 11,914, 1,390 people were resident but absent, that is, working elsewhere, and 1,203 of those were overseas.

The only data for Bousselam are based on the 1973 census survey done by the Ministry of Agriculture. The only analysis available is offered as part of the comparative study done by the same authors who did Besbès, Souagui, and F'kirina.[82]

Table 4.33 (Agricultural census, 1973, for residents only) shows only a low level of inequality of land distribution. The reform agents in this area set ten to twenty hectares of dry land as the amount needed to support a family, with the ceiling on private holdings at twenty-five to forty-five hectares. Therefore, none of the holdings registered with the Ministry of Agriculture was touched by the reform.

There is no alternative evidence to suggest a more unequal distribution of lands. However, the authors provide evidence of the importance of market-oriented, as opposed to subsistence, agriculture and the unequal distribution of other means of production. In Table 4.33 there appears to be an association between size of holding and land use: those units reporting larger

TABLE 4.32--Combination of Activities and Resources among Farmers of the Hodna Mountains, 1974

	Farm Units of More Than 20 hectares	Farm Units of 5 to 20 hectares
No. of farmers surveyed	178	107
No. benefitting from overseas remittances	97	18
No. of tractors owned	47	2
No. of sheep and goats per farm unit	36	15

SOURCE: de Villers, Pouvoir politique, p. 313.

NOTE: Table is based on a sample survey.

TABLE 4.33--Distribution of Private Agricultural Land, Animals and Crops, Bousselam 1973, by Size Category of Farm Unit

Size Category of Farm Unit (ha.)	Farm Units No.	%	Total Land Area Ha.	%	Distribution Cereals Ha.	%	Fallow Ha.	%
Less than 1	706	36	342	10	195	10	44	13
1-< 5	1,096	57	2,171	62	1,217	61	212	64
5-< 10	115	6	707	20	423	21	63	19
10-< 20	18	1	217	6	129	6	10	3
20 and up	3	0.2	70	2	27	1	1	0.3
Subtotal landed units	1,938	100	3,507	100	1,991	100	330	100
Landless units	23		. . .		. . .		. . .	
Total all units	1,961		. . .		. . .		. . .	

SOURCE: Benattig and de Villers, 'Emploi en milieu rural," "Bousselam," p. 42.

[a]Includes orchards, e.g., of olives and figs.

[b]Includes pulse and market gardens.

holdings have a much higher proportion of the land in use in "permanent cultures" (for example, tree crops and vegetables) than in cereals, as compared to other units. Since tree crops and vegetables require irrigation, and irrigated land is much more productive than non-irrigated land (by a factor of at least five), there emerges a higher level of concentration of the more productive land: 1 percent of the units report having ten or more hectares, which adds up to 8 percent of total hectares, but 11 percent of the hectares in permanent cultures. These same units report having only 5 percent of their land fallow, while units under ten hectares have around 10 percent in fallow.

The agricultural census reported practically no use of chemical fertilizer or mechanical traction in Bousselam. It found that three-fourths of all units reported using animal traction, one-half of them owning their own animals and the other half renting them from the first, but this was not checked against size of holdings. The landless and the landpoor (under ten hectares) have the vast majority of the animals. It is reasonable to surmise, then, that the twenty-one larger units (having greater than ten hectares and virtually no animals) must be the ones to use mechanical

TABLE 4.33--Continued

| of Land by Crop Type | | | | Distribution of Animals | | | | | |
| Perm. Cultures[a] | | Other Uses[b] | | Cattle | | Sheep | | Goats | |
Ha.	%	Ha.	%	No.	%	No.	%	No.	%
95	8	8	13	115	18	219	19	349	33
698	62	44	71	416	64	717	64	592	56
214	19	7	11	94	14	153	14	89	8
75	7	3	5	14	2	5	0.4	7	0.7
42	4	0	0	2	0.3	0	0	0	0
1,124	100	62	100	641	99	1,094	97	1,037	98
. . .		. . .		9	1	32	3	26	2
. . .		. . .		650	100	1,126	100	1,063	100

traction. This surmise would fit with the survey data on the Hodna region given in Table 4.32 above.

The authors report that the state has been encouraging private farmers to expand fruit tree plantations in Bousselam. In 1976, the national bank lent 246,300 dinars to twenty-four private farmers (who had requested 451,300 dinars) to buy motorized irrigation pumps, cattle, and draft animals for use in their orchards. Table 4.34 shows the distribution of these funds by size category (unfortunately irrigated is not distinguished from non-irrigated land). Medium-sized and larger farms seem to have concentrated the larger credit for equipment, while smaller units got most of the short-term loans for staying alive until harvest time. However, only 130,000 dinars of the equipment funds were actually used, by thirteen farmers, because the desired equipment was not available on the market. In the following year, the national bank awarded only 34,000 dinars for equipment purchases to seven farmers, on grounds that previous recipients had not used their funds for the agreed-on purposes. By this evidence, only those farms which have their own independent capital sources would be able to expand cultivation of fruit trees.

The evidence on "credits for the growing season" in Table 4.34 confirms this interpretation. These credits, either in money or in kind (seeds, cereals, fodder, etc.), are made for one season only, to hold the producers over until the next harvest, when the

TABLE 4.34--BNA Credits to Private Farmers at Bousselam, 1976-1978, by Size Category of Farm Unit and Amount of Loan

Size Category of Farm Unit (ha.)	No. of Credits Awarded							
	Credits for Heavy Equipment, 1976 (DA)				Credits for Growing Season, 1977-78 (DA)			
	5,000 DA	5-10,000	10,000 & Up	Total	200 DA	200-500	500-1,000	Total
1- <5	0	3	0	3	24	17	0	41
5- <15	2	4	12	18	0	0	3	3
15 and up	0	2	1	3	0	0	0	0
Total all units	2	9	13	24	24	17	3	44

SOURCE: Benattig and de Villers,"Emploi en milieu rural,""Bousselam," pp. 44, 46.

loans must be repaid. Small farm units (less than fifteen hectares) are much more likely to need them than larger farms, and they were the ones to receive them, as the table confirms. Before 1977, the service cooperative supplied these. However, now the national bank has suspended the marketing cooperative's credit lines in Bousselam, because it could not recover the loans, and taken over this function itself. The bank is much more strict about which farms receive credit, based on expected profitability of the various units.

Using the same typology as for Besbès, Souagui and F'kirina, the authors argue that at Bousselam even the Type I farms ("rich peasants") can hardly make ends meet without recourse to employment outside the farm. No "peasants" at Bousselam surpass the ceiling income officially allowed for a rural private family in 1975-76, 11,500 to 17,000 dinars. Indeed, these people can hardly be called "peasants" because of their integration into wage labor (see below Tables 4.35 and 4.36).

A Type I household might have fifteen hectares, part in cereals and part (irrigated) in figs, and would market the figs to buy other food and perhaps even some cereal for family consumption. It would own one draft animal, use no chemical fertilizer, hire seasonal wage labor, and have a net annual revenue of 2,500 dinars. Often it has members employed elsewhere.

A Type II or Type III ("middle to poor peasant") farm would have two hectares, half in barley, half in figs, and own no farm equipment and no draft animals (or it might have three hectares in figs and one cow for which they must buy fodder). Some household members would have to go out to work. Such a household might receive remittances and/or pensions from abroad equalling 8,000 dinars per year.

The reform had virtually no impact on the structure of private property here. In the first phase, sixty hectares of communal lands were given to four individual beneficiaries and five others were confirmed on the lands on which they were already employed. In the second phase, thirty-four hectares of lands belonging to absentees were given in individual title to four more beneficiaries. After the reform, the distribution of usable agricultural land became: self-managed farms, 20 percent; private farms, 79 percent; and reform cooperatives, 1 percent. The marketing cooperative barely functions here, not even possessing farm equipment to lend to the beneficiaries.

The dependence of the population on outside employment can be seen from Table 4.35. For every size category, there are many more "farmers" with outside employment than farmers without. Adding columns 4, 6, 7 and 8 gives a rate of outside employment equal to 38 percent of the adult population and 60 percent of the adult male population.[83] Table 4.36 shows that even though the average size of household increases with the size of the farm, the number of persons per household employed outside the farm does not decrease--that is, in the case of Bousselam, even "rich peasants" must sell labor power in order to support the family. For all size categories, almost all jobs held outside the farm are non-agricultural and across the board about 28 or 29 percent of those jobs are overseas. Of the 2,422 farmers and their family aids who work outside the farm, 75 percent are wage earners and most are full-time permanent workers (defined as those who work more than two hundred days per year).

Table 4.37 reveals the level of unemployment in Bousselam. Only units having more than ten hectares need more labor than the family can supply, but this adds up to only two jobs. Meanwhile, there are 1,936.5 unemployed agricultural workers. Overall, this yields a rate of disguised unemployment of 44 percent.

The reform itself has done little to alter this reality. One hundred ninety-three people applied to become beneficiaries (106 agricultural workers, 31 unemployed agricultural workers, and 49 small peasants), of whom 134 were deemed acceptable. However only eight of them ever actually received land, while five more were allowed to keep religious-endowment lands on which they were already working. In comparison,

TABLE 4.35--Distribution of Adult Population, Bousselam 1973, by Size Category of Farm Unit and Economic Activity

| Size Category of Farm Unit (ha.) (1) | Economic Activity of Farmers | | | Family Helpers Who Work Solely on Own Farm (5) |
	No. of Farmers[a] (Col. 3 & 4) (2)	Farmers who Work Solely On Own Farm (3)	Farmers with Other Activity Part-Time (4)	
Less than 1	723	150	573	1,440
1-< 5	1,109	257	852	2,801
5-< 10	107	30	77	349
10 and up	23	6	17	76
Subtotal landed farmers	1,962	443	1,519	4,666
Landless farmers	26	5	21	61
Total all farmers	1,988	448	1,540	4,727

SOURCE: Benattig and de Villers, "Emploi en milieu rural," "Bousselam," p. 6.

[a]The number of "farmers" in Tables 4.35 and 4.36 is different from the number of farm units in Table 4.31 due to leasing and indivision.

non-agricultural employment has increased by 315 full-time jobs (of two hundred days per year each) since 1974, with the establishment of public workshops in Bousselam.

Wage labor continues to be a relatively attractive alternative to becoming a beneficiary to the reform. Candidates to the reform who did not receive allotments and went into wage labor instead earn a much higher income, 6,600 dinars per year on average, than the beneficiaries of the reform, while self-managed farm workers got from 6,800 to 11,900 dinars in 1975-76 in this region.

In Bousselam, then, the reform has had very little impact. The push of the small agricultural producers off the land and into wage labor continues as before. The only possibility of change comes from the state-promoted program to spur the growth of fruit orchards using irrigation. While this might turn out to be a serious arena for farm expansion and intensive capital investment in the future, there is no evidence that it has succeeded so far.

Guenzat, Babor and Salah Bey. Like Bousselam, Guenzat and Babor are in the Kabyle mountains, wilaya of Sétif, north of the city of Sétif. (Babor is fifty kilometers to the east of Bousselam, and Guenzat is thirty kilometers to the southwest.) Salah Bey is in the same wilaya, but south of the city in the Saharan Atlas range, overlooking the Zone III plains in which

TABLE 4.35--Continued

Economic Activity of Farm Family Members					
Fam. Helpers With Other Activity Part-Time (6)	Wage Workers, Off Own Farm (7)	Non-Agric. Non-Wage Workers, Off Own Farm (8)	Econ. Active Adult Pop. (Col. 2, 5 6, 7 & 8) (9)	Housewives and Inactive (10)	Total Adult Pop. (Col. 9 & 10) (11)
214	171	3	2,551	552	3,103
556	485	27	4,978	994	5,972
87	60	2	605	130	735
16	9	1	125	15	140
873	725	33	8,259	1,691	9,950
9	6	0	102	21	123
882	731	33	8,361	1,712	10,073

TABLE 4.36--Size of Household and Number of Economically Active Persons outside of Farm Unit, Bousselam 1973, by Size of Farm Unit

Size Category of Farm Unit (ha.) (1)	No. of Farmers (2)	Total Farm Population (3)	Avg. Size of Household, per Farmer (Col. 3 ÷ 2) (4)	Ttl. No. of Persons Working Off Own Farm[a] No.	Ttl. No. of Persons Working Off Own Farm[a] (% of Econ. Active Pop.)	Avg. No. of Persons Working Off Own Farm per Farmer (Col. 5 ÷ 2)
Less than 1	723	5,037	7.0	961	38	1.3
1- < 5	1,109	9,816	8.9	1,920	39	1.7
5- < 10	107	1,279	12.0	226	37	2.1
10 and up	23	256	11.1	43	34	1.9
Subtotal landed farmers	1,962	16,388	8.4	3,150	38	1.6
Landless farmers	26	189	7.3	36	35	1.4
Total all farmers	1,988	16,577	8.3	3,186	38	1.6

SOURCE: Benattig and de Villers, "Emploi en milieu rural," "Bousselam," pp. 7, 8.

[a]These totals for each size category are equal to the addition of columns 4, 6, 7, and 8 in Table 4.35. Column 9 in Table 4.35 gives the Economically Active Population.

TABLE 4.37--Employment Furnished by Farm Units and Estimated Rates of Disguised Unemployment, Bousselam 1973, by Size Category of Farm Unit

Size Category of Farm Unit (ha.) (1)	Equiv. of No. of Persons Available for Full-time Work (2)	Equiv. of No. of Active Persons Working Full-time Off Own Farm (3)	Equiv. of No. of Active Persons Working Full-time On Own Farm (Col. 2 − 3) (4)	Ttl. Employment (No. of Full-time jobs) Furnished on Farm (5)	Employment Shortage (+) or Surplus (−) (Col. 4 − 5) (6)	Rate of Disguised Unemployment (Col. 6 ÷ 2) (7)
Less than 1	1,338	567.5	770.5	54.5	716	54
1- < 5	2,600	1,216	1,384	282.5	1,101.5	42
5- < 10	316	144	172	79	93	29
10 and up	56	26.5	29.5	31.5	−2[a]	...
Subtotal landed units	4,310	1,954	2,356	447.5	1,908.5	44
Landless units	51	21	30	2	28	55
Total all units	4,361	1,975	2,386	449.5	1,936.5	44

SOURCE: Original data from Benattig and de Villers,"Emploi en milieu rural," "Bousselam," p. 14. See Appendix C for methodology.

[a] Only the ten-hectare-or-more farms generate jobs equal to the number of workers on hand to fill them, with only a marginal need to employ wage labor.

Ras el-Oued and Ain Djasser are located. These communities, mentioned briefly in the CREA pilot study, are slated for full-scale investigation by the CREA researchers later.[84]

As in Bousselam the reform has had a negligible impact on these communities. The few reform beneficiaries were mostly small peasant farmers on public lands, who are now doing exactly what they did before. In Babor, the reform has absorbed 3.2 percent of the reported usable agricultural land, and 0.6 percent of the workforce. In Salah Bey, the reform has 0.4 percent of the agriculturally useful land and 0.1 percent of the workforce. Between 1 and 5 percent of the needs of the landless have been met by the reform here.

    Collo and Arris. The community of Collo, despite being located on the coast, is part of the "petite Kabylie," the eastern extension of the Kabyle range. Arris (directly south of Collo, about 215 kilometers) is high up in the Aurès section of the Saharan Atlas range. While land is unequally distributed here (see Table 4.38), there is by no means as extensive a development of local commercial agriculture as in other zones. The maximum reported holding is two hundred hectares. Most holdings are small, fragmented properties producing a meagre subsistence, and heavily subsidized by the remittances from emigrant wage labor.

    These communities are treated briefly by the author of the comparative study that includes El-Arrouche, Ain Djasser, and El-Khroub.[85] At Collo, the self-managed farms have only 1 percent of the agriculturally usable land, the post-agrarian-reform private sector retains 98 percent, and the reform sector has 1 percent (half from public lands, half from private absentees). At Arris, there are no self-managed farms at all, the private sector retains 98 percent, and the reform sector has 2 percent (all from public lands).

    For Guenzat, Babor, Salah Bey, Collo and Arris, the reform wrought little change and the existing opportunities for market-oriented agriculture and the existing inequality of holdings have been untouched. As in Bousselam, it is likely that market-oriented farmers are intensifying their production of "mountain" cash crops such as figs and olives, which are known to be grown in Guenzat, with the encouragement of the Ministry of Agriculture and the national bank.

ZONE V. DESERT OASES

    Two studies are available on Zone V, one major study of the highest calibre, which compares three

TABLE 4.38--Distribution of Private Agricultural Land, Collo 1973,
by Size Category of Farm Unit (in percent)

Size Category of Farm Unit (hectares)	% of Farm Units	% of Land Area
0- < 5	85	49
5- < 20	14	41
20- < 50	1	6
50- < 100	0	3
100 and up	0	1
Total	100	100

SOURCE: Cote, "Le cas de l'est," p. 177.

NOTE: Percentages are approximate as data were culled from bar graph.

communities of the Oued Rhir region (Touggourt, M'Ghaier, Djemaa), and one minor study of a neighboring community, Oumache, which is comparable with the first but of only marginal usefulness.

For the Sahara as a whole, the reform took about 800,000 palm trees out of a registered total of 7,000,000 or 11 percent.

The Oued Rhir

The Oued Rhir is a region in the province of Oasis known internationally for the fine quality of the dates it produces. Capitalist date production was encouraged here first by the French settlers starting in 1855, when they began to introduce modern techniques for drilling and raising water, and second by the opening up of the European market to Algerian dates in 1915 through the creation of a railroad link from Touggourt through Biskra to the coast. The increase in the number of date-palm trees in Oued Rhir shows the growing importance of this commodity:

1855	360,000
1880	600,000
1925	610,000
1970	2,250,000[86]

Even under the French, an absentee Algerian landed gentry existed on this economic base, at first

employing sharecroppers, then gradually turning to wage
labor.   After   the   colonizers departed, most of their
estates were taken over as   part   of   the   self-managed
sector   and   the   new   Algerian   state   took   over   the
lucrative date export   market.   Yet   Oued   Rhir   still
retained   the   strongest   concentration of agricultural
means   of   production   in the   country   on   the   remaining
private properties, and its gentry continued to control
the extensive and also lucrative domestic date   market.
Prior   to the reform the private sector held 79 percent
of   the   date   palms   (EDN)[87]   of   Oued   Rhir,   while
self-managed farms held 21 percent.

The Oued Rhir   study   is   the   most   reliable   and
carefully   done   of   all   the   investigations   reviewed
here.[88]   The   researchers   (professional   economists,
statisticians and other social scientists employed by a
research   office   of   the   Secretary   of   State)   were
meticulous   about   defining   terms   and   self-conscious
about methodology.   They conducted their   own   survey[89]
of   land   and palm trees owned and of social relations,
pointing out the discrepancies between their   work   and
the   official agricultural census results, and offering
explanations   of   these   discrepancies.   Further,   they
explicitly   examined   the   impact   of the reform on the
socio-economic structure they found.

At Oued Rhir there are   three   dimensions to   the
socio-economic   structure   that   affect   the   economic
strength   and   competitiveness   of   the   date-palm
plantations.   One   factor   is   the   location   of   the
particular community.   The second factor is the size of
the   plantation   and   its   command   over   means   of
production, including numbers and types of   palm   trees
and   water.   And   the   third   factor   is the system of
production,   involving   differences   in   technology,
methods   of   operation   and   social   relations   of
production.

Location of Communities.   Of the three communities
at   Oued   Rhir,   Touggourt,   the   southernmost,   is the
oldest and has the most serious problems with   lowering
of   the   water   table   and soil salination, Djemaa, the
central community, is second oldest and M'ghaier,   the
northernmost,   is   the   newest   and least problemmatic.
This   shows   up   in   productivity   differentials: the
average   rate   of   output   per   palm   tree is 0.0023 at
Touggourt, as compared to 0.0026 at Djemaa   and   0.0027
at M'ghaier.[90]   Table 4.39   presents these differences
and the data used in calculating them for a sample palm
grove (a subgroup of plantations selected for intensive
study) within each community.[91]   In   response   to   this
productivity difference,   the   Ministry of Agriculture
set a minimum of 115 EDN to provide   an   annual   family
income   of   at least 3,000 dinars at Touggourt but only
100 EDN at Djemaa and M'ghaier.

TABLE 4.39--Number of Plantations and Distribution of Factors of
Production among Three Palm Groves at Oued Rhir, 1973
(private sector only)

	Sidi Khelil (M'ghaier)	Tiguedidine (Djemaa)	Blidet Amor (Touggourt)	Total
No. of planta- tions	560	598	580	1,738
Date palm trees[a]				
Number	70,100	59,200	108,700	238,000
% of 3 groves	31	24	45	100
Avg. No. per plantation	125	99	187	137
% Deglet nour of palm trees at each grove	60	48	57	. . .
% immature trees of palm trees at each grove[b]	32	25	21	. . .
Rate of output of dates, in litres per second[c]	190	152	252	. . .
Rate of output[d] per palm tree	0.0027	0.0026	0.0023	. . .

SOURCE: SEP, Oued Rhir 4:106.

[a]Includes trees of all types, including fruit bearing adults and non-
fruit bearing immature trees.

[b]These trees do not yet bear fruit.

[c]This is a "fictive continuous rate" obtained by distributing the
total harvest over the time it takes to grow and reap the fruit.

[d]This figure is obtained by dividing the total number of trees into
the fictive continuous rate of output.

Size of Plantation and Command over Means of Production. Table 4.40 shows the broadest classification of private property holders in terms of the size distribution of palm tree holdings and their associated income levels in three Oued Rhir communities. There is a wide disparity between the average income of a medium plantation, which is just enough to support a family, and the average income of a large plantation, which is much more than the 9,000 dinars per year set by the Ministry of Agriculture to define a "rich peasant" household. The small and micro plantations cannot support a family and must rely on wage employment or sharecropping to generate additional income.

Based on classification of holdings by size distribution, a concentration ratio can be calculated for large plantations in each community and in each sample palm grove. In general, large plantations hold almost one-third of all adult, fruit-bearing trees at Oued Rhir. Table 4.41 shows that large plantations (those having three hundred EDN or more) possess 37 percent of the total number of adult, fruit-bearing palm trees in M'Ghaier commune (31 percent at Sidi Khelil palm grove), 31 percent in Djemaa commune (27 percent at Tiguedidine grove), and 27 percent at Touggourt commune (40 percent at Blidet Amor grove).

A more refined understanding of the extent of concentration based on the quality, as well as the

TABLE 4.40--Classification of Private Properties in Three Oued Rhir Communes, 1973

	M'Ghaier, Djemaâ	Touggourt[c]	Avg. Equiv. Income Level per year (dinars)
Large plantations	300 EDN[a] and up	345 EDN and up	20,000-30,000
Medium plantations	100-299 EDN	115-344 EDN	3,000-4,400
Small plantations	20 palms[b]-99 EDN	20 palms-114 EDN	3,000 or less
Micro plantations	1-19 palms	1-19 palms	. . .

SOURCE: SEP, Oued Rhir 4:45.

[a]The deglet nour is the finest quality date produced, so a tree that produces them is used as a standard measure. "EDN" is the equivalent of one tree producing deglet nour dates.

[b]A common, full-grown palm tree is considered to be worth approximately one-third of a deglet nour tree.

[c]Productivity at Touggourt is generally lower than at M'Ghaier and Djemaâ because, first, this commune in the south has lost water as the other two regions (center and north) expanded, and, second, its plantations have a consistently higher rate of irrigation equipment out of order.

TABLE 4.41--Holdings of Mature, Fruit-bearing Palm Trees by Large Plantations at Oued Rhir, 1973

	Commune M'Ghaier	Palm grove Sidi Khelil	Commune Djemaâ	Palm grove Tiguedidine	Commune Touggourt	Palm grove Blidet Amor	Total Oued Rhir
1. Total EDN of private sector	203,000	34,700	344,000	28,800	440,000	58,100	987,000
2. EDN belonging to large plantations	75,000	12,000	107,000	8,300	117,000	23,100	299,000
3. EDN belonging to large plantations as % of ttl. EDN (line 2 ÷ line 1)	37%	35%	31%	29%	27%	40%	30%

SOURCE: SEP, Oued Rhir 4:85 (adapted).

quantity, of palm trees at Oued Rhir can be gleaned
from the microdata offered in Table 4.42. In contrast
to Table 4.41 here all palm trees (both adult
fruit-bearing and unproductive trees, djebbars) are
included. While this provides a lower overall
concentration ratio (for example, 2 percent of
plantations at Sidi Khelil are large and have 16
percent of all trees, as opposed to 31 percent of
adult, fruit-bearing trees), large and medium
plantations have much higher percentages of deglet nour
trees than do small plantations, (see line six of Table
4.42) and large and medium plantations have lower
proportions of unproductive trees than the small
plantations (see line seven of Table 4.42).

Water control is even more concentrated than tree
possession (line 8 of Table 4.42). Since this is an
oasis region, water supply is the single most crucial
constraint on production. The large plantations at
Sidi Khelil (2 percent of all plantations) control 30
percent of the water, at Tiguedidine 3 percent control
28 percent of the water, and at Blidet Amor 7 percent
control 43 percent.

The association between size of holding and
productivity, and thus economic security of the
property owner, is shown in line nine of Table 4.42
(output per fruit-bearing tree). The large plantations
at Sidi Khelil and Tiguedidine have more than double
the output per tree of the small plantations, with the
medium plantations falling in between. At Blidet Amor,
the differentials are much smaller but the pattern is
the same.

The explanation for these productivity
differentials lies not only in technical economies of
scale (for example, possession of more efficient
motorized pumps by large plantations and thus more
reliable access to water) but also in the social
organization of production. The researchers argue that
the benefits of specialization and division of labor
seem to be captured on the large plantations, since the
owners employ others to work instead of working alone.
Furthermore, large plantation owners are politically
better connected and thus are assured privileged access
to water. Table 4.43 demonstrates the direct
reflection of these productivity differences in incomes
attained, measured in dinars per EDN.

The majority of plantations cannot provide their
holders with an adequate income. Table 4.42, line
five, "Average No. of Trees per Plantation," shows that
about 80 percent of all plantations are smaller than
what the Ministry of Agriculture set as the minimum
necessary to support a family. These, as well as
holders of micro plantations and non-property holders,
were then all technically eligible to apply to become

TABLE 4.42--Respective Weights and Characteristics of Large, Medium and Small Plantations in the Palm Groves Studied at Oued Rhir[a], 1973

	Sidi Khelil				Tiguedidine				Bidet Amor			
	Large	Medium	Small	Total	Large	Medium	Small	Total	Large	Medium	Small	Total
1. Ttl. no. of plantations[b]	9	60	391	460	7	31	202	240	33	66	371	470
2. % of plantations	2	13	85	100	3	13	84	100	7	14	79	100
3. Ttl. no. of trees (EDN, inc. unproductive)	10,896	16,344	40,860	68,100	10,661	14,027	31,422	56,110	40,899	23,679	43,052	107,630
4. % of trees	16	24	60	100	19	25	56	100	38	22	40	100
5. Avg. no. of trees per plantation	792	228	82	115	737	198	69	103	892	245	78	158
6. % deglet nour of adult fruit-bearing trees	77	81	45	60	68	45	43	48	66	66	45	57
7. Ratio of unproductive over fruit-bearing trees	14	28	37	31	11	16	23	20	19	25	20	21
8. % of water	30	35	35	100	28	25	47	100	43	19	38	100
9. Output per fruit-bearing tree	0.005	0.0039	0.0016	0.0027	0.0048	0.0027	0.0023	0.0029	0.0028	0.0021	0.0020	0.0023

SOURCE: SEP, Oued Rhir 4:110.

[a] All the concentration indicators would be higher if the Zaouia (religious order) holdings were counted in. However, this would have distorted the picture, because these have been practically abandoned at Bidet Amor but are still important producers at Sidi Khelil and Tiguedidine.

[b] Does not include microplantations. The holders of microplantations are not included in the table because their weight in ownership of productive factors is small. At Sidi Khelil, 100 of them (18 percent of all plantations) have 2,000 EDN and djebbars (4 percent of all trees); at Tiguedidine 258 of them (43 percent) have 3,090 trees (8 percent); and at Bidet Amor 110 (9 percent) have 1,070 trees (1 percent).

reform beneficiaries.[92]

In contrast to the small plantations, the medium plantations (less than 15 percent of all plantations) mainly fall above the Ministry of Agriculture's minimum but below the official ceiling (190 EDN).[93] They thus would remain untouched by the reform. Note, however, that this means their share of palm trees, 25 percent, and their otherwise generous share of factors of production (for example, their share of water is everywhere greater than their size in the population) also were untouched by the reform.

Types of production systems. A critical virtue of this study is the explicit recognition that there are three distinct systems of production at Oued Rhir, which are not merely a function of physical size of plantation (the primary focus of the reform), but also of methods of operation and social relations. This typology differs from the one used by Benattig and de Villers for Besbès, Souagui, F'kirina and Bousselam because it distinguishes between capitalist and traditional units at all size levels.

Type I are the capitalist plantations. The owner does no manual work himself; he or a hired manager directly supervises the work of day laborers and controls the factors of production.[94] Profits from the sale of the product are reinvested to enlarge or improve the plantation. This form occurs on both large and medium plantations.

Type II are the middle and poor peasant plantations. The members of the family unit work their property directly, sometimes with the aid of seasonal day workers or labor exchange. They do not employ permanent wage labor. They are not self-sufficient units in the sense of producing everything they need; rather, they grow vegetables and dates for their own consumption and sell surplus dates to market to earn

TABLE 4.43--Average Revenues at Three Oued Rhir Palm Groves, 1973, by Size Category of Plantation

Size Category of Plantation[b]	Revenue (in dinars) per EDN[a]		
	Sidi Khelil	Tiguedidine	Blidet Amor
Small	11	19	20
Medium	24	21	24
Large	30	45	28

SOURCE: SEP, Oued Rhir 4:138.

[a]Find definition of EDN in note to Table 4.40.

[b]Find boundaries of categories in Table 4.40.

enough income to purchase the other commodities they
need. With luck, such a unit manages to reproduce
itself from one year to another. Without luck, its
members must sharecrop for other owners and go into
wage labor, at least temporarily.

Type III are the traditional landlord-sharecropper
plantations. An absentee owner employs a resident
manager to supervise sharecroppers on the plantation.
Such units usually have lower average productivity per
tree than either Type I or Type II units. But, because
they are usually of larger size, the total product is
adequate to provide a rentier income to the owner, an
income used for luxury consumption, urban investment,
or for loans to the less well-endowed date producers.

For Oued Rhir as a whole, the Type I plantations
make up 50 percent of all large and medium plantations,
while Type II and Type III each have 25 percent. Type
II, however, has fewer trees per plantation than Type I
or Type III, and owns no trees in other palm groves as
do the Type I and Type III owners. The most striking
contrast is between Types I and III in all locations,
especially at Tiguedidine.

The relationship between type of production
system, use of yield-improving techniques, productivity
and profitability is illustrated in Tables 4.44, 4.45,
and 4.46, based on detailed accounts kept on the
economic activities of all types of plantations in the
three palm groves. The data for Type II are included
in these tables for Blidet Amor, but not for Sidi
Khelil or Tiguedidine, for a special reason. The
researchers had expected productivity to be lower for
Type II than for Types I and III at all locations,
based on the logic of their typology. The expectation
turned out to be correct for Sidi Khelil and
Tiguedidine and was not considered worthy of further
study. The fact that Type II surpassed both Type I and
Type III as Blidet Amor required more explanation.

Table 4.44 shows that Type I plantations are much
more likely than Type III plantations to use
yield-improving technologies (no data was available for
Type II on this dimension). This translates into
investment costs that are three to four times higher
for the Type I plantations than for the Type III. Type
I at Tiguedidine is the absolute highest. At Blidet
Amor, the Type II plantations have investment costs
comparable to the Type I, but the funds are used much
more to complement labor-intensive methods (fertilizer)
than for purchase or rental of machinery. The
researchers also report that the less productive Type
II plantations at Blidet Amor have been systematically
abandoned in recent years, so that only the ones
undergoing new investment remain.

Table 4.45 shows that Type I plantations in all

TABLE 4.44--Use and Costs of Yield-Improving Technology in
Three Palm Groves at Oued Rhir, 1972-73 Season, by
Type of Production System

	Sidi Khelil		Tiguedidine		Blidet Amor		Blidet Amor
	I	III	I	III	I	III	II
No. of plantations	13	10	8	6	10	6	6
Use of technology (% of plantations)							
Pruning	53	0	77	4	85	46	...
Drainage	39	21	93	17	31	0	...
Sand/gravel management	88	6	90	30	58	24	...
Material costs (DA/EDN, except for water)	3.35	1.13	4.07	0.85	3.30	0.4	3.60

SOURCE: SEP, Oued Rhir 4:146.

groves and Type II in Blidet Amor have higher productivity than the Type III, even though they have fewer trees per worker. This seems to reflect the greater intensity of work, and materials applied to each tree. Type I at Tiguedidine has the highest output per tree.

Table 4.46 shows that higher productivity seems to translate into higher revenues, gross and net, and higher profits for the Type I plantations than the Type III at all groves. Again, Type I at Tiguedidine is in the lead. The showing of Type II on the profitability dimension is a bit misleading, because Type II plantations hire as little non-family labor as possible and do not subtract the costs of their own family labor before reporting "profit."

The authors interpret their cross-sectional comparison as evidence of a historic process of the general decline of Type III and the general ascendancy of Type I plantations prior to the land reform. They do not speculate on the place of the relatively successful Blidet Amor Type II plantations in this process. Whether the Type IIs are in the throes of a competitive shake-out and those which remain will shift toward the Type I model, or whether the peculiar situation of Blidet Amor (with the severe decline of water sources and soil salination) encourages highly labor-intensive family farming and creates diseconomies of scale, are as yet unanswered questions.

Impact of the land reform. By the terms of the reform, only those owners not living at their plantations or having substantial non-agricultural incomes were subject to total expropriation. Those

TABLE 4.45--Productivity Indicators in Three Palm Groves at Oued Rhir, 1972-73 Season, by Type of Production System

| | Sidi Khelil | | Tiguedidine | | Blidet Amor | | Blidet Amor |
	I	III	I	III	I	III	II
No. trees per permanent worker	319	329	250	326	170	190	165
Total product in litres/second	6,690	6,460	6,720	5,190	8,570	5,530	10,130
Rate of output per tree	0.0052	0.0042	0.0081	0.0028	0.0029	0.0028	0.0039

SOURCE: SEP, Oued Rhir 4:146.

TABLE 4.46--Value of Production and Profitability in Three Palm Groves at Oued Rhir, 1972-73 Season, by Type of Production System

| | Sidi Khelil | | Tiguedidine | | Blidet Amor | | Blidet Amor |
	I	III	I	III	I	III	II
Total product (DA/EDN)[a]	43	32	58	20	33	24	47
Net value added (DA/EDN)[b]	34	27	52	16	25	18	38
Profit (DA/EDN)[c]	25	20	43	12	18	13	37

SOURCE: SEP, Oued Rhir 4:146.

[a]Total value of product in dinars after subtracting costs of harvest and merchants' profit.

[b]Net value added equals total product minus costs of materials (water, manure, chemical fertilizer) and amortization of equipment.

[c]Profit equals net value added minus explicit costs of employed labor (either permanent or temporary). The implicit costs of the labor of the owner and family workers are not subtracted.

TABLE 4.47--Estimates of Nationalizable Properties, Oued Rhir 1973, by
Palm Grove and Size Category of Plantation (in percent)

A. Strict Application of Reform Criteria, with no exceptions

	Nationalizable Properties, as % of total properties		
	Sidi Khelil	Tiguedidine	Blidet Amor
Large plantations	95	92	89
Large & medium plantations	71	79	78
All plantations	39	50	76

B. Strict Application of Reform Criteria, but allowing exceptions
foreseen by the reform texts

	Nationalizable Properties, as % of total properties		
	Sidi Khelil	Tiguedidine	Blidet Amor
Large plantations	66	76	69
Large & medium plantations	44	59	56
All plantations	25	37	48

C. Allow APCE to define as "resident" and non-expropriable those
owners who entrust their plantation to an overseer, while they
live at the palm grove and do not have significant non-agricultural income

	Nationalizable Properties, as % of total properties		
	Sidi Khelil	Tiguedidine	Blidet Amor
Large plantations	50	59	50
Large and medium plantations	33	40	38
All plantations	20	29	32

D. Actual Application of Reform by APCEs: % of total properties
finally nationalized in whole or in part

	Sidi Khelil	Tiguedidine	Blidet Amor
Large plantations	36	28	37
Large and medium plantations	24	22	29
All plantations	15	21	25

SOURCE: SEP, Oued Rhir 4:227, 235, 237, 239.

living on their plantations and dependent on them for most of their income were liable, at most, to partial expropriation.

Of proprietors who did not manage to avoid the reform altogether, Type III owners were more likely to be affected than Type I. The researchers found that 45 percent of all large-scale proprietors at Oued Rhir resided outside their plantations. However, within the class of large proprietors, there was a distinct pattern not taken into account by the reform: whereas 62 percent of Type I owners live at the grove where they own a plantation (38 percent live outside), only 20 percent of Type III owners do so (80 percent live outside). Furthermore, whereas only 34 percent of Type I owners have significant non-agricultural income, 71 percent of Type III owners do so, especially in commerce, and that is not counting outside economic activity of other than the head of household.

Though the researchers calculated that about 90 percent of the large plantations should have been affected by the reform, only about one-third finally experienced some effects. At Sidi Khelil two-thirds of large Type I owners and one-third of Type III owners were left intact. All large Type I owners and one-quarter of Type III owners were left intact at Tiguedidine. Fourteen out of seventeen large Type I plantations and seven out of nine Type III plantations were left intact at Blidet Amor. All medium sized Type I plantations were left intact at all locations. Based on their own survey data, the authors were able to

TABLE 4.48--Reasons for Discrepancy between Properties Nationalizable and Properties Nationalized, Oued Rhir 1973, in % of EDN (immature trees included)

	Sidi Khelil	Tiguedidine	Blidet Amor
1. Proprietor's name does not appear on any APCE list.	64	15	50
2. Proprietor is listed, but with fewer trees than (s)he actually owns.	7	11	17
3. Proprietor's challenge was accepted by APCE after publication of lists as in Table 84, c.	29	63	11
4. Other (such as listing more dependents than proprietor really has).	0	11	22
Total	100	100	100

SOURCE: SEP, Oued Rhir 4:240.

reconstruct how these modest results came out of the reform.[95] Table 4.49 (based on Tables 4.47 and 4.48) shows the difference between the properties registered during the reform and the authors' estimates of the real total of nationalizable properties and the proportion of missing trees.

Political power of the Type I plantation owners. These modest results were obtained from the reform partly because the local rural bourgeoisie, owners of large and medium Type I plantations, kept control of the communal political apparatus (the communal assembly and the reform service cooperative) that is responsible for, on one hand, the supply of water and, on the other hand, enforcement of the reform itself. They not only control existing water supplies, but also make decisions concerning new forages, irrigation and circulation systems. They continue to control the domestic date market. They are also linked through kinship, marriage and political alliance to the officials in the public sector who govern the self-managed plantations, the date processing plants, and the state marketing agency.

The researchers found that this influence takes two specific forms. First, in the committee of mandataires (the local water authority in each commune), one-half of the members are large plantation proprietors and the other half are mainly medium plantation proprietors. Second, large and medium proprietors dominate the communal assemblies. At Sidi Khelil, the large and medium owners are 13 out of 19 members (while non-owners have only 2 seats). At Tiguedidine, out of 13 seats, the big and medium proprietors have 7, while non-owners again have only 2. At Blidet Amor, out of 16 seats, large and medium proprietors have 6, while small proprietors have 8 and non-owners have 2. In all three communes, the non-owners holding seats in the communal assemblies are permanent wage workers employed outside private sector agriculture. No simple sharecroppers or agricultural day workers are represented at all.

Impact of the agrarian reform on agricultural employment. Sixty percent of all men of working age were employed in agriculture (essentially date production) in the whole of Oued Rhir prior to the reform. Touggourt registered a much lower rate (49 percent) than M'Ghaier (66 percent) and Djemâa (73 percent) because of availability of non-agricultural wage employment in light industry, date processing and crafts in that community.

Most of the permanent agricultural workers on both the Type I and Type III plantations were classified by the Oued Rhir researchers as sharecroppers, rather than wage workers, although day laborers do most of the

TABLE 4.49--Estimates of Number of Date Palms Missing from Communal Lists and Their Nationalizable Proportion, Oued Rhir 1973

	Commune M'Ghaier	Palm grove Sidi Khelil	Commune Djemaâ	Palm grove Tiguedidine	Commune Touggourt	Palm grove Blidet Amor
Total trees-number						
1. On APCE lists	374,000	44,000	390,000	47,500	535,000	63,600
2. In authors' survey	423,000	70,100	685,000	64,200	840,000	108,700
No. of missing trees (line 2 minus line 1)	49,000	26,000	295,000	16,700	305,000	45,100
% of trees missing (line 3 ÷ line 2)	12%	37%	43%	26%	36%	41%
Proportion nationalizable of missing trees (on criteria of Table 85-B)		up to 1/3		3/10		up to 4/5

SOURCE: SEP, Oued Rhir 4:241.

actual work. These are the characteristics of the
traditional Muslim sharecropping relationship. (1) The
sharecropper (_khammes_)[96] brought nothing to production
but his labor power. (2) Whereas the wage of the
proletarian is fixed in advance, the _khammes_ was
supposed to receive a portion of the total crop--at
Oued Rhir, one-fifth of the dates (the production of
which is commercialized) and one-third of the
vegetables planted under the date palms (for own
consumption). With three-fifths of the product going
to cover expenses paid by the owner, and one-fifth of
the total product as "profit" to the owner, this
yielded a rate of exploitation of 100 percent. (3) The
sharecropper had autonomy over his day-to-day work
activity and a material interest in the product
itself--he could plant in unused beds, for example, or
negotiate with the owner over the amount of other work
he needed to do. (4) The sharecropper had to perform
personal services for the owner, such as domestic
labor, cutting wood and carrying water, in return for
gifts or loans from the owner.

This type of social relationship was already in
decline before the reform. There had been a steady
increase in the use of temporary laborers paid by the
day on the big and medium plantations. Because the
wages of temporary laborers are low, this had lowered
the share of revenue going to labor and increased that
going to the owners. The researchers estimated that in
1973 the actual ratio of profits to labor costs was at
least 2.6 (260 percent), much higher than the
traditional 100 percent. Day workers, who average only
600 dinars per year, have thus been added on beneath
the sharecropper as the lowest-ranking stratum.

The role of the former "sharecroppers," the
permanent workers, had accordingly evolved into that of
overseers or managers of dayworkers. This conversion
was accompanied by a decline in the paternalistic
aspects of the owner/sharecropper relationship,
especially on the Type I plantations, and the expansion
of the impersonal contractual aspects. The former
sharecroppers interviewed perceived this, on one hand,
as a loss of former security, but, on the other hand,
as an opportunity to absolutely increase their incomes,
as the technological innovations on Type I units allow
them to increase the number of trees they supervise and
the productivity of each tree. However, all also
stated that they would prefer stable wage employment
outside agriculture if it were available. These
overseers generally receive a higher income on big and
medium than on small plantations, and higher on Type I
than on Type III units. The overseers' income was
highest on the large Type I units at Tiguedidine,
although even there they get no more than one-tenth of

TABLE 4.50--Effect of Reform on Employment, Oued Rhir 1974

	Commune M'Ghaier	Palm grove Sidi Khelil	Commune Djemaâ	Palm grove Tiguedidine	Commune Touggourt	Palm grove Blidet Amor	Total Oued Rhir
Active agric. population							
1966 census	3,627	288	5,356	489	6,413	684	15,396
1974 government estimate	4,570	363	6,749	616	8,080	862	19,399
Authors' survey		478		682		1,021	
Reform beneficiaries	698	60	591	63	855	128	2,144
Beneficiaries as % of active agric. pop.	15%	13%	9%	9%	11%	13%	11%

SOURCE: SEP, Oued Rhir 4:244.

TABLE 4.51--Trees Allotted to Reform Beneficiaries, Oued Rhir 1974

	Commune M'Ghaier	Palm grove Sidi Khelil	Commune Djemaâ	Palm grove Tiguedidine	Commune Touggourt	Palm grove Bidet Amor	Total Oued Rhir
CAPRA							
No. of beneficiaries	430	0	332	32	181	128	943
No. of EDN[a] per bene-ficiary	130	0	95	61	130	140	
Ttl. EDN attributed	55,900	0	31,540	1,952	23,530	17,920	110,970
GMV							
No. of beneficiaries	268	60	259	31	674	0	1,201
No. of EDN[a] per bene-ficiary	134	140	122	74	110	0	
Ttl. EDN attributed	35,912	8,400	31,598	2,294	74,140	0	141,650

SOURCE: SEP, Oued Rhir 4:244.

[a]Immature trees are included in this calculation.

the total product.[97]

One of the stipulated goals of the reform was to eradicate the landlord/sharecropper relationship. Table 4.50 shows that the reform has affected only 11 percent of the active agricultural workforce at Oued Rhir as a whole. Table 4.51 shows the distribution of palm trees to reform beneficiaries, in some cases (the CAPRA in Djemaa and the GMV at Touggourt) in insufficient quantities to support a family. If the beneficiaries of the reform were drawn first from the true sharecroppers of the properties nationalized and only second from the wage laborers on those properties, then some progress would have been made in dealing a final blow to the already decaying sharecropping system. But the wage-labor system would have been left intact.

All in all, at Oued Rhir then, we see that the capitalist agricultural sector was increasingly important prior to the reform and that the pre-capitalist tenures were contracting. The reform mounted a serious attack on the remaining pre-capitalist tenures (Type III) but mainly left the capitalist tenures (Type I) intact. The fact that the Type I owners seem to dominate the local political apparatus may indicate that the reform benefited the further development of capitalist agriculture at Oued Rhir, but the evidence is only suggestive. There is no evidence on the social dynamics of the cooperative sector for Oued Rhir like we have seen for other localities, but there is evidence that the reform has enhanced the conversion of the small independent producers (Type II) and sharecroppers into wage laborers.

Oumache.

Information on Oumache, done as part of the same comparative study by Cote on El-Arrouche, El-Khroub, Ain-Djasser, Collo and Arris, shares the same limitations as these other community descriptions.[98] Unlike the Oued Rhir authors, Cote fails to question the validity of the government data he uses.

Oumache is a commune just south of the city of Biskra, and north of Oued Rhir, on the rail line from Touggourt to the coast. As in the other date palm growing communities, with the introduction of modern technology to raise water in the twentieth century, those who had the financial wherewithal to purchase the water-pumping machinery were better able to appropriate the common water supplies in order to enhance their individual plantations. Hence, concentration of the means of production proceeded apace, as those who did not have such financial resources were forced into becoming sharecroppers or wage laborers on either European or native Algerian large-scale plantations.

At Oumache, the self-management movement captured 4 percent of the palm trees on European estates on the eve of independence. But this did not stop the flow of petty producers into wage labor, the subsequent new workers becoming non-member employees of the self-managed permanent farm workers themselves. Concentration of means of production continued in the private sector as it had before independence.

As in the high plains (Zone III) where self-managed farms are important but not overwhelming (in contrast to Zone I where they are centrally important), and where there are few real independent peasants left, the reform had a significant impact at Oumache, but without destroying the existing structure of private landholding and capitalist agriculture. The reform now controls 26 percent of the palm trees (some _deglet_ _nour_ included) registered on the local government lists, as compared to 70 percent for the private sector. Most of the nationalized properties (20 percent) came from the private sector, while the other 6 percent came from public holdings.

CONCLUSION

Table 4.52 presents a summary of statistics that bear on the impact of the reform in each community and allow some comparisons by zone.

It was in Zone III, the high plains, that the impact of the reform was the greatest. In two communities, El-Khroub and Ain Nehala, the private sector became smaller than the reform sector. The proportion of the agriculturally useful land incorporated into the reform sector ranged from 11.5 up to 35 percent in this zone. Reform beneficiaries constituted only 3 or 4 percent of the economically active population, but in one community, F'kirina, they represented 89 percent of the poor and landless farmers, and in El-Khroub a majority of reform beneficiaries reported an improvement in their income as a result of the reform.

Although the majority of reform lands in most cases came from the former public holdings, in one case, El-Khroub, 57 percent came from private absentees and this had a marked effect on the concentration of holdings there. However, El-Khroub also had the greatest presence of capitalist farms, which held 93 percent of the land among resident private owners. Capitalist farms in other Zone III communities held 40 to 50 percent. These relatively high levels of concentration are due, first, to the economies of scale associated with highly mechanized cereal production on large farms here and, second, to the shift on the part of the medium-scale farms (20 to 50 hectares) to the production of vegetables and dairy farming. This zone was highly commercialized to start with, and the reform enhanced that tendency, leaving most of the commercial family farms and resident capitalist farms intact.

Zone V, the date-producing desert oases, was affected somewhat less than Zone III. Between 11 and 26 percent of the date palms were incorporated into the reform. Reform beneficiaries came to constitute 11 percent of the economically active population. Although the private sector was left with about 70 percent of the date palms, most of those taken by the reform came from private absentee holdings. Yet, as in Zone III, the resident capitalist subsector retained its influence among private holders, with about 24 percent of all trees, and there remains an important contingent of medium-sized commercial family farms using labor-intensive techniques.

Zone II, the foothills and river valleys of the coastal mountain range, was the third hardest hit by the reform: from 6 to 16 percent of the agriculturally useful land was absorbed, and, in three cases out of four, the majority of the reform lands came from the holdings of private absentees. However, the capitalist sector retained its influence among resident private farmers, with a range of 26 to 46 percent of the lands under its control. There is a wide scope for the further development of commercial family farms in this zone, because the most lucrative opportunities at present are in fruit trees and market garden vegetables, where economies of scale are not important, and because most resident families have members working elsewhere and remitting their incomes to maintain the family. Reform beneficiaries constituted between 2 and 5 percent of the landless and landpoor. In only one case, that of Merad, did the beneficiaries report an increase in their income as a result of the reform.

The impact on Zone I, the coastal region, was somewhat less than on Zone II, the reform absorbing from 4 to 14 percent of the agriculturally useful land. In three cases out of four, the reform lands came directly from the former public holdings and made very little impact on either private holdings or the number of people who became beneficiaries. In two of these three, the resident capitalist sector is small but significant, retaining from 15 to 25 percent of the private lands. Besbès is the exception: most of the reform lands were taken from private absentees and its resident private sector was reduced to only 8 percent of the total lands, less than that of the reform

TABLE 4.52--Summary Statistics on Impact of Reform,
by Community and Zone

	Share of Agricultural Lands (%)	Origin of Reform Lands (%) Public	Private	Share of Agricultural Lands in Private Sector After Reform (%)
I. Coastal Plains				
Besbès	14	6	94	8
Zemmouri	5	86	14	35
Thénia	4	most		63
Cheraga (Zeralda)	7.4	67	33	8
II. Foothills				
Souagui	6	14	86	88
Merad	9[a] / 7[b]	33	67	16[a] / 37[b]
Berrouaghia	16[a] / 14[c]	7	93	40[a] / 49[c]
El Arrouche	15	33	67	54
III. High Plains				
F'kirina	35	81	19	61
Ain Djasser	29	83	17	61
El Khroub	35	43	57	20
Ain Nehala (Tlemcen)	31	79	21	29
Ras el Oued	11.5	-	-	23
Sour el-Ghozlane	-	-	-	-
IV. High Mountains				
Bousselam	1	64	36	79
Guenzat	-	-	-	-
Babor	3.2	-	-	-
Salah Bey	0.4	-	-	-
Collo	1	50	50	98
Arris	2	100	0	98
V. Desert Oases				
Oued Rhir	11		most	68
Oumache	26	23	77	70

[a]official   [b]Benbarkat   [c]Bouzebra
[d]Ait-al-Hadj   [e]land   [f]permanent cultures
[g]EDN

TABLE 4.52--Continued

Share of Capitalist ("Type 1") Farms in Private Holdings, Residents Only, After Reform (%)			Number of Reform Beneficiaries
% of Units	Size (Ha)	% of Land	
3	>20	58	c.350
1	>10	15	29
–	>50	25	49
–	–	–	–
5	>20	26	67
3	>15	46	57
1	–	33	–
–	–	–	–
{ 8	{ >50	{ 40^a	
{ 12	{ >70	{ 46^d	950
6	>50	49	–
57	>50	93	900
–	–	–	111
–	–	–	–
–	–	–	–
1.2	>10	{ 8^e { 11^f	13
–	–	–	–
–	–	–	–
1	>20	10	–
–	–	–	–
6	>100^g	24^g	2,144
–	–	–	–

TABLE 4.52--Continued

	Reform Beneficiaries as % of Economically Active Population	Reform Beneficiaries as % of Landless and Landpoor Farmers	Majority of Reform Beneficiaries Report Increased Income After Reform
I. Coastal Plains			
Besbès	13	29	no
Zemmouri	-	-	-
Thénia	-	-	no
Cheraga			
(Zeralda)	4.6	-	no
II. Foothills			
Souagui	-	2	no
Merad			
	-	5	yes
Berrouaghia			
	-	-	-
El Arrouche	-	-	-
III. High Plains			
F'kirina			
	-	89	no
Ain Djasser	-	-	-
El Khroub	-	-	yes
Ain Nehala			
(Tlemcen)	4	-	no
Ras el Oued	3.4	-	-
Sour el-			
Ghozlane	-	-	-
IV. High Mountains			
Bousselam			
	-	1	no
Guenzat	-	-	-
Babor	0.6	-	-
Salah Bey	0.1	-	-
Collo	-	-	-
Arris	-	-	-
V. Desert Oases			
Oued Rhir	11	-	-
Oumache	-	-	-

sector, while the number of beneficiaries reached 13 percent of the economically active population, or 29 percent of the landless and landpoor. However, within the private sector that remained, the capitalist farms controlled 58 percent of the land, and, as in Zone I in general, all farms were highly commercialized, producing fruits, vegetables, dairy products and poultry for the urban markets. As in Zone II, there remains scope for the further development of commercial family farming in these specialties.

The impact on Zone IV, the high interior mountains, was the smallest of all. A maximum of 3.2 percent of the total agricultural land went to the reform, most of that from public holdings. The beneficiaries amounted to less than 1 percent of the economically active population, and about 1 percent of the landless and landpoor. Because of the poor quality of the land in this zone and the lack of opportunities for capturing economies of scale, resident capitalist farms controlled only 8 to 10 percent of the lands. There is a small but limited scope for commercial family farming here, unless irrigation and reforestation projects are undertaken and new crops (such as tree fruits) are quickly expanded.

Overall, the communities examined in all five zones [9] showed a relatively high degree of commercialization and specialization in their agricultural production before the reform. "Self-sufficient" peasant producers, in the sense of families producing solely for their own consumption, were already rare, if not extinct. Farm families in all zones were already linked into markets, at least through the sale of their labor power and the renting out of their lands, if not through the sale of agricultural output they produced themselves. What the reform did was to reorganize these market relationships along six dimensions.

First, the reform eliminated private absentee landholding, public land rentals, and sharecropping. Its major impact on the private tenure system was to encourage the direct working of lands by those who held title to them.

Second, the reform awarded de facto legitimacy to the remaining inequalities in the private sector with regard to landholdings, the distribution of means of production, the employment of wage labor, and income distribution.

Third, markets in land sales, in means of production, in wage labor, and in agricultural products have been enhanced. The service cooperatives' success in replacing the private markets was limited.

Fourth, the reform enhanced commercialization of agricultural products, but, so far, has stimulated increased production only of highly profitable crops such as fruits, vegetables, meat and poultry, not grains.

Fifth, the reform decreased rural unemployment very little, but facilitated the shift of surplus labor from agriculture to industry and services. Four zones still produce surplus labor and export it out of agriculture. Only Zone I does not.

Sixth, the reform replicated private sector structures and inequalities in the new cooperative farms, which, unequally endowed and under competitive pressure, must function as profit-maximizing businesses.

Through all of this, power relations in the countryside were modified: the commercial family farms had their material base strengthened and the capitalist farms were legitimized, so that these groups can now promote their interests directly and openly. There were also some real achievements for reform beneficiaries in some communities, such as Besbès and El-Khroub, but on the whole this did not amount to a "revolution" by or for petty producers and workers. The reform succeeded in its hidden agendas, to increase commercialization of agriculture and to transfer surplus labor from agriculture to industry. However, the reform failed in its overt agendas, to increase national self-sufficiency in basic food production and to eradicate the "exploitation of man by man."

NOTES

1. Most of the authors of the works cited approached the reform from a different perspective. Hoping for an egalitarian, "socialist" reform (with a "land to the tiller" orientation), they decry the continued inequalities, and the broad scope that remains for capitalist agriculture to develop, as signifying the failure of the reform. They did not generally consider the possibility that the transformation to capitalist agriculture was an implicit goal of the reform all along, and that, in this at least, the reform may have succeeded.

2. The inspiration for this methodology is from Vladimir I. Lenin, The Development of Capitalism in Russia, following the text of the 2d ed., 1908 (Moscow: Progress Publishers, 1974); and Mahmoud Abdel-Fadil, Development, Income Distribution, and Social Change in Rural Egypt (1952-1970): A Study in the Political Economy of Agrarian Transition (New York: Cambridge

University Press, 1975).

3. Terminological note: Algeria is divided into thirty-one wilayat (provinces). Each wilaya is in turn divided into dairat (the equivalent of counties). Each daira is in turn divided into communes, in the French sense of local administrative communities, townships, not in the English sense of socialist common-property-owning units. Algeria does not have "communes" in the latter sense. While the agrarian reform was initiated at the national level, and the final authority rests there, the tools for actual execution were placed in the hands of the communal government.

4. Claudine Chaulet et al., "Projet de recherche sur la révolution agraire" (Algiers: CREA Equipe de la Révolution Agraire, 1976), mimeographed proposal based on pilot project; Rachid Benattig and Gauthier de Villers, "Enquête socio-économique sur la situation de l'emploi et des revenus en milieu rural" (Algiers, 1978), mimeographed; and Marc Cote, "Révolution agraire et sociétés agraires: le cas de l'est algérien," Annuaire de l'Afrique du Nord, 1975 (1976), pp. 173-184.

The growth of capitalism always involves uneven development, among production units, among firms, among localities and among regions. While uneven development also occurs in other modes of production, it is a necessary feature of capitalist development due to the dictates of production for profit and the anarchy of decisions.

5. Rachid Benattig and Gauthier de Villers, "Enquête socio-économique sur la situation de l'emploi et des revenus en milieu rural" (Algiers: 1978), mimeographed.

The two persons responsible for this study were associates of the Chaulet team at CREA in Algiers. I was able to interview one of them, Rachid Benattig, several times. He provided me with their unpublished research results and explained that the Ministry of Labor had forbidden their publication because of the unfavorable light cast on the government's employment policies, even though the research had been commissioned jointly by the Algerian Ministry of Labor and the International Labor Organization.

Each section of the study was paginated separately. Therefore page references cited also include the relevant section, for example, "Besbès."

6. The landless units seem to be mainly small herders, but it is possible that cattle rearing is a local capitalist specialty.

7. One hundred thirty-one properties were wholly expropriated, and sixty-five were limited. The owners are reputed to be mainly landlords with properties in

other regions and/or government functionaries.

8. "Associated" means they work the land together as a unit, although for the agricultural census they registered as separate units.

9. "Full-time" is defined as 250 days per year, which leaves plenty of time for work on a small family plot.

10 Recall that this was mainly absentee-owned land not included in the land distribution tables offered here.

11 Two-thirds of the beneficiaries were older than forty-five years, a higher proportion than in the male population at large. Their previous occupations were: 59 percent day-laborers, 17 percent associates of farmers (for example, family aids), 11 percent permanent wage laborers, 7 percent poor peasants, and 6 percent sharecroppers. These data suggest that only those who have few options elsewhere in the labor force chose to become beneficiaries in this region.

12. The three failures to cover costs are attributed to CAPCS inefficiency, for the harvest was not marketed quickly enough (crops rotted in the storehouses in this case). This goes a long way toward explaining, first, why the beneficiaries plant for domestic consumption, and, second, why the private farmers prefer to market through private channels.

13. Hildebert Isnard, La réorganisation de la propriété rurale dans la Mitidja (Algiers: A. Joyeux, 1947); George Mutin, La Mitidja: décolonisation et espace géographique (Algiers: Office des Publications Universitaires, 1977).

14. Georges Mutin, "L'agriculture en la Mitidja ou les difficultés d'une réconversion," Annuaire de L'Afrique du Nord 1975 (1976), pp. 152-154, 161-163.

15. Smail Arbadji, "L'impact de la révolution agraire sur le revenu des attributaires" (Master's Thesis, University of Algiers, 1977).

16. These figures on registered lands seem to be minimum estimates. Without explanation, the author provides alternative data from an unspecified source (apparently his own calculation from observation) that show the private sector to have a total of 4,830 hectares under cultivation in 1974, as compared to 5,182 for the self-managed farms and 372 for the reform sector. Over 1,500 hectares of private land simply disappeared between the 1974 and 1975 counts.

17. In fact, because of the availability of industrial jobs, even the self-managed farm sector has experienced withdrawal of members here--the average age of the permanent self-managed farm worker is old by national standards.

18. Fatma Diabi, "La décision dans les coopératives de la révolution agraire" (Master's

Thesis, University of Algiers, 1977); interviews with
Fatma Diabi, at Algiers, April-May 1979; and Chaulet
et al. (including Diabi), "Projet de recherche."

19. Only one half of an irrigated hectare is
needed to support a family here, and irrigation is the
norm.

20. Thénia's poultry farms had 45,000 chickens at
the time of Diabi's study.

21. Meat markets are not controlled by the state;
Diabi thinks that the state implicitly condones the
meat producers' privileged position.

22. Only 0.5 irrigated hectares are needed to
support a family here, so these are well-to-do farmers.
Also, travel to Mecca is quite expensive, and can only
be undertaken by the well-to-do.

23. In another case, the bank granted credit to a
cooperative to drill a new well, but the state
engineers refused to carry through because it would
have drained water from the supply of a neighboring
self-managed farm.

24. In 1974: 2 to 5 years at 2.5 percent; 5 to
10 years at 2 percent; 10 to 20 years at 1.5 percent.
Before 1975, interest was calculated from time of
grant; after 1975, from time of use.

25. In one case, a beneficiary who had been the
guardian of the communal lands before the reform keeps
the equipment locked away from his fellow cooperative
members.

26. The only family to have a television owns ten
goats and a cow, and sells the milk products in the
private market.

27. Centre Nationale pour la Recherche sur
l'Economie et Sociologie Rurale (CNRESR), Equipe de
Cheraga, "Début de la révolution agraire dans la daïra
de Cheraga" (Algiers, 1975); and Chaulet et al.,
"Projet de recherche." These two projects were
affiliated.

28. At Zeralda, 86 percent of those who became
reform beneficiaries were formerly wage workers.

29. The gap between Douera and Staoueli is due to
the latter having richer soil with more highly
intensive cultivation.

30. In fact, representatives of all sectors
complain of the shortage of seasonal wage labor due to
opportunities for other employment.

31. Benattig and de Villers, "Emploi en milieu
rural," "Souagui"; and R.A.D.P., Ministry of
Agriculture, Centre National de Recherche sur
l'Economie et Sociologie Rurale (CNRESR), "Agriculture
de Subsistance?" (Algiers, 1973), mimeographed. The
pilot study was never followed up because the CNRESR
research institute, sponsored by the Ministry of
Agriculture, was disbanded when it consistently came up

with embarrassing results such as these. The researchers regrouped into a relatively more independent institute, only indirectly receiving public monies for its work, called the CREA. It was at the CREA that I got access to most of the first-hand studies I analyze here. A new series of projects is being undertaken there now that pick up on the CNRESR work; we recall that it was the CREA team who also provided some of the aggregate summing up of reform results presented in Chapter 3.

32. Apparently, owners hoped to avoid expropriation by registering their land as worked rather than fallow.

33. It is possible that these small holdings are gardens maintained by households that basically rely on wage employment for their living.

34. Elsewhere, Benattig estimates that the rate of subemployment may be as high as 70 percent in Souagui. Rachid Benattig, "Impact of the Agrarian Revolution on Employment" (Algiers, 1979), CREA internal working document, p. 13.

35. They had the following distribution of former occupations:

366	landless peasants
180	poor peasants
118	sharecroppers and wage workers
25	veterans of the national

liberation war.

36. This may or may not be true of the private sector as well. The text is unclear.

37. Some migrated while others declined in social status. As of 1954, there was only one Muslim "notable" family here, having thirty hectares (twenty-two in vines), whose sons were employed in the French administration.

38. Houria Benbarkat, "Les relations sociales dans une commune rurale en mutation (Merad-Mitidja occidentale)" (Master's Thesis, University of Algiers, 1978).

39. It was 8,399 in 1966. With a 3 percent natural rate of increase (Algeria as a whole has a slightly higher rate than this), it would have been almost 11,000 in 1975. However, as outmigration is common here, 11,000 is the upper limit.

40. Furthermore, the self-managed farms not only rely on but help to generate dispossessed wage labor as well: when a CAPAM (a self-managed farm for war veterans) was set up on communal lands in Merad in 1968, the ninety full-time agricultural workers who had worked the land until then were literally forced off. When they petitioned to be rehired, the CAPAM director refused, on grounds that the unit could employ seasonal

wage labor more cheaply.

41. There was widespread burning of houses and crops, the expropriation of animal herds, and collective punishment administered for harboring guerillas or aiding the liberation army, or for cutting the colonizer's vines.

42. Khelifa Bouzebra, "Impact socio-économique des coopératives agricoles de production dans les campagnes: cas de la commune de Berrouaghia" (Master's Thesis, University of Algiers, 1975).

43. Other forms of exploitation (such as sharecropping and association) do not yield as good returns.

44. Cote, "Le cas de l'est: El-arrouche." This is an anthropological approach focusing on the indigenous cultural structures rather than on the development of colonial capitalist economic structures. Although Cote's approach is not logically incompatible with ours, we will simply use his data without summarizing his whole work.

45. Fierce resistance was finally violently suppressed only thirty years later.

46. Cote does not tell us from which size category of farm units the nationalizations were made.

47. This author is totally unquestioning of the government statistics available and of the "socialist" mission of the reform.

48. The number of hectares in cereals now is lower than in 1854 due to the lack of irrigation and widespread soil erosion.

49. Benattig and de Villers, "Emploi en milieu rural," "F'kirina"; and Yvette Ait-el-Hadj, "Village de la révolution agraire et restructuration de l'espace rural dans les hautes plaines de l'est algérien: F'kirina" (Master's Thesis, Institute of Earth Sciences, Constantine, Algeria, 1975).

50. Ait-el-Hadj estimates that: of the 10 to 25 hectare category, only 49 percent of working units are owned by those who work them; of the 25 to 70 hectare category, only 24.4 percent of working units are owned by those who work them; and of the more-than-70 hectare category, only 46 percent of working units are owned by those who work them.

51. The greater number is also due to a "working unit" being physically visible and socially known, while an "owned unit" is merely a legal status, sometimes officially recorded and sometimes only conventional, the latter being much easier to hide when the census taker comes.
   The number 51,105 hectares was obtained from Table 4.17 by multiplying the number of farm units worked by the minimum number of hectares in each size category and adding up the products across size categories.

52. Wool rugs and blankets woven by local women are also sold to urban markets--but the nature of the production process (for example, simple commodity production versus cottage industries) is not described.

53. As many as half of the properties may be run by tenant farmers, but these too can be capitalist farmers employing wage labor.

54. The decline between the last two categories suggests that some of the very large units (more than fifty hectares) may be of the low-productivity, absentee owned, traditional landlord type, while some of the medium-sized units (twenty to fifty hectares) may be of the high-productivity, intensive capitalist type. No other evidence is provided in these studies to substantiate this possibility.

55. The authors quote Jean Claude Karsenty's calculation for 1973-74 that the cost of plowing land with wage labor and animal traction is 66 percent greater than with rented mechanized traction, and 138 percent greater than with an owned tractor. Of course, the unit must have capital saved out of profits to be able to purchase a tractor or even rent one. Apparently, the large-scale farms are capturing economies of scale. The relatively high degree of mechanization here may be related to the type of crop, cereals, and the relative cheapness of using machines in cereal production as compared to production of other crops.

56. This is according to Ait-el-Hadj. Benattig and deVillers say it was 5,100 hectares, but it is not clear that this is all usable agricultural land, or that all of it was disbursed as part of the reform.

57. Large-size animal herds were supposed to be nationalized in the 3rd phase of the reform, to be started in 1975. As of 1979, when these case studies were gathered, no significant redistribution of animals had yet taken place.

58. Associated lands are those which, for example, are registered as belonging to a collectivity, such as an extended family, which allegedly works them in common.

59. These authors did not see a traditional absentee landlord class left at F'kirina after the second phase of the reform, although not all large-scale absentee land was expropriated.

60. Benattig, "Impact on Employment," p. 13, goes on to estimate sub-employment (which includes this full-time unemployment) at 57 percent for F'kirina.

61. A sample of beneficiaries gave this distribution of previous occupations: 57 temporary wage workers (52 percent), 22 sharecroppers and herders (20 percent), 23 renters of communal lands, i.e., farmers and herders (21 percent), 3 permanent wage

workers (3 percent), 5 merchants (4 percent), 10 no response. It is noteworthy that 60 percent were wage workers and only 45 percent were "traditional" farmers and herders, either sharecroppers or independents, that is, that wage labor was predominant over traditional tenures.

62. 559 were organized into production cooperatives on agricultural land, 182 into 34 production cooperatives on pasture land, and 23 into one reclamation cooperative on land they were to make cultivable themselves.

63. The cooperatives' accounts are kept by a state agency, the Coopérative Agricole de Comptabilité et de Gestion, and the "profits" distributed by the national bank at Ain-el-Beida. However, as the amortization of equipment is not accounted for before this profit is paid, and the cooperatives still have to pay the bank back for the equipment loans it granted them, the actual spendable income of the individual cooperative members is overstated in these accounts.

64. The average reform beneficiary here got 2,100 to 3,800 dinars per year in 1975-76, while the state farm worker got 6,600 to 10,500 dinars. Those candidates to the reform who did not receive allotments but went into wage labor instead earned, on average, 5,400 dinars that year.

65. The remainder of Ait-el-Hadj's study reports on the proposed "new villages" where these factories would be located and on the largely suspicious reaction of the local populace to the project. This will be the fourth time since the French colonization began that many F'kirina families will be moved--so much for the "traditional" agricultural sector.

66. Gauthier de Villers, Pouvoir politique et question agraire en Algérie (Louvain, Switzerland: Université Catholique de Louvain, Institut des Sciences Politiques et Sociales, 1978).

67. R.A.D.P., Centre Universitaire de Recherches, d'Etudes, et de Réalisations (C.U.R.E.R.), "Structures foncières et sous-emploi rural dans le secteur privé de la commune de Oum-el-Bouaghi" (Algiers, 1974), mimeographed manuscript, no pagination.

68. Cote, "Le cas de l'est," pp. 174-175, 181-182. See also Rezig Abdelouahab, "La réproduction du capital agraire en Algérie au cours des années 1920" (doctoral dissertation, University of Algiers, 1977), pp. 104-106; Andre Nouschi, Enquête sur le niveau de vie des populations rurales constantinoises de la conquête jusqu'en 1919 (Paris: Presses Universitaires de France, 1961), pp. 268-301.

69. Cote, "Le cas de l'est," pp. 179, 182.

70. R.A.D.P., C.U.R.E.R., "La propriété foncière des habitants de Constantine" (Algiers, 1973),

218

unpublished manuscript, no pagination. This is the
same research unit that provided the Oum el-Bouaghi
data above.
    71. The relevant limitations of the agricultural
census data published in 1973 are: (1) they do not
control for the number of trees on the properties (a
crucial aspect of land wealth in Constantine); (2)
they do not control for irrigated versus non-irrigated
lands; (3) the declarations are neither exact nor
honest; (4) the data reflect properties held better
than concentration of proprietors, because with
"indivision" one property can belong to more than one
person, and so can be recorded more than once, or one
person can record only his share so that properties
appear smaller than they are; and (5) changes in
administrative units have led to confusions in land
registration records.
    72. The "CAPAM" is a self-managed farm for
veterans of the war of national liberation.
    73. Cherif Benguergoura, "Village agricole et sens
d'une mutation (Le cas du village de Ain-Nehala)"
(Master's Thesis, University of Algiers, 1975).
    74. As compared to less than 12 percent in fallow,
more than 50 percent in cereals, and the rest in cash
crops on the self-managed farms; 12 percent fallow,
one-third cereals, and the rest in cash crops for
CAPAM; 20 percent fallow, 20 percent cash crops and
the rest in cereals for the reform sector.
    75. At this time, of the thirteen cooperatives
studied, three had purchased tractors, three owned
mowers, eight had ploughs, three had trailers, and two
had cisterns.
    76. However, the families are generally not
extended in form: 38 percent of households have
grandparents in residence; 6 percent have married
children in residence.
    77. Chaulet et al., "Projet de recherche,"
pp. 64-80.
    78. land nationalized = 57.5 percent
         total private
    79. R.A.D.P., CNRESR, "Sour el-Ghozlane, La
première année des CAPRA dans une daïra céréalière"
(Algiers, 1973), unpublished manuscript; and Nelly
Jazra, "Révolution agraire et organisation de la
production," Terre et Progrès (Algiers: Ministry of
Agriculture, February 1976), pp. 4-12. The author was
affiliated with the CNRESR research project on the
reform. Her outspoken critique of the malfunctionings
of the reform, some published in the MARA's own vehicle
Terre et Progrès, was one of the factors that motivated
MARA to finally disband the CNRESR and suspend
publication of Terre et Progrès.
    80. However, only two of these units used

purchased fertilizer and none of the area producers rotated their crops on more than a two-part, sown/fallow cycle, an indication that not all were heavily capital intensive farmers.

81. De Villers, Pouvoir politique, p. 313.

82. Benattig and de Villers, "Emploi en milieu rural," "Bousselam."

83. Only 25 percent of adults at Bousselam are classified as housewives and inactive, as compared to 51 to 61 percent in other communes, because women, youths, and the elderly here keep the farms going while the adult men go off to work elsewhere.

84. Chaulet et al., "Projet de recherche," pp. 68-80. No statistics are provided for Guenzat.

85. Cote, "Le cas de l'est," pp. 174-176, 181.

86. This growth in the number of trees must be qualified by acknowledgement of a decline in productivity between 1940 (when output averaged six tons per hectare) and 1970 (when output averaged four tons per hectare). The explanation for this decline is that while the development of extensive monoculture was accompanied by the use of the most advanced irrigation technology on each plantation, this was undertaken without coordination among plantations, which resulted in the overall depletion of the water table in the west and south and in soil salination.

87. The deglet nour is the finest quality date produced, so a tree that produces them is used as a standard measure. "EDN" is the equivalent of one tree producing deglet nour dates.

88. R.A.D.P., Sēcretariat d'ētat au plan (SEP), Enquête socio-économique sur l'Oued Rhir, 4 vols., (Algiers, 1974), Vol. 4: Systèmes de production et révolution agraire..

89. The researchers found that proprietors were predictably reticent about giving out information. However their employees, the sharecroppers and wage workers, turned out to be excellent alternative informants, for three reasons: (1) they often knew the plantation better than the owners themselves did (number of trees, date output, water input, and so on); (2) the sharecroppers' mode of payment (set by Muslim tradition at one-fifth the harvest) allowed calculation of the total product and the rate of return to owners; and (3) their high mobility among plantations allowed internal checks to be run on the reliability of the data gathered.

90. This figure is obtained by dividing the total number of trees into the rate of output of dates, in litres per second. The numerator here is a "fictive continuous rate of output" obtained by distributing the total harvest of one year over the time it takes to grow the trees and reap the fruit. This method was

adopted in order to control for the factors (a) that the fruit is not reaped all at once during the year, (b) that trees take several years to mature and do not bear fruit until then, and (c) that there are different varieties of trees producing different qualities of dates.

91. These groves were chosen because they are representative of their respective communities' overall economic structure. The Blidet Amor grove contains 12 percent of trees in Touggourt. Tiguedidine possesses 10 percent of Djemâa's trees. Sidi Khelil possesses 14 percent of M'Ghaier's trees.

92. Furthermore, the small producers at Blidet Amor seem to be under more pressure than at the other two palm groves. Whereas at Sidi Khelil and Tiguedidine most of the small plantations are worked directly by their owners, 68 percent of those at Blidet Amor are rented out to be worked by others, while their owners work as sharecroppers or wage laborers off their own plantations.

One of the few serious flaws in this study is the lack of data on the leasing in/leasing out of plantations, which can significantly alter concentration ratios and size of holdings (usually in a more unequal direction).

93. Established as the maximum one family could work directly with only seasonal help from temporary laborers.

94. The authors of the Oued Rhir study argue that wage labor is more important than, and growing in importance relative to, sharecropping on the Type I plantations. But they do not give numerical estimates to the relative proportions of the two.

95. The steps are presented in Tables 4.47 and 4.48. They were estimated as follows. (a) First the authors estimated the total of potentially nationalizable property (in terms of EDN, including unproductive trees) based on their own criterion of size holdings, and allowing no exceptions. Small properties are included in the total because they were expropriated under the reform if not worked directly. Over 70 percent of medium properties and over 89 percent of large properties would have been affected by the reform by this schema. (b) They revised the calculation, allowing for legal exceptions foreseen by the reform texts, for example, for properties owned by the aged, women and minors, or held in "indivision,". About two-thirds of large properties and one-fifth of medium properties are still nationalizable by this calculation. (c) Then (and here is the rub), they revised the calculation again to allow Type I owners (residents without significant extra-agricultural income) to be excepted. The ratio of nationalizable

properties goes down to one-half of large holdings and under 40 percent for medium holdings. Total nationalizable property falls to under one-third. (d) Finally, they compared this last calculation to the actual application of the reform by the communal governments, where about one-third of large properties and one-fourth of medium properties were affected by nationalization. The differences are explicable by four factors, the relative importance of which is shown in Table 4.48.

96. Literally, "taker of one-fifth" of the crop.

97. It was also among full-time workers on the large Type I units at Tiguedidine that the researchers found the greatest degree of class consciousness and awareness of and enthusiasm for the reform.

98. Cote, "Le cas de l'est," pp. 174-175, 179, 181.

99. Since the research for this book was finished, four more community studies have been published which look explicitly at the effects of the reform on the private sector:

S. Abda and H. Khaldoun, Etude sur le secteur privé agricole: Caracteristiques socio-économiques, Daïra d'El Attaf (Chlef) (Algiers: Institut National d'Etudes et d'Analyses pour la Planification, INEAP, 1982);

Abdelkrim Hemmam, Etude du secteur privé agricole: Caracteristiques socio-économiques, Daïra de Sig-Wilaya de Mascara (Algiers: Association Algérienne pour la Recherche Démographique, Economique et Sociale, AARDES, 1980);

Hamid Khaldoun, Etude sur le secteur privé agricole: Caracteristiques socio-économiques, Daïra de Chelghoum Laïd, Constantine (Algiers: Institut National d'Etudes et d'Analyses pour la Planification, INEAP, 1982);

(No author), Etude sur le secteur privé agricole: Caracteristiques socio-économiques, Daïra de Dréan, Wilaya de Annaba (Algiers: Institut National d'Etudes et d'Analyses pour la Planification, INEAP, 1980).

These works confirm the conclusions reached in this chapter, in particular that the major achievement of the reform was to eliminate tenure on public lands and archaic absentee tenures, but that the inequalities within the private sector remain. The authors stress that, although the middle-size family farms and larger-scale capitalist farms are highly commercialized and specialized in what they produce for market, land and labor are still underutilized and there is much opportunity for technical improvements to raise productivity. They suggest that absenteeism was not the only cause of stagnation in Algerian agriculture, and that it is necessary to develop other explanations and new strategies to correct the problem.

Two areas of further research are germane. One is to examine the larger context of state economic policy. A preliminary attempt to do so is offered in Chapter 5 below. The second is to examine farm family strategies for achieving material security in an environment which integrates agricultural with other types of economic activity. Both of these are areas in which I hope to complete further work in the near future.

5
State Policy Towards Agriculture Since 1974: An Interpretation

1974-1979, LIBERALIZATION PHASE ONE

Starting in 1974, the national leaders developed a set of policies designed to solve some of the problems of Algerian agriculture by changing the incentive structure to allow retention of profits by farms that increased their output. The major thrust of these policies was to downplay central planning and the focal role of the state bureaucracy in economic governance in favor of treating the agricultural production units in all three subsectors as autonomous, individual profit-maximizing units responding directly to a going set of relative prices. The coordination of production, through indicative planning, allocation of "credit envelopes," marketing of output, and distribution of means of production to be purchased or rented by the units, was still to be done by governmental organizations. These were to be community and provincal organizations rather than national agencies. Overall pricing policies (which ultimately govern the set of relative prices in effect at any one time) were still to be decided by planners at the national level, at least until the new system was fully in operation.

Investment and mechanization

While the national rulers desired to encourage increased agricultural productivity through investment in capital intensive modern technology, they wished to have the enterprises themselves make the decisions about the nature and amount of the investment. This was the first plank in the new policy and it explains why there was only a minor growth of public investment in agriculture accompanying the land reform. Current expenditures for agriculture by the central government declined from over 4 percent to less than 3 percent of total expenditures from 1970 to 1977. Investment expenditures for agriculture by the central government rose to a peak of 17.6 percent in 1973 (during the reform) and then declined to 6.7 percent in 1977. While gross fixed investment by the public sector in agriculture had merely doubled in the first six years of the land reform (1970-1976), investment in hydrocarbons increased sevenfold and in manufacturing sixfold. The establishment of community-level plans in 1975 and their subsequent growth to one-sixth of central government investment expenditure in 1977 also showed the trend toward increasing local autonomy.[1]

Instead of centrally planned public investment then, the state planning agency and the Ministry of Agriculture encouraged the production units in all three subsectors to engage in autonomous investment out of their own accumulated capital, if they had it, or by borrowing from the national bank. The method they used was, on one hand, to increase the supply of inputs (machines, tools, fertilizer, seeds, young animals) produced by public industrial enterprises for sale to the service cooperatives. The agricultural producers were expected to play their part in a growing domestic market for industrial goods.[2] Then, on the other hand, the bank was assigned to provide credit at low interest rates; given an annual average rate of inflation of 13.9 percent in the 1970s,[3] real rates of interest were negative for loans and, in effect, constituted subsidies to agricultural producers. This subsidization must have resulted in a total investment by the government in agriculture higher than the direct outlays cited above.

As of June 1977, these annual money rates of interest were applied to agriculture:[4]

short-term (less than one year)	4.0%
medium-term (1-5 years, 2 years grace)	3.5
long-term (5-10 years, 2 years grace)	3.0
long-term (11-20 years, 2 years grace)	2.5
long-term (to reform cooperatives only)	2.0

The rate falls with the length of term of the loan. In the examples found in community studies cited in Chapter 4 above (for example, Bousselam), where term of loan was examined relative to size category of land holding, it was found that short-term loans went mainly to the smaller units operating at the margin between success and failure, that is, those units which needed cash loans to tide them over until the next harvest. Long-term loans went mainly to larger units investing in new capital equipment, that is, those units which could afford to be accumulating capital and expanding production and whose credit rating was higher. The

structure of interest rates charged in 1977 appeared to
have marginally favored the larger, more successful
units which are already accumulating capital over the
smaller, less credit-worthy units.

The strategy underlying the government policy was
to induce the production units to increase marketable
output over time. The sole inducement was an increase
in net revenue to the unit, which was then shared among
its members. The subsidized credit program in effect
encouraged capital-intensive, mechanized investment by
the units.This is because reform cooperative members,
self-managed farm workers, and private farmers could
maximize personal income by using more efficient
machinery (purchased at negative credit cost) to
increase output and save on labor costs. In fact, when
some members of the reform cooperatives or the
self-managed farms withdrew, the remaining members
tended to benefit from not replacing them with new full
members: it was cheaper to buy machinery on credit and
employ day workers as needed, and it was more
remunerative to the remaining individuals to share
profits among their reduced numbers. By the same
token, the unemployed and temporary workers who were
not successful private farmers, or members of
self-managed farms or of reform cooperatives, did not
benefit from this credit policy. Furthermore, there
was no direct complementary program to absorb these
laborers into alternative employment. Rural and urban
labor markets saw to that instead.

State price policies

Up to 1973-74, the state authorities had tried to
implement a relative-prices policy that would favor
industrial capital accumulation over agricultural:[5]
most input prices were allowed to rise at a much more
rapid rate than agricultural output prices. Table 5.1
shows some examples of how the prices of heavy farm
equipment and superphosphate fertilizer rose in those
years. The price of ammonitrate fertilizer was kept
stable due only to state subsidies. Furthermore, the
price of cereal seeds (all domestically produced) rose
30 percent from 1970 to 1973 and that of potato seeds
rose 92 percent from 1970 to 1975. In addition, the
costs of obtaining animals and equipment to house and
care for them rose 200 percent between 1969 to 1973.
Meanwhile the wholesale prices that producers were
allowed to charge in the public distribution networks
rose more slowly (see Tables 5.2 and 5.3). The
consequence was a severe falling off of agricultural
investment in those years, as we saw in Chapter 2 (no
doubt compounded by the announcement of the land reform

TABLE 5.1--Evolution of Price Indices of Selected Factors of Agricultural Production 1968-1976 (base = 100 in 1969)[a]

	1968	1969	1970	1971	1972	1973	1974	1975	1976
TSP 45%	100	100	100	100	103	103	127	127	127
Ammonitrate fertilizer	100	100	100	100	103	103	100	100	100
Wheeled tractor									
65 horsepower	...	100	...	...	...	180	180	180	180
Thresher-harvester	...	100	...	...	...	135	135	135	135
Sowing machine 6 m.	...	100	...	...	...	205	205	205	205

SOURCE: Abdellatif Benachenhou, L'exode rurale en Algérie (Algiers, 1979), p. 81.

[a]For the absolute prices on which these indices are calculated, see Chap. 3, footnote 62.

TABLE 5.2--Agricultural Producer Prices, 1964-1978 (in dinars[a] per quintal)

	1964	1965	1966	1967	1968	1969	1970	1971	1972	1973	1974	1975	1976	1977	1978
Durum wheat	50	50	50	50	50	53	53	53	53	54	54	64	76	86	100
Soft wheat	41	41	41	41	41	44	44	44	44	48	48	58	68	78	90
Barley	30	30	30	30	30	32	32	32	32	32	32	41	50	55	60
Maize	...	...	...	...	...	...	...	...	...	...	...	48	48	50	80
Rice	...	...	...	...	...	...	...	...	...	...	...	112	122	122	130
White lentils	98	...	...	98	...	...	90	...	...	90	...	75	160	250	270
White beans	102	...	...	140	...	...	149	...	...	151	...	161	205	270	...
Chick peas	81	...	...	...	...	...	...	...	...	80	...	...	...	200	...
Fava beans	55	...	...	...	...	...	...	...	...	40	...	...	...	150	...

SOURCES: Fahme, "Mécanismes des prix," pp. 116, 122; Benachenhou, Exode rurale, p. 78; World Bank, Prospects of Algeria (1978), Table 7-4.

[a]The dinar was officially equal to U.S. $ .25 in 1979.

TABLE 5.3.--Evolution of Indices of Selected Agricultural Producer Prices, 1966-1976

A. Base = 100 in 1965 for the following products.

	1966	1967	1968	1969	1970	1971	1972	1973	1974	1975	1976
Soft wheat	100	100	100	108	108	108	108	118	118	144	192
Durum wheat	100	100	100	106	106	106	106	108	108	128	172
Barley	100	100	100	105	105	105	105	105	105	135	165
Alfa	100	100	100	100	100	156	156	156	156	156	156
Sugarbeets	...	...	100	127	127	127	127	127	139	139	139
Olives for oil	...	...	...	...	100	...	...	...	...	183	183

B. Base = 100 in 1971 for the following fruits and vegetables.

	1970-71	1971-72	1972-73	1973-74	1974-75	1975-76
Oranges	100	100	109	130	161	226
Table grapes	100	100	110	130	130	240
Melons	100	112	125	150	155	175
Potatoes	100	100	150	275	300	350
Onions	100	100	110	130	130	240
Tomatoes	100	125	156	219	281	375

SOURCE: Benachenhou, Exode rurale, p. 79.

in 1971), with the exception of fertilizer use, perhaps because it is labor intensive.[6] Table 5.4 shows a decline in the rate of growth of tractors and combines in operation, and wide swings in fertilizer use oscillating around a rising secular trend.

The state planners made a major switch in pricing policy in 1974 in order to raise net revenues to agricultural producers providing cash crops to market. This was the second plank in the new policy. As Tables 5.2 and 5.3 show, prices for raw agricultural output rose dramatically after 1974. Overall, they rose by about 90 percent from 1973 to 1976. But these were not passed on directly by the marketers as increased retail prices for food, which rose only 30 to 40 percent in the same years, because that would have forced urban industrial wages up sooner or later as well.[7] Rather, the central government covered most of the difference out of its current budgets in the form of subsidies from general revenue to the processor agencies, OAIC (for cereals), ONAPO (for sugar and vegetable oils), and SN-SEMPAC (for flour milling).[8] This allowed the processors to hold down the prices they charged to retail marketers.

The choice of this policy had consequences for rural class structure and income distribution among agricultural producers. We have seen that costs of production continued to rise for all agricultural producers. After 1974, farmgate prices were allowed to rise too, thus raising the share of total revenues going to agriculture. If the state wished to prevent increased farmgate prices in agriculture from being passed on as increased retail prices, then it could have intervened at any one of three places:

(1) The state could have subsidized retail marketers who in turn would have paid the full costs of production and processing, but charged retail prices less than costs. This would have benefited the retailers by giving them control of the state's subsidy fund. As this type of mercantile power in the distribution networks was one of the fetters on the earlier development of Algeria's economy, having been the province of the merchant-absentee-landlord class, the state was not likely to follow this course in conjunction with a land reform aimed in part to curtail the power of this "exploitative" class

(2) The state could have subsidized the direct producers, who in turn would have charged the processors less than the full cost of production, allowing the processors to pass all their costs on to the retailers. This would have benefited all agricultural producers in the same manner; but it would have been very difficult for the state to force the producers to market their output through the new

TABLE 5.4 --Usage of Selected Agricultural Factors of Production, 1965-1977

	1961-65	1969	1970	1971	1972	1973	1974	1975	1976	1977
Tractors in use (number)	27,620	45,000	47,637	48,878	49,000	49,500	50,000	51,000	52,000	52,000
Harvester-threshers in use (number)	4,870	5,700	6,000	6,300	6,500	6,700	6,900	7,000	7,100	7,200
Nitrogenous fertilizer used (1000 m. tons)	...	42	29	68	85	94	65	63	70	66
Phosphate fertilizer used (1000 m. tons)	...	57	57	74	77	84	68	77	92	93

SOURCE: United Nations, Statistical Office, Statistical Yearbook (1978), pp. 100, 104, 643, 646.

networks being set up in order to insure urban
consumption, or for the state to prevent home
consumption and hoarding of output. There would not
necessarily have been a disintegration of the
subsistence production system that the agrarian reform
was implicitly geared to eradicate.

(3) If the state were to subsidize the processors
of agricultural products (highly concentrated and easy
to control), who are by definition embedded in a market
system, purchasing raw materials from the producers and
selling output to retailers, then the pitfalls of the
first two alternatives could be avoided; indeed the
state would be better able to curtail the power of the
retailers, on the one hand, and increase the proportion
of marketed output, on the other hand. Only those
agricultural producers who were already integrated into
the market structure, the yeomen and gentry, or those
who were capable of raising marketable output quickly,
would consistently be able to raise their net revenues
by selling to the subsidized processors. Those who
were organized for subsistence production, or who
produced small quantities inefficiently for sale to the
market, would suffer from rising input costs, would not
be able to take full advantage of rising farmgate
prices, and thus would suffer declining net revenues.

The choice by the state of the third method of
intervention had the consequence, then, of undermining
the independent economic power of the retailers and
favoring market-oriented over subsistence-oriented
agricultural producers. These results fully conformed
to the agrarian reform's agenda of increased
commercialization and eradication of archaic
exploitative social structures.

State marketing policies

As in the case of price policy, the state's
marketing policy in the 1966-1973 period was geared to
maximizing capital accumulation in industry at the
expense of agriculture. While the state farms were
tightly bound to those policies, private farmers
producing cash crops were able to circumvent them by
working through private marketing networks. These
private networks were legal, and the planners did not
attempt to subject them to its policies in those years.
The prices of oranges and onions (in dinars per
kilogram) provide an example:[9]

1967-68	Public Market	Private Market
Oranges	.27	.49
Onions	.53	.57

1968-69

Oranges	.18	.42
Onions	.25	.32

The private sellers could allow themselves this differential because of the constricted domestic supplies that developed out of the state marketing agency's (OFLA) program to export fruit and vegetables to Europe (selling in competition with other, more efficient, Mediterranean producers at their lower prices).

Although the state policies were changed in 1974 in order to benefit cash-crop producers in all three agricultural subsectors and to bring the retailers under tighter rein, private food processing and private wholesale and retail marketing of food remained very important. In 1974, private commerce controlled 65 percent of fruit and vegetable distribution and almost all of meat and fish distribution. There was a complementarity and interpenetration, rather than substitution, between the state and private institutions. Privately-owned factories that processed fruits and vegetables, for example, could buy their raw materials from OFLA (one state agency) at cost, and then sell their processed output back to a state-run consumer goods distributor at a profit.[10]

The merchants and wholesalers who controlled the private processing and marketing of food based their power on both backward and forward links. They acted as creditors and monopsonists to the petty producers of fruits, vegetables, meat and fish, on the one hand, and as creditors and monopolistic suppliers to the overwhelmingly small-scale retail dealers, on the other hand. Small producers (for example, of olive oil) often preferred to sell to the private wholesalers, in spite of their usurious rates, because they generally offered better final prices than the state agency and paid immediately in cash.[11] Although the data available do not allow the calculation of a concentration ratio, they hint at the possibility that the wholesaler-processors were organized in a power hierarchy among themselves, mainly in the Wilaya of Algiers.[12]

Cereal processing and distribution provided a particularly crucial example of the interlacing of the private and public economic structures. The assigned role of the OAIC (Office Algérien Interprofessionel des Céréales) was to collect domestic grain and to import foreign-produced grain as needed, which it transferred to processors to be made into flour, pasta, and couscous. The OAIC was charged with the rationalization of the relationship between agricultural producers and industries processing agricultural outputs, assuring the first of a buyer and the second of a supplier. The major processor to which OAIC sold was SN-SEMPAC,[13] the national miller. There ramained, besides, private millers who sold their grain products either back to OAIC or on private markets. State pricing policy benefitted the private processors as part of its rationalization program after 1974. OAIC's policy was to charge the processors prices less than its own costs, in effect subsidizing the costs of transport and storage, and taking a loss which it recouped out of general state revenues.[14]

In addition to the interweaving of some private processing and public marketing of cereals, there remained an extensive private network completely outside the state's control. As of 1973, less than half of all cereals produced moved through the OAIC-supervised chain. The institutions set up by the agrarian reform were originally intended to ensure that this proportion increased, insofar as reform beneficiaries were technically required to market their grain only through the public marketing cooperative (CAPCS), although they were able to get around it, as we saw in Chapters 3 and 4. By the end of the decade, as described below, even this constraint on private processing and marketing was lifted.

There were two structural problems with the OAIC marketing structure. First, the production and processing of cereals did not grow fast enough to keep up with the increase in demand, as we saw above in Chapter 2. Therefore imports continued to be crucial in the 1970s, much to the frustration of the state planners. Second, the state agencies were unable to plan ahead for world market purchases and processing goals, because each agency (OAIC, SN-SEMPAC) and each state farm, reform cooperative, and private farm was an autonomous enterprise.[15] The whole system was thus subject to wide and unpredictable fluctuations in supply on both the world grain market and the domestic market; furthermore, while relative prices were controlled on the domestic market, they could not be controlled on the world market and the domestic system was forced to continually adjust to accomodate them. This made "planning" at best tenuous.

This analysis suggests that these price-management and marketing techniques, following on the state's "autonomous" investment policies in agriculture, represented links in the chain binding Algerian agriculture to capitalist relations of production. As in other capitalist societies--United States farm policies are an example--the role of the state was not to lead in organizing agricultural production to fit in with a higher plan. Rather it was to redress, on an ad hoc basis, the imbalances devolving out of the lack of coordination in investment decisions in a system of market-and-profit-oriented food production. It was not "central planning."

1979-1984, LIBERALIZATION PHASE TWO

Since 1979, the role of central planning in governing Algeria's economy has been reduced further and market forces have been allowed more scope.[16] This tendency began first as the simple removal of government strictures on the provision of credit to private farmers. The next step, still in 1979, was to lift the monopsonist power of the state marketing cooperatives on the gathering of agricultural produce, and to allow private merchants full legal rights, for the first time since independence, to market all agricultural products. This was a direct reversal of the policy established for the service cooperatives (CAPCS) in the early years of the agrarian reform.

Wide-ranging debates took place within the FLN over the development program from 1978 to 1980, a two year period for which there was no "Four-Year Plan" in operation. The resolution was to systematize these ad hoc liberalization policies and elevate them to the level of a full program for the period 1980-1984, that is for what would have been a "Four Year Plan" if planning were still in effect. The further pursuit of the agrarian revolution was unceremoniously abandoned. Hopes for renewed agricultural development, including increased production for both the domestic market and the export market, were shifted onto the private sector, for the first time since independence. In order to encourage the private sector,[17] a new bank for agriculture and rural development was entrusted with the job of constraining the credit system to respond solely to profit criteria and to apply those criteria uniformly to all farms in all subsectors. Tax-exempt joint ventures with foreign capital as minority partners were made legal, again for the first time since independence. Full free rein has been given to producers of poultry, eggs, meat, dairy products, fruit and vegetables, in order to curb imports and promote exports through the market mechanism.

The sectors formerly controlled by the state have been as deeply affected as the private sector. State monopolies on imports and exports of foodstuffs were curtailed. This was done, first, so that higher-income urban consumers would be better able to find what they needed in the markets, provisioned if need be by imports. Second, following advice from the World Bank, it was believed that the influx of competition from foreign products would stimulate the Algerian producers to improve their products and processes of production. And, third, it was argued that the expansion of agricultural exports would serve to meet the need for a diversification of sources of foreign exchange earnings as well as an increase in their volume. This last became increasingly important as oil prices declined in the 1980s, given that hydrocarbons had already climbed to 99 percent of Algeria's exports. Concern with national self-sufficiency in basic grain production has been swept aside.

Even state-governed production units have been affected by the policy changes. Companion legislation has decreed the reconstitution of the self-managed farms, breaking them up into a much larger number of smaller units in competition with one another on the input, credit and product markets. Sales of marginal or underused public farmland to the private sector have become legal. 450,000 hectares of land nationalized during the agrarian revolution has been redistributed to individuals as their private property, another direct reversal of the original agrarian reform policy. Prices for agricultural output have been decontrolled in general, and both self-managed farms and reform producer cooperatives have been released from their quota supply obligations to the public marketing cooperatives. All of these changes were symbolically reflected in the decision in early 1984 to alter the name of the Ministry of Agriculture and the Agrarian Revolution to "the Ministry of Agriculture and Fishing". This was taken as the final word that the agrarian reform, limited as it was, was over.

In spite of declarations that national attention in the 1980s would focus on agriculture as a top economic priority, little is being done by the state to invest directly in farming. Nor is any other aspect of agriculture to be the beneficiary of large-scale public spending. The 1980-84 Plan allocated 12 percent of total investment to agriculture, only slightly higher than previous plans, as compared to 39 percent for industry. Of that 12 percent, half went to water resources, only two-fifths went to farming and the remainder went to forestry and fishing.[18] In the 1984 yearly budget, agriculture accounted for 1.3 percent of current spending and under 2 percent of development spending,[19] less than 1983 in relative and in absolute terms. The policy is intended to let market forces direct new investment in agriculture and to rely on private sector profit-maximizing decisions to allocate resources and determine type and quantity of output.

STATE CAPITALISM AND AGRARIAN REFORM: PROMISE
FULFILLED AND PROMISE BREACHED

State capitalism in the 1960s in Algeria
represented a promise of all things to all Algerians,
high rates of investment and income growth, economic as
well as political independence from the capitalist
West, and equality and fraternity through Arab
socialism.

In several dimensions the state capitalist
development program succeeded in fulfilling this
promise to a significant degree. The nationalization
of hydrocarbons and the rising revenues obtained from
their export allowed major structural changes to be
undertaken. In only twenty years, transportation,
communications, utilities and basic industry were all
developed far beyond the levels attained under
colonialism. Sophisticated technology was adopted in
industry and major strides were taken in education and
basic services such as health care. A new material
base was created, in which both the means of production
and the labor force were profoundly changed, and the
foundation of a modern economy was laid.

Once this "revolution" in infrastructure and
industry was underway, a similar reconstruction of
agriculture was proposed via the agrarian revolution.
Here too there were important successes. The
commercialization of both inputs to and outputs of
agricultural production was enhanced. Absentee
ownership and archaic rental tenures were abolished,
thus removing some of the fetters on increasing
investment and productivity in agriculture.

The ability of the state to continue to deliver on
its promises was constrained by the necessity for
economic growth and capital accumulation to proceed
apace. As the 1970s wore on, however, threats to
growth and accumulation became more serious. These
threats arose out of the blossoming of contradictions
in the development program. Each of them affected one
or another of the class forces balanced in the state
capitalist equation in a different way and the
cumulative effect of the mounting criticisms threatened
to upset that balance. The result by the end of the
decade was that no class force was satisfied with
"state capitalism", and the economic crisis was
translated into a political crisis over what course
Algeria would subsequently follow.

From the point of view of the urban capitalist
class, state enterprises had come to dominate the
economy too thoroughly by the end of the 1970s,
substituting for instead of complementing them.
Potentially profitable opportunities for expanded
investment were constrained by the national banks'

allocation of too much credit to basic industry and too
little to final goods production and distribution.
Furthermore, rigid legal restraints on the rights of
foreign capital to invest in the Algerian economy were
curtailing possibilities for joint ventures to cater to
the expanding domestic market. One important outcome
was secret capital flight for investment in Europe and
North America.

The planning mechanism itself came under fire from
both intellectuals on the left (especially economists)
and private capitalists on the right. Since 1965, the
development program had promised economic independence
and the pursuit of technical efficiency in industry.
However, by 1978 it had become apparent that the
Algerian economy was more dependent than ever on the
import of ever more expensive foreign capital goods and
foreign technology, foreign management and foreign
technicians, in order for its "modern" industry to
operate at all. Still worse, the operations in place
functioned at low levels of capacity utilization and
low or negative rates of profit. This led to
accusations of bureaucratic inefficiency and
mismanagement, and to the curtailment of new investment
in basic industry.

From the point of view of urban workers, state
capitalism succeeded in creating new job opportunities,
educating the labor force and raising income levels,
but the effects of these were glaringly limited.
Unemployment remained a serious problem, due to the
highly capital-intensive nature of the state investment
program, due to the state's failure to deal directly
with the reorganization of the labor force (this was
left to the market almost entirely), and due to the
dispossession of small peasants from rural agriculture.
Furthermore, the bureaucratic undermining of the
workers' self-management structure and of the
independent trade union federation was hotly resented,
as workers' experienced an erosion of their influence
on government economic policy decisions. This
resentment was exacerbated by the widening realization
that income distribution was becoming more unequal, as
privileged strata in the state apparatus and in private
enterprise ostentatiously pulled ahead of everyone
else.

All urban classes became increasingly disturbed in
the 1970s by the contradiction between their rising
average incomes and the extreme dearth of consumer
goods, including food. In combination with challenges
around the other problems, already described, these
frustrated expectations led to questioning of the most
basic premise of the development program: the
apparently interminable postponement of improvements in
consumption in favor of yet more investment in

underutilized, inefficient basic industry.

Agricultural classes experienced these contradictions somewhat differently. To the extent that they or members of their families did not participate in the urban boom, peasant producers, agricultural workers (on both self-managed and private farms) and agrarian capitalists all suffered a relative decline in their income from agricultural pursuits in the 1960s and early 1970s. Under state capitalism, they were expected to serve the needs of urban accumulation without obtaining much help from the state or any of the benefits of growth in the near future. They resisted by simply not producing the needed crops in the needed quantities. Because oil revenues had been used mainly to invest in urban economic activities and thus were funneled into rising urban incomes, rural people chose whenever they could to abandon the lower-valued agricultural pursuits and to place one or more family members into civil service or commerce (if they were educated and well-connected) or into wage employment. This tendency was exacerbated by the state's further use of oil revenues to subsidize food imports. The distribution of the oil rent, in other words, steadily raised the opportunity cost of expanding production of basic price-controlled foodstuffs.

The agrarian revolution was intended to change this pattern. Again a state capitalist program embodied a promise to be all things to all people: the revolution was supposed to raise total production, raise rural incomes, reduce unemployment, decrease inequality and eradicate exploitation, all in one blow. Furthermore, in response to criticism that rural housing, welfare, education and infrastructure had been neglected in favor of public investment in the urban sphere, the government declared that, alongside the agrarian reform, it would simultaneously build 1000 "socialist villages" for beneficiaries of the agrarian reform to inhabit. These were to be brand-new communities, constructed from scratch, incorporating all the services and amenities rural people would need to be part of the modern economy without moving to the cities.[20]

As in the overall development program, the agrarian reform was not without its achievements, as we saw above. Yet here too the emergence of problems and irreconcilable contradictions has led to the disenchantment of all rural classes touched by the changes. More scope had been provided to agrarian capitalists and to commercialized family farms as the pre-modern tenures were abolished by the reform. Yet they required much more in the way of credit facilities and removal of price ceilings, and, like urban capitalists, felt constrained by the state's presence in input and credit provision, in output marketing, and on 40 percent of the land in the form of self-managed farms and reform cooperatives.

The response of commercial farmers was to continue to reduce investment in basic food production and to switch to the higher-profit, less-controlled products such as poultry, dairy, fruit and vegetables for export as well as for the urban domestic market, to invest in non-agricultural activities such as commerce, and to place more family members in non-agricultural occupations. One of the reform's achievements was to enlarge the scope for family farms in this context, but whether these yeomen will be able to hold their own in competition with capitalist farms as competition and accumulation intensify is yet unknown. One thing that is clear to the yeomen is that the reform has not eradicated inequality in holdings of land and other means of production, and that only a minority of small holders benefited from the reform directly.

From the point of view of agricultural workers and landless peasants, the reform had only limited benefits. Rural unemployment was not significantly reduced, nor did the basic inequalities among rural classes decrease. Furthermore, the new production cooperatives that were established by the reform, as well as the self-managed farms, were treated by the state as profit-maximizing business enterprises, rather than as internally egalitarian, equally-endowed socialist units. They themselves became exploiters of non-member wage labor. Furthermore, only 171 of the new socialist villages had actually materialized by the end of 1981, and those that did were roundly criticized for their failure to make up in modern services for the sense of community and social meaning that was lost in reorganizing the inhabitants, many of them strangers to the region and to each other.[21]

By the end of the 1970s, state capitalism in Algeria was being attacked from both the left for its inequities and the right for its inefficiences. A struggle ensued over what direction to take, more socialism versus more capitalism. While it was not a foregone conclusion which road would be taken, the outcome was affected by two factors. First, the domestic pro-capitalist forces had been building their strength within the state and party apparatus for years, and they were able to get their man, Chadli Benjadid, into the presidency in 1979. The subsequent purge of the state planners, outlawing of the opposition Socialist party (the PAGS), and reorganization (including firing) of personnel opposed to a pro-capitalist direction, reflected the shift in the balance of political forces in their favor. The

second factor was the foreign exchange crisis which
resulted from falling oil revenues, leading to a
curtailment of new public investment and increased
influence for the World Bank and the international
capitalist banks, always pushing for more scope for
private enterprise, free markets and a more direct role
for foreign capital. The shift was codified in the FLN
party decisions of December 1983.

The unleashing of private capitalist agriculture
via the agrarian reform in the 1970s and recent changes
in state policy conform to the overall pattern of
socio-economic transformation in independent Algeria.
State capitalism effectively served as a cocoon within
which the capitalist mode of production was nurtured.
It would be premature to argue that the Algerian social
formation is now characterized by the clear
predominance of capitalism. The baggage of
underdevelopment from the colonial era and
anti-imperialist, anti-capitalist ideas from the period
of the war of national liberation and post-independence
is too heavy to allow such a characterization at this
stage. Yet motion in the direction of unqualified
capitalist transformation is undeniable and it is this
direction that is setting the framework for future
development.

NOTES

1. World Bank, Memorandum on the Economic
Situation and Prospects of Algeria, (1978), Tables 2.6,
5.4, and 5.5, all in current prices.
2. For example, fertilizer production was
expanded: in 1969, 25,000 metric tons of nitrogenous
fertilizer and 16,000 metric tons of phosphate
fertilizer were produced. In 1977, the amounts
produced were 42,000 and 70,000 metric tons,
respectively (United Nations, Statistical Office,
Statistical Yearbook (1978), pp. 302 and 304). This
should be compared to fertilizer consumption in Table
5.4 below.
3. World Bank, World Development Report (1984),
p. 219.
4. World Bank, Prospects of Algeria (1978), Table
6.5.
5. Such a policy has been common in the East
European centrally planned economies, and in other
Middle Eastern economies such as Egypt.
6. Paule Fahme, "Mecanismes et portée des prix
dans l'agriculture algérienne" (Master's Thesis.
University of Algiers, 1976), pp. 106, 109, 114, 116.

7. While wholesale prices rose 31 percent for processed foodstuffs, 33 percent for textiles and 12 percent for leather goods between 1973 and 1976, consumer prices rose 37 percent for foodstuffs and 14 percent for clothing and shoes in the Greater-Algiers region, 39 percent for food and 26 percent for clothing and shoes in all urban regions, and 31 percent for food and 29 percent for clothing and shoes in the rural areas.

Officially, wages have kept up with price increases in this same period: the legal minimum wage in non-agricultural occupations was raised from 2.08 to 2.90 dinars per hour, and the legal minimum wage in agriculture was raised from 12.25 to 19.90 dinars per day, between 1973 and 1977. (The dinar was officially equal to U.S. $ .25 in 1979.) "Officially" remains different from "actually," due to continuing problems of enforcement and sub- and unemployment, especially in private agriculture. (Data source: World Bank, Prospects of Algeria (1978), Tables 9.1, 9.2, 9.3, 9.5, 9.7.)

8. World Bank, Prospects of Algeria (1978), Table 5.3. The amount of the subsidies was 280 million dinars in 1974, 3,422 million in 1975, 2,338 million in 1976, and a planned 1,311 million in 1977.

"OAIC" stands for Office Algérien Interprofessionel des Céréales. "ONAPO" stands for Office Nationale des Produits Oléicoles. "SN-SEMPAC" stands for Société Nationale des Semolines, Pâtes Alimentaires et Couscous.

9. Fahme, "Mecanismes des prix," pp. 132-133, 139-140.

10. Furthermore, it is reputed that finished consumer goods imported by the state agency often could not be found at the state supermarkets at official prices, but turned up in the private markets at higher prices (Ali Boukrami, "Politique et structures commerciales de l'Algérie" (Ph.D. Dissertation, University of Algiers, 1977), pp. 10-12.

11. There were 65,274 retailers in 1967, of whom 47,319 dealt in agricultural or processed food products. Boukrami, "Structures commerciales," p. 95.

12. On the one hand, there were many small-scale wholesale dealers: 68 percent of wholesale dealers were individual enterprises, and about 1,200 of them did an annual volume of business worth less than 500,000 dinars. More than 40 percent did less than 50,000 dinars worth of business per year. On the other hand, 7.6 percent of them had a volume of more than one million dinars per year, and these were the ones that dominated the field. Retail trade seemed to be less concentrated within itself, but functionally dependent on wholesale trade. Boukrami, "Structures

commerciales," pp. 38-39.

13.   Société Nationale des Semoules, Pâtes Alimentaires, et Couscous, which was created in 1964 through the nationalization and amalgamation of the colonial millers.

14.   While wholesale prices of agricultural products increased up to 1977, this policy allowed retail prices of grain products to remain constant, and thus provided a brake on the rise of wage costs to the rapidly expanding industrial sector.   Mokrane, "Relations OAIC-SN SEMPAC," p. 115, concludes: "Thus one cannot confirm the thesis that says that the industrial sector realizes an accumulation on the basis of a surplus produced in agriculture, at least as far as cereals are concerned" (my translation).

15   Mokrane, "Relations OAIC-SN SEMPAC," pp. 97-101.

16.   This tendency is documented in: Economist Intelligence Unit, Quarterly Economic Review of Algeria, No. 2 (1984, London), pp. 8-9;   United States Department of Commerce, "Algeria" Foreign Economic Trends (December 1983);   "Algeria: FLN Outlines Development Policy," Middle East Economic Digest (January 6, 1984), p. 9;   "Algeria's Economic Liberalization," Africa Contemporary Record (1982), p. B16.

These changes in policy and their relationship to Algeria's overall development program are the subject of current research by the author.

17.   This is meant to apply to industry and services as well as to agriculture.

18.   Economist Intelligence Unit, "Algeria, the Giant Market of North Africa" (London, EIU Special Report, 1982), p. 20.

19.   Economist Intelligence Unit, "Quarterly Economic Review of Algeria" (no. 2, 1984), p. 8.

20.   See Keith Sutton, "Algeria's Socialist Villages - a Reassessment," The Journal of Modern African Studies, 22, 2 (1984), pp. 223-248.

21.   Sutton, "Socialist Villages," p. 234.   The author goes on to argue that the whole program, like the agrarian revolution, may be abandoned.   Instead, the government has substituted a program of support for construction of private housing, which "mainly favors the middle and upper strata in rural society, rather than the poorer reform beneficiaries" (pp. 246-247).

Appendixes

Appendix A

VOLUME AND VALUE OF MAIN FOODSTUFF IMPORTS, 1970-1976

	1970	1971	1972	1973	1974	1975	1976
Dairy products							
Millions of dinars	134	163	267	218	358	459	419
Thousands of tons	113	132	160	112	114	128	131
Wheat, hard and soft							
Millions of dinars	125	256	298	341	1,264	1,242	1,079
Thousands of tons	330	713	1,154	775	1,697	1,328	1,175
Other cereals							
Millions of dinars	7	14	36	43	82	77	58
Thousands of tons	24	39	121	63	110	91	98
Cereal products							
Millions of dinars	14	15	18	14	25	292	446
Thousands of tons	20	19	24	16	18	189	361
Sugar							
Millions of dinars	118	168	228	293	593	1,692	647
Thousands of tons	214	266	266	256	291	453	346
Oil seeds							
Millions of dinars	57	41	85	64	84	240	121
Thousands of tons	70	49	64	57	58	121	86
Oil, fat and wax							
Millions of dinars	116	128	125	130	392	497	324
Thousands of tons	82	94	101	89	138	181	165
Total							
In millions of dinars	571	785	1,057	1,103	2,798	4,499	3,094

SOURCE: World Bank, Memorandum on the Economic Situation and Prospects of Algeria (February 17, 1978), Table 3.7, based on Ministère des Finances, Direction des Douanes.

Appendix B

EQUIPMENT AND OPERATIONS OF SERVICE COOPERATIVES (CAPCS)

As compared to 1973, the CAPCS had acquired a relatively large amount of heavy agricultural equipment by 1977:

	1973	1977
Wheeled tractors	473	2,627
Caterpillar tractors	178	1,215
Automatic reaper-threshers	138	1,234
Heavy trucks and lorries	203	1,309
Light trucks	245	948

Between 83 and 91 percent of these machines were in working order in 1977, most of them less than five years old. They are particularly numerous in Tiaret, Sidi-bel-Abbès, El-Asnam, and Annaba.

Other equipment possessed by CAPCS included machines and tools for:

Soil preparation	Ploughshares	1,548	
	Disk ploughs	1,647	20 percent
	Stubble/cover-crop ploughs	2,459	out of order
	Soil preparation tools	1,109	
Planting	Seeders	628	
	Fertilizer spreaders	495	Less than 10%
	Pulverizers	552	out of order
	Dusters	83	
Harvesting	Mechanical mowers	1,079	
	Hay rakes	631	From 12 to
	Pressure harvestors	1,028	41% out of
	Other	179	order
Transport	Trailers and tows	1,400	
	Reservoirs, bulk carriers	936	
	Tank carriers	55	

Of the 643 CAPCS surveyed, these operations were ongoing:

Administrative, accounting services	627
Pens and buildings for animals	626
Purchasing of inputs and transmission	617
Marketing	590
Extension services	240
Provision of credit in kind to private farmers	107
Repair shops	91
BNA branch	386
OAIC branch[a]	42
Retail shops	411
Other services[b]	52

SOURCE: R.A.D.P., Ministry of Agriculture, Enquête sur les coopératives de la révolution agraire, campagne 1975-76 (Algiers, 1978), pp. 53-57, 65, 68.

[a]Office algérien interprofessionnel des céréales.

[b]Includes butchers, butane gas sales, grain-feed shops, some bathhouses, and insurance.

Appendix C

METHODOLOGY OF TABLES 4.5, 4.12, 4.21 AND 4.37,
EMPLOYMENT FURNISHED ON FARM UNITS
AND ESTIMATED RATES OF UNEMPLOYMENT

The original tables on which tables 4.5, 4.12, 4.21 and 4.37 are based were constructed by Benattig and de Villers in their comparative study to show the high levels of disguised unemployment in all four communities (Besbès in Zone I, Souagui in Zone II, F'kirina in Zone III, and Bousselam in Zone IV), and to show the differences among them.[a] In that presentation, the authors used survey data on the possession of land and animals and types of crops to show how much labor was demanded at each level of size category of farm unit, in comparison to how much labor was supplied.

Implied, but not explicated, in the original data tabulation is evidence that the different size categories (basically, small and landless, medium, and large) represent different types of production systems. This has a critical impact on employment which the authors fail to draw out (although they offer similar concepts elsewhere in their analysis).

(1) The small and landless units (with the exception of intensive irrigated farms, for example, market gardens) generally have more archaic techniques, lower productivity and lower incomes. They generate disguised unemployment and surplus labor.

(2) The middle sized units tend to be self-sufficient, producing a product and income adequate to support the farm family, on one hand, and generating enough employment to absorb most of the labor available from the farm family, on the other hand. Their rates of disguised unemployment are thus lower than those of the small and landless units.

(3) The large-scale units, and some of the smaller ones with a significant amount of irrigated land, operate as capitalist farms, concentrating land and modern means of production in their

---

[a]Rachid Benattig and Gauthier de Villers, "Enquête socio-économique sur la situation de l'emploi et des revenus en milieu rural" (Algiers: Ministry of Labor and International Labor Office, 1978).

I have corrected these tables for typographical, arithmetic and transposition errors to make them internally consistent and consistent with other data presented for these communities by Benattig and de Villers.

hands, with higher productivity and higher incomes than other farms, and generating a demand for labor beyond what the farm family itself can supply. This is manifest in the employment surpluses, that is labor shortages, expressed as negative numbers in the next-to-the-last column of each of the tables. The large-scale units must therefore employ some of surplus labor generated by the smaller units. (The remainder of the surplus labor may then either be "disguised unemployed" in agriculture or join the migratory flow to the cities or overseas.)

In all cases, the first column is the standardized "Size Category of Farm Units" used for classifying holdings throughout the book.

The second column is the "Equivalent of Number of Persons Available for Full-time Work." The researchers constructed these estimates based on direct interviews with farmers and farm family members. What each estimate represents is the number of actual persons who said they were available for full-time work (defined as two hundred or more days per year) plus the sum of fractions of persons who said they were available for varying amounts of part-time work.

Column 3 is the "Equivalent of Number of Persons Working Full-time off own Farm." In the originals, the authors simply used the column "Total Number of Persons Working off own Farm" (column 7 from Table 4.4 for Besbès, column 6 in Table 4.11 for Souagui, column 7 in Table 4.20 for F'kirina, and column 5 in Table 4.36 for Bousselam). The problem here is that while they estimated only the equivalent number of persons available for full-time work in column 2, they included in column 3 the actual number of persons working outside of own farm both full-time and part-time as though all were full-time.

I have corrected for this in the text tables by making two simple assumptions about active persons who work off of their own farms. First, I have assumed explicitly (as the authors did implicitly) that "Wage Workers off Own Farm" and "Non-wage, Non-agricultural Workers off Own Farm" (columns 7 and 8 in Tables 4.3 for Besbès, 4.10 for Souagui, 4.19 for F'kirina, and 4.35 for Bousselam) all work full-time. From other statements the authors make, this is a reasonable assumption.

Second, I have assumed that farmers and farm family members who both work on their own farm and have other economic activity part-time (columns 4 and 6 of Tables 4.3 for Besbès, 4.10 for Souagui, 4.19 for F'kirina, and 4.35 for Bousselam) do each activity 50 percent of their time on average. So I have counted only half of them into the "Equivalent of Number of Active Persons Working Full-time off Own Farm" (column 3 of text tables).

For example, column 3 of Table 4.5 for Besbes was constructed as follows (based on figures from columns 4, 6, 7, and 8 from Table 4.3):

Less than 1 ha $\frac{447}{2} + \frac{2}{2} + 217 + 11 = 452.5$

1 - 5 ha $\frac{38}{2} + \frac{0}{2} + 32 + 2 = 53$

. . . and so on.

Column 4, "Equivalent of Number of Persons Available to Work on Farm Full-time," is column 2 (Equivalent of Persons Available for Work Full-time) minus column 3 (Equivalent of Persons Working Full-time off Own Farm). Column 4 is therefore an estimate of the supply of farm labor.

Column 5 is "Total Employment Furnished on Farm." It is derived by adding together estimates for the number of full-time jobs generated by the various land qualities and types of crops and animals held by the farm units.

For Besbès for example, this was the method used. Assume that 5 hectares of non-irrigated land, or .75 hectares of irrigated land, or 10 cattle, or 50 sheep, or 60 goats, generate one full-time job. Then, using the land and animal distributions (see Table 4.2), divide the amount held by each size category by the number that generates one full-time job to get an estimate of how many jobs are provided in that activity in that size category. For example, Besbès farm units of less than 1 hectare hold .57 hectares of irrigated land. That, divided by .75, yields one full-time job (rounded). They hold 34 hectares of non-irrigated land; that divided by 5 yields 7 full-time jobs. They hold 361 cattle, which, divided by 10, yields 36 jobs. Their 229 sheep and 72 goats, divided by 60, yield 4 and 1 jobs, respectively. So altogether the Besbès farm units of less than one hectare generate 1 + 7 + 36 + 4 + 1 = 49 jobs.

For Souagui, assume that 15 hectares of non-irrigated land (no irrigated was registered) = 10 cows = 60 sheep = 60 goats = 1 full-time job.

For F'kirina, assume that 24 hectares of non-irrigated land (no irrigated was registered) = 10 cows = 100 sheep = 100 goats = 1 full-time job. (Differing assumptions among areas reflect different on-site observations by the original researchers.)

For Bousselam, assume that 2 hectares irrigated land = 11 hectares in olives = 6.5 hectares in figs = 3 hectares in "other" (market-garden) = 15 hectares in non-irrigated land = 10 cows = 60 sheep = 60 goats = 1 full-time job.

The column "Total Employment Furnished on Farm" is the sum of all jobs generated in these various activities. It is an estimate of the demand for farm labor.

The column "Employment Shortage [or Surplus]" (the next-to-the-last column) is the supply of labor minus the demand for labor on the farms. When a negative number shows up, it represents the number of jobs available that are unfilled by farm unit members in that size category. To get the work done, then, those units must employ labor from outside in the same amount. When a positive number results, it is the equivalent of the number of persons available for full-time work who are not employed. This number, divided by the total number of persons available for work full-time, yields a rate of "disguised unemployment" (last column in all tables) as distinguished from a simple rate of unemployment, because many of the actual persons work only part-time or unproductively, especially on the less efficient small units, and are not officially counted as unemployed.

The resulting overall rates of unemployment may be

significantly overestimated due to a fundamental inadequacy of
the basic data: as Benattig and de Villers and many others point
out over and over again, these data were gathered under the cloud
of the impending land reform, so the possession of high quality
land, irrigation, orchards, market gardens, animals, and other
modern   means   of production were underreported.   As   the
calculation of jobs generated is directly a function of these
factors (for example, irrigated land and orchards generate a much
higher demand for labor than dry land per hectare), the estimate
of the demand for labor must be on the low side.   The rates of
disguised unemployment must therefore be on the high side.   This
is confirmed by the widespread complaints of shortages of wage
labor in agriculture in areas like Besbēs and F'kirina.

Glossary

AARDES. Association algérienne pour la recherche démographique, économique et sociologique.

ALN. Armée de la libération nationale.

APC. Assemblée populaire communale.

APCE. Assemblée populaire communale élargie.

APN. Assemblée populaire nationale.

APW. Assemblée populaire de la wilaya [province].

Berger. A shepherd or tender of farm animals.

BNA. Banque nationale de l'Algérie.

CACG. Coopérative agricole de comptabilité et de gestion.

CAEC. Coopérative agricole d'exploitation en commun.

CAPAM. Coopérative agricole de production des anciens mujahidins.

CAPCS. Coopérative agricole polyvalent de commercialisation et de service.

CAPRA. Coopérative agricole de production de la révolution agraire.

CNRA. Commission nationale de la révolution agraire.

CNRESR. Centre nationale de recherche sur l'économie et sociologie rurale.

COFEL. Coopérative des fruits et legumes.

Commune. A village or local community; it is both a residential and an administrative unit.

CREA. Centre de recherche en économie appliquée.

CUV. Comité universitaire de volontariat.

Daira. An administrative unit at a level midway between the local community and the province; the equivalent of a county.

Dinar. The basic unit of currency in Algeria. In 1978, the official rate of exchange was four dinars algériens (DA) to one United States dollar.

FLN. Front de la libération nationale.

GEP. Groupement d'entraide paysanne.

GI. Groupement indivisaire.

GMV. Groupement pré-cooperative de mise en valeur.

Hectare. The basic unit of land area measurement. One hectare equals 2.471 acres.

MARA. Ministère d'agriculture et de la révolution agraire.

OAIC. Office algérien interprofessionel des céréales.

OFLA. Office des fruits et legumes d'Algérie.

ONAB. Office national des aliments du betail.
ONACO. Office national de commercialisation.
ONAMA. Office national du matériel agricole.
ONAPO. Office national des produits oléicoles.
RADP. République algérienne démocratique et populaire.
RGA. Recensement générale d'agriculture.
SAP. Société agricole de prévoyance.
SEP. Sécretariat d'état au plan.
SIP. Société indigène de prévoyance.
SN-SEMPAC. Société nationale des semoules, pâtes alimentaires, et
    couscous.
UNPA. Union nationale de la paysannerie algérienne.
Wilaya. An administrative unit equivalent to a state or province.

Bibliography

BOOKS

Abda, S. and H. Khaldoun. <u>Etude sur le secteur prive agricole:</u>
   <u>Caracteristiques socio-economiques, Daïra d'El Attaf</u>
   <u>(Chlef)</u>. Algiers: Institut National d'Etudes et d'Analyses
   pour la Planification (INEAP), 1982.
Abdel-Fadil, Mahmoud. <u>Development, Income Distribution, and</u>
   <u>Social Change in Rural Egypt (1952-1970): A Study in the</u>
   <u>Political Economy of Agrarian Transition</u>. New York:
   Cambridge University Press, 1975.
Amin, Samir. <u>The Maghreb in the Modern World</u>. Baltimore: Penguin
   Books, 1970.
_____. <u>Unequal Development</u>. New York: Monthly Review Press,
   1976.
Andreyev, Igor L. <u>The Noncapitalist Way. Soviet Experience and</u>
   <u>the Liberated Countries</u>. Moscow: Progress Publishers, 1977.
Bedrani, Slimane. <u>L'agriculture algerienne depuis 1966,</u>
   <u>etatisation ou privatisation?</u> Algiers: Office des
   Publications Universitaires, 1981.
Benachenhou, Abdellatif. <u>L'Exode rural en Algerie</u>. Algiers, 1979.
Bennamane, Aissa. <u>The Algerian Development Strategy and</u>
   <u>Employment Policy</u>. Swansea, Wales: Centre for Development
   Studies, University of Wales, University College of Swansea,
   1980.
Berberoglu, Berch. <u>Turkey in Crisis: From State Capitalism to</u>
   <u>Neo-Colonialism</u>. London: Zed press, 1982.
Bourrinet, Jacques. <u>Salaires et revenus des travailleurs</u>
   <u>agricoles en Tunisie et en Algerie</u>. Geneva: International
   Labor Office, 1975.
Clegg, Ian. <u>Workers' Self Management in Algeria</u>. New York:
   Monthly Review Press, 1971.
Comite Universitaire du Volontariat (CUV). <u>La revolution agraire,</u>
   <u>bilan et perspectives</u>. Algiers, 1978.
Cooper, Mark N. <u>The Transformation of Egypt</u>. Baltimore: The Johns
   Hopkins University Press, 1982.
de Bernis, G. Destanne. <u>L'Afrique, de l'independance politique a</u>
   <u>l'independance economique</u>. Paris: Editions Maspero, 1975.
de Villers, Gauthier. <u>Pouvoir politique et question agraire en</u>
   <u>Algerie</u>. Louvain, Switzerland: Universite Catholique de
   Louvain: Institut des Sciences Politiques et Sociales, 1978.
Economist Intelligence Unit. <u>Quarterly Economic Review of</u>
   <u>Algeria</u>, no. 2 (1984).
<u>Etude sur le secteur prive agricole: Caracteristiques socio-</u>
   <u>economiques, Daira de Drean, Wilaya de Annaba</u>. Algiers:
   Institut National d'Etudes et d'Analyses pour la
   Planification (INEAP), 1980.
Haider, Fadela. <u>Les attributaires de la revolution agraire:</u>

VI. Emplois et revenus des populations candidates à la
révolution agraire. Algiers: Institut National d'Etudes et
d'Analyses pour la Planification, 1980.

Hemmam, Abdelkrim. Etude du secteur privé agricole:
Caracteristiques socio-économiques, Daïra de Sig-Wilaya de
Mascara. Algiers: Association Algérienne pour la Recherche
Démographique, Economique, et Sociale (AARDES), 1980.

Hersi, Abdurahman. Les mutations des structures agraires en
Algérie depuis 1962. Algiers: Office des Publications
Universitaires, 1981.

Hussein, Mahmoud. Class Conflict in Egypt, 1945-1970. New York:
Monthly Review Press, 1973.

Isnard, Hildebert. La réorganization de la propriété rurale dans
la Mitidja. Algiers: A. Joyeux, 1947.

Keyder, Caglar. The Definition of a Peripheral Economy: Turkey
1923-1929. New York: Cambridge University Press, 1981.

Khaldoun, Hamid. Etude sur le secteur privé agricole:
Caracteristiques socio-économiques, Daïra de Chelghoum Laïd
(Constantine). Algiers: Institut National d'Etudes et
d'Analyses pour la Planification (INEAP), 1982.

Launay, Michael. Les paysans algériens. Paris: Editions du Seuil,
1963.

Lazreg, Marnia. The Emergence of Classes in Algeria: A Study of
Colonialism and Socio-political Change. Boulder, Colorado:
Westview Press, 1976.

Lenin, Vladimir I. The Development of Capitalism in Russia.
Moscow: Progress Publishers, 1974 (following text of 2d ed.,
1908).

Lewis, Bernard. The Emergence of Modern Turkey. London: Oxford
University Press, 1968.

Mutin, Georges. La Mitidja, décolonisation et espace
géographique. Algiers: Office des Publications
Universitaires, 1977.

Nouschi, André. Enquête sur le niveau de vie des populations
rurales constantinoises de la conquête jusqu'en 1919. Paris:
Presses Universitaires de France, 1961.

Ottaway, David and Marina Ottaway. Algeria, The Politics of a
Socialist Revolution. Berkeley, California: University of
California Press, 1970.

Popov, Yuri. The Developing Countries from the Standpoint of
Marxist Political Economy. Moscow: Novosti Press Agency
Publishing House, 1977.

Raffinot, Marc and Pierre Jacquemot. Le capitalisme d'état
algérien. Paris: Maspéro, 1977.

Sayigh, Yusuf. Economies of the Arab World. New York: St.
Martin's Press, 1978.

Solodovnikov, Vasily and Victor Bogoslovsky. Non-capitalist
Development, An Historical Outline. Moscow: Progress
Publishers, 1975.

Tidafi, Tami. L'agriculture algérienne et ses perspectives de
développement. Paris: Maspéro, 1969.

Touat, Ammar. Villages socialistes et révolution agraire: Les
problèmes de l'emploi et des revenus. Algiers: Institut
National d'Etudes et d'Analyses pour la Planification

(INEAP), 1981.

Yacono, Xavier. La colonisation des plaines du Chélif. 2 volumes. Algiers: Imprimerie Imbert, 1955.

ARTICLES

Abdi, Nourredine. "La réforme agraire en Algérie." Maghreb/ Machrek no. 69 (July-September 1975):33-41.

Ahmed, Feroz. "Military Intervention and the Crisis in Turkey." MERIP Reports no. 93 (January 1981):5-24.

"Algeria: FLN Outlines Development Policy." Middle East Economic Digest (January 6, 1984):9.

"Algeria's Economic Liberalization." Africa Contemporary Record (1982):B16.

Amara, Aît. "Algeria: The Agrarian Revolution; Reorganization of the Rural World, Condition and Result of the Economic Breakthrough." Ceres 7 (July-August 1974):41-44.

Benabdelkrim, Ahmed. "Agrarian Revolution in Algeria." World Marxist Review 19 (October 1976):118-126.

Cleaver, Kevin M. "The Agricultural Development Experience of Algeria, Morocco, and Tunisia." Washington, D.C.: World Bank, Staff Working Papers no. 552.

Cote, Marc. "Révolution agraire et sociétés agraires: Le cas de l'est algérien." Annuaire de l'Afrique du Nord, 1975 (1976):173-184.

Delorme, Hélène. "L'Algérie: Importations de céréales, blocage de la production et développement de l'état." Maghreb/Machrek no. 91 (January-March 1981):7-21.

Durand, Jean Paul. "Exacerbation des contradictions sociales et reserrement des alliances politiques en Algérie." Annuaire de l'Afrique du Nord, 1977 (1978):123-140.

Economist Intelligence Unit. "Algeria, the Giant Market of North Africa." (London: EIU Special Report, 1982).

Grandguillaume, Georges. "Algeria." In Commers, Climbers and Notables, A Sampler of Studies on Social Ranking in the Middle East, pp.175-195. Edited by C.A.O. Van Nieuwenhuijze. Leiden: E.J. Brill, 1977.

Griffin, Keith. "Algerian Agriculture in Transition towards Socialism." In Land Concentration and Rural Poverty, pp. 22-72. New York: Holmes and Meier Publishers, Inc., 1976.

Jacquemot, Pierre and Michel Nancy. "Chronique économique: Algérie." Annuaire de l'Afrique du Nord, 1973 (1974):535-558.

Jazra, Nelly. "Révolution agraire et organisation de la production." Terre et Progrès, Algiers: Ministry of Agriculture (February 1976):4-12.

Karsenty, Jean Claude. "Les investissments dans l'agriculture algérienne." Annuaire de l'Afrique du Nord, 1975 (1976):115-142.

_____. "La politique agricole algérienne." Maghreb/Machrek no. 77 (July-September 1977):31-39.

Kielstra, Nico. "Algeria's Agrarian Revolution." MERIP Reports no. 67 (May 1978):5-11.

Knauss, Peter. "Algeria's 'Agrarian Revolution': Peasant Control
or Control of Peasants?" African Studies Review 20 (December
1977):65-78.
Landau, Jacob. "Some Soviet Works on Algeria." Middle East
Studies 17, 3 (July 1981):408-412.
Mutin, Georges. "L'agriculture en Mitidja ou les difficultés
d'une reconversion." Annuaire de l'Afrique du Nord, 1975
(1976):143-171.
Nancy, Michel. "Chronique économique: Algérie." Annuaire de
l'Afrique du Nord, 1976 (1977):545-567.
Okyar, Osman. "The Concept of Etatism." Economic Journal no. 297
(March 1965):98-111.
Ollivier, Marc. "Place de la révolution agraire dans la strategie
algérienne de développement." Annuaire de l'Afrique du Nord,
1975 (1976):91-114.
Pamuk, Sevket. "The Political Economy of Industrialization in
Turkey." MERIP Reports no. 93 (January 1981):26-32.
Pfeifer, Karen. "The History of Algerian Agriculture, 1830-1970."
Research in Economic History 11 (1986), forthcoming. Edited
by Paul Uselding. Greenwich, Conn.: JAI Press, Inc.
_____. "Three Worlds or Three Worldviews? State Capitalism
and Development." MERIP Reports no. 78 (June 1979):3-11, 26.
Prenant, André. "La propriété foncière des citadins dans les
régions de Tlemcen et Sidi-Bel-Abbès." Annales Algériennes
de Géographie 3 (1967):2-94.
Schliephake, Konrad. "Changing the Traditional Sector of
Algeria's Agriculture." Land Reform, Land Settlement and
Cooperatives 1 (1973):19-28.
Smith, Tony. "Political and Economic Ambitions of Algerian Land
Reform, 1962-1974." Middle East Journal 29 (Summer
1975):259-278.
Sutton, Keith. "Agrarian Reform in Algeria--The Conversion of
Projects into Action." Afrika Spectrum 1 (1974):50-68.
_____. "Algeria's Socialist Villages--A Reassessment."
Journal of Modern African Studies 22, 2 (1984):223-248.
Temam, Abdelmalek. "La contribution de la banque nationale
d'Algérie à la révolution agraire." Terre et Progrès
(Algiers: Ministry of Agriculture), 1976.

PUBLIC DOCUMENTS

Association Algérienne pour la Recherche Démographique,
Economique et Sociale (A.A.R.D.E.S.). Etude socio-économique
sur les attributaires de la première phase de la révolution
agraire. 1975.
_____. Etude sur le secteur privé agricole, Wilaya de
Tlemcen. 3 volumes. 1975.
International Labor Office. Yearbook of Labor Statistics. 1979.
République Algérienne Démocratique et Populaire (R.A.D.P.),
Centre Universitaire de Recherche, d'Etude, et de
Réalisation (CURER). "La propriété foncière des habitants de
Constantine." Algiers, 1973, mimeographed.
_____. "Structures foncières et sous-emploi rural dans le

secteur privé de la commune de Oum el-Bouaghi." Algiers,
1974, mimeographed.

République Algérienne Démocratique et Populaire (R.A.D.P.),
Direction des Statistiques. Algeria in Numbers, 1962-1972.
1972.

_____. L'Algérie en quelqueschiffres. 1977, 1978, and 1982.

_____. Annuaire statistique de l'Algérie. 1970, 1975, and
1976.

_____. Tableaux de l'économie algérienne. 1960 and 1973.

République Algérienne Démocratique et Populaire (R.A.D.P.), Front
de Libération Nationale. La charte nationale. 1976.

République Algérienne Démocratique et Populaire (R.A.D.P.),
Ministère d'Agriculture et de la Révolution Agraire
[Ministry of Agriculture]. Enquête sur les coopératives de
la révolution agraire, campagne 1975-1976. 1978.

République Algérienne Démocratique et Populaire (R.A.D.P.),
Ministère du Travail et des Affaires Sociales [Ministry of
Labor]. Evolution des problèmes de l'emploi en Algérie.
1976.

République Algérienne Démocratique et Populaire (R.A.D.P.),
Secrétariat d'état au plan (S.E.P.) [Secretary of State for
Planning]. Balances Regionales. Document II: "Elements de
synthèse sur les secteurs agricoles." 1978.

_____. Enquête socio-économique sur l'Oued Rhir. 4 volumes.
Volume 4: Systèmes de production et révolution agraire.
1974.

United Nations, Statistical Office. Statistical Yearbook. 1976,
1978, 1979, and 1981.

United States, Department of Commerce. "Algeria." Foreign
Economic Trends (December 1983).

World Bank. World Development Report. Washington, D.C., 1984.

_____. Memorandum on the Economic Situation and Prospects of
Algeria. 1978.

UNPUBLISHED REPORTS AND INTERVIEWS

Abdelouahab, Rezig. "La réproduction du capital agraire en
Algérie au cours des années 1920." Doctoral dissertation.
University of Algiers, 1977.

Ait el-Hadj, Yvette. "Village de la révolution agraire et
restructuration de l'espace rural dans les hautes plaines de
l'est algérien: F'kirina." Master's thesis. Institute of
Earth Sciences, Constantine, Algeria, 1975.

Arbadji, Smaïl. "L'impact de la révolution agraire sur le revenu
des attributaires." Master's thesis. University of Algiers,
1977.

Bedrani, Slimane. Interview. Algiers: Centre de Recherche en
Economie Appliquée, May 1979.

Benattig, Rachid. Internal working document on "Impact of the
agrarian reform on employment." Algiers: Centre de
Recherche en Economie Appliquée, 1979.

_____. Interview. Algiers: Centre de Recherche en Economie
Appliquée, May 1979.

260

Benattig, Rachid and Gauthier de Villers. "Enquête socio-
économique sur la situation de l'emploi et des revenus en
milieu rural." Algiers: Ministry of Labor and International
Labor Office, 1978.
Benbarkat, Houria. "Les relations sociales dans une commune
rurale en mutation (Merad--Mitidja occidentale)." Master's
thesis. University of Algiers, 1978.
Benguergoura, Cherif. "Village agricole et sens d'une mutation
(Le cas de village de Ain Nehala)." Master's thesis.
University of Algiers, 1975.
Bessaoud, Omar. "Le mouvement coopératif dans le processus de la
révolution agraire en Algérie." Master's thesis. University
of Algiers, 1976.
Boukella, Mourad. "Le thème du dualism dans la politique agraire
en Algérie." Master's thesis. University of Algiers, 1976.
Boukhari, Ahmed Lotfi. "Stratégie de développement et financement
de la révolution agraire." Master's thesis. University of
Algiers, 1976.
Boukrami, Ali. "Politique et structures commerciales de
l'Algérie." Ph.D. dissertation. University of Algiers, 1977.
Bouzebra, Khelifa. "Impact socio-économique des coopératives
agricoles de production dans les campagnes: Cas de commune
de Berrouaghia." Master's thesis. University of Algiers,
1975.
Centre Nationale de Recherche sur l'Economie et le Sociologie
Rural (C.N.R.E.S.R.). "Agriculture de subsistance?" Algiers,
1973. (Mimeographed)
_____. "Début de la révolution agraire dans la daïra de
Cheraga." Algiers, 1975. (Mimeographed)
_____. "Etude socio-économique de la zone de modernisation
rurale de Beni-Slimane." Algiers, 1971. (Mimeographed)
_____. "Sour el-Ghozlane, La première année des CAPRA dans
une daïra céréalière." Algiers, 1973. (Mimeographed)
Chaulet, Claudine. "Paysans et collectifs de producteurs dans la
'révolution agraire' algérienne." Paper delivered at Fourth
World Congress for Rural Sociology, Torun, Italy, 1976.
_____. Interviews, Algiers: Centre de Recherche en Economie
Appliquée, April-May 1979.
Chaulet, Claudine et al. (anonymous) "Projet de recherche sur la
révolution agraire." Algiers: Centre de Recherche en
Economie Appliquée, 1976.
_____. "Bilan de la révolution agraire." Algiers, 1979.
(Mimeographed)
Diabi, Fatma. "La décision dans les coopératives de la révolution
agraire." Master's thesis. University of Algiers, 1977.
_____. Interviews, Algiers: Centre de Recherche en Economie
Appliquée, April-May 1979.
Fahme, Paule. "Mecanismes et portée des prix dans l'agriculture
algérienne." Master's thesis. University of Algiers, 1976.
_____. Interviews, Algiers: Centre de Recherche en Economie
Appliquée, April-May 1979.
Foreign Broadcast Information Service. Washington, D.C., 25
October 1974.
Mokrane, Arab Si. "Analyse des Relations OAIC--S.N. SEMPAC."

261

Master's thesis. University of Algiers, 1977.
Ollivier, Marc. "La politique agraire de l'Algérie." Ph.D.
dissertation. University of Grenoble, 1972.

Index

263